PRAISE FOR *THE TEEN HEALTH REVOLUTION*

"*The Teen Health Revolution* is a powerful, heartfelt, and urgently needed call to action for young people everywhere. Written with authenticity, lived experience, and deep compassion, this book empowers teens to take ownership of their health and future. It's more than a guide—it's a movement that speaks directly to a generation desperately ready for change."
—David Perlmutter, MD, FACN, author of the #1 *New York Times* bestseller *Grain Brain*

"*The Teen Health Revolution* proves that when children make empowered choices today, they hold the power to transform the future of health for us all."
—Mona Sharma, celebrity nutritionist, podcast host of *Rooted in Wellness*

"*The Teen Health Revolution* is the empowering guide every teen needs right now. Written *for* teens, *by* teens, Abdullah, Zain, Emaad, and Qasim don't just talk the talk—they live it. With humor, heart, and honesty, they give teens practical tools to tackle the teen health crisis head-on—one powerful, yet simple, lifestyle shift at a time. They show teens that fatigue, anxiety, acne, and brain fog do not have to be a way of life. This book will change lives—it's a must-read for every teen ready to take charge of their health and spark a health revolution of their own."
—Elisa Song, MD, integrative pediatrician and bestselling author of *Healthy Kids, Happy Kids*

"As an integrative pediatrician, I've read countless health books—but never one written *by kids* that speaks so clearly to the next generation's power to heal. These kids aren't just authors—they're leaders in a movement our world desperately needs. This book proves what I've long believed: kids aren't the problem—they're the solution."
—Joel "Gator" Warsh, MD, MSc, integrative pediatrics and medicine, author

"*The Teen Health Revolution* is nothing short of extraordinary. Written by teens, for teens—with the wisdom of trusted experts—this book is a beacon of empowerment, hope, and healing for a generation in need. Their message is not only timely—it's transformative. This book will ignite a revolution in teen health, and adults would be wise to read it, too."
—Deanna Minich, PhD, CNS, IFMCP, nutrition scientist, educator, and author of *The Rainbow Diet*

"I'm thrilled about *The Teen Health Revolution* by Abdullah, Zain, Emaad, and Qasim Ansari, along with their mom and functional medicine physician, Dr. Madiha Saeed. This book is an excellent resource that tackles a vital topic and provides young adults with the tools they need to achieve their healthiest selves. It presents information in a straightforward, actionable way while addressing common issues such as depression, anxiety, and acne. By highlighting the power of simple lifestyle changes and daily habits, the book offers practical advice on how to improve well-being, prevent common health conditions, and just feel better."
—Elizabeth W. Boham, MD, MS, RD, physician and nutritionist

"More than ever our teens are struggling with little good guidance around emotions, relationships, and exercise and nutrition. Rather than turn to the questionable advice of peers of social media, the Ansari/Saeed family offers sound advice in a fun format for teens, future teens, and their families and caregivers!"
—Chris Willard, PhD, Harvard professor and author

"As a physician, author, and mom, passionate about environmental health and disease prevention, I was deeply moved by this unique collaboration between a physician-mother and her sons. Their honest, thoughtful voices bring a refreshing perspective to wellness in today's complex world. This book is not only informative—it's inspiring. A testament to the power of family, education, and empowerment."
—Aly Cohen, MD, FACR, integrative rheumatologist and author of bestselling books *Detoxify* and *Non-Toxic*

"I love that this book puts the power in teens' hands to understand and direct their own health choices! Absolutely packed with resources and actionable advice. . . . I'm a huge fan!"
—Katie Wells, author, podcaster, and founder of Wellness Mama

"The Holistic Kids have created an easy-to-understand formula for teens to follow that will support their health—mind, body, and spirit. By sharing the practical everyday things that they do to stay healthy, they are leading the way for an entire generation to thrive."
—Beth Lambert, author of *A Compromised Generation*, founder of Documenting Hope

"A much-needed wake-up call for today's youth. This book cuts through the noise and provides real, science and expert-backed solutions to everyday teen health issues and overall wellness."
—Kashif Khan, bestselling author of *The DNA Way*

THE TEEN HEALTH REVOLUTION

Unlocking Lifestyle Secrets for the Mind, Body, and Soul

ABDULLAH, ZAIN, EMAAD, AND QASIM ANSARI

WITH MADIHA SAEED, MD

BLOOMSBURY ACADEMIC
NEW YORK • LONDON • OXFORD • NEW DELHI • SYDNEY

BLOOMSBURY ACADEMIC
Bloomsbury Publishing Inc, 1359 Broadway, New York, NY 10018, USA
Bloomsbury Publishing Plc, 50 Bedford Square, London, WC1B 3DP, UK
Bloomsbury Publishing Ireland, 29 Earlsfort Terrace, Dublin 2, D02 AY28, Ireland

BLOOMSBURY, BLOOMSBURY ACADEMIC and the Diana logo are trademarks of Bloomsbury Publishing Plc

First published in the United States of America 2025

Copyright © Abdullah Ansari, Zain Ansari, Emaad Ansari, and Qasim Ansari, with Madiha Saeed, MD, 2026

Cover design: Amanda Wilson
Cover image: © istock/karandaev
Interior illustrations: Zain Ansari and Anna Cunningham

All rights reserved. No part of this publication may be: i) reproduced or transmitted in any form, electronic or mechanical, including photocopying, recording or by means of any information storage or retrieval system without prior permission in writing from the publishers; or ii) used or reproduced in any way for the training, development or operation of artificial intelligence (AI) technologies, including generative AI technologies. The rights holders expressly reserve this publication from the text and data mining exception as per Article 4(3) of the Digital Single Market Directive (EU) 2019/790.

Bloomsbury Publishing Inc does not have any control over, or responsibility for, any third-party websites referred to or in this book. All internet addresses given in this book were correct at the time of going to press. The author and publisher regret any inconvenience caused if addresses have changed or sites have ceased to exist, but can accept no responsibility for any such changes.

A catalog record for this book is available from the Library of Congress.

ISBN: HB: 978-1-5381-9590-1
ePDF: 979-8-7651-6058-9
eBook: 978-1-5381-9591-8

Typeset by Deanta Global Publishing Services, Chennai, India
Printed and bound in the United States of America

For product safety related questions contact productsafety@bloomsbury.com.

To find out more about our authors and books visit www.bloomsbury.com and sign up for our newsletters.

To Our Future

CONTENTS

Foreword ix

Introduction 1

PART ONE Time for a REVOLUTION!

1 We Have an Emergency! 11
2 Our Lives Influence Our Bodies 23

PART TWO The R.E.V.O.L.U.T.I.O.N.

3 R—Revolutionize the Gut 39
4 E—Eat Real Food 63
5 V—Vanquish Toxins 97
6 O—Optimize Stress Management 109
7 L—Love Nature 121
8 U—Unite with Others 129
9 T—Tech Limits 139
10 I—Invest in Sleep 147
11 O—Open to Gratitude and Purpose 155
12 N—Navigate Decisions with Mindfulness 163

PART THREE Real-Life Revolution

13 Revolutionize Your Physical Health 175
14 Revolutionize Your Mental Health 215
Conclusion 229

Appendix A: The Teen Health Revolution Resources 235
Appendix B: Sample Shopping List 238
Appendix C: Holiday Swaps 241
Appendix D: Teen Health Revolution Recipes 242
Notes 260
Acknowledgments 277
Index 280
About the Authors 292

FOREWORD

There are some health books that are especially important—*The Teen Health Revolution* is one of them. This book takes on the important topic of teen nutrition and its relationship to mental and physical health. I can't think of a more important topic. And this book is written by four boys, Abdullah, Zain, Emaad, and Qasim Ansari, who know a lot about this topic—in fact, they produce their own successful podcast on the subject that is frame shifting. This book is a "must-read" for both parents and adolescents alike and is a manifesto for better nutrition and health. The authors have grown up in a family that "walks the talk" of bringing food and nutrition to the forefront in their lives. The boys bring their positive personal experiences with good eating and healthy foods on every page of the book. This is a unique book that is written by four adolescent boys whose mother and co-author Madiha Saeed, MD, is a leading physician in the Functional Medicine movement. The combination of the boys' experiences growing up in a time where social media, food advertising, and culture norms for teenagers steer adolescents into making poor nutrition and health decisions and how they have found their own paths to physical, emotional, and mental health is truly inspiring. It provides real solutions as to how a teenager can chart their own path to health and wellness through making good choices about what to eat, think, and act. It is a book that provides real-world solutions to problems that teenagers and their parents are experiencing.

Jeffrey Bland, PhD
President of the Personalized Lifestyle Medicine Institute
Founder of Functional Medicine

Introduction

What do you want to be in this world? What do you want to accomplish? Where do you want to go? Everything matters in life until you get sick. Then your health is the only thing that really matters. What would happen if we start to worry about our health *before* it becomes a cause for concern? We are guessing many of you want to change your life—as that is why you picked up this book. Change is possible. Change starts the moment we open our eyes.

The Unfortunate Reality for Most Teens

Beep. Beeeep. Beep. Face smashed against the pillow; I turn around to slap my alarm clock's snooze button. Another minute, another hour, another day. Did I get all my assignments in? What classes do I have today? Is it shorts day, jeans day, or sweatpants day? Thoughts consume my every moment. I force myself out of bed, getting ready for the day ahead.

All this may sound familiar to each and every one of you—we have all been there. But while each of our days may start in a similar way, the rest of the day goes by very differently. Some deal with asthma, depression, eczema, fatigue, anxiety, ADHD/ADD, and digestive issues—and if you look at the current statistics, you are not alone.

One in ten US children have ADHD or a behavioral problem.[1] One in three teen girls have seriously thought of suicide. One in five kids have eczema. One in two kids have at least one persistent health issue.

There has been a steady increase in suicides among US teens over the past two decades. One in eight kids have tried to commit suicide, and every eleven minutes someone dies of suicide. Close to 30 percent are prediabetic, and more than 40 percent are overweight or obese. Diabetes in kids have doubled during the pandemic. Our brains, bodies, and souls are suffering silently. These numbers are going to continue to rise unless we do something today. Teen health is becoming a big worry.

We Were Part of Those Statistics

We were also in your shoes. We have seen firsthand the power of healthy living. We were not always healthy. Like most kids, we did not feel well. Despite both our parents being doctors, we were getting sicker and sicker.

Let us start at the beginning. Our parents completed their medical training together. With Abdullah as a newborn, they each worked eighty hours a week. High stress, lack of sleep, and terrible food, our mother got sick. She continued on the hamster wheel like everyone else until one day she walked into a nightmare.

During noon conference one day, our dad asked our mom to check up on Abdullah in day care (he was ten months old at the time). Our mom walked in and saw the day care provider almost suffocating Abdullah to death. Amid the close call, she recognized her blessings. Our mom made a promise to take care of her children the best she knew how, but if her body was falling apart, then how could she take care of us? Beginning her mission, she looked for answers on how to keep us healthy. The more she learned, the more she taught us, and the more we implemented as a family.

Our dad continues to practice traditional family medicine, and our mom specializes in integrative, holistic, and functional medicine. Like with every path toward health, there were hurdles along the way.

Emaad, born six years after Abdullah, dealt with severe sinus issues. He could not even sleep because he would sneeze every five seconds. With excessive drainage, he slept at the sink, as the drainage would not stop, even waking to have an entire "waterfall" of drainage. Qasim, eight years younger, had severe patches of eczema all over his body that even discolored his skin. Zain was dealing with emotional instability, rage, and eczema. Even Abdullah had several periods of time when he was unable to function. He could not read, memorize, or go to school. His brain did not work properly. He suffered from severe dizziness, terrible headaches, brain fog, could not walk, and could only move around with a walker. This lasted for months!

We all saw countless physicians, despite our parents being medical doctors. No one could really help us or tell us why we were dealing with these issues at such an early age. We found out very quickly that conventional medicine was great for acute care, like when you break your arm or have an infection. We were dealing with chronic problems (problems that last a long time); conventional medicine did not help us get to the root cause. The only solutions we were given were medications. We needed to take matters into our own hands. This was our life. Not our parents. Not our aunts. Not our grandparents. This is our life. We needed to take charge.

Time to Stop Following Blindly

You are probably wondering, if most people and doctors are not worried, then why should we?

Our great-grandfathers were physicians, our grandfather is a physician, our parents are physicians, our aunts and uncles are physicians . . . so we can tell you that they were never taught how to really take care of us, so we can heal and *prevent* chronic disease. Time to take matters into our own hands. We need to start asking the questions:

- Why are we getting sicker?
- Why are our brains not working the way they should?
- Why did the chicken cross the road? Okay, maybe not that one.
- What is going on with all the acne and rashes?

Over the last five years, we have asked the questions and received expert advice. These statistics are the result of how adults took care of our health and needs . . . but they are failing us!!! They have failed to make any real change in this teen health crisis. Our lives are becoming less bright.

WE are suffering. We are entering a world where we will be living fewer total years on this planet than our parents.[2] Our lives are shortening—not theirs.

We are the future leaders, we are the future caregivers, we are the future police, doctors, politicians, engineers, and artists. If we are sick, what will happen to our future? This is why we need the Teen Health Revolution TODAY! We are the future! We need to get back into the driver's seat for our own health, of our own body, of our own brain, of our own soul. We need to start acting! Now!

Why We Need a Teen Health Revolution

Teens are living in a world where we are running from one class to the next, from one activity to the next. Stuffing whatever our hearts desire into our mouths, staying up late at night scrolling through reels, shorts, and TikTok. The few reels turn into hundreds. Soon enough we look at the clock again, and hours have passed by, making us numb to reality.

We are overconsuming processed artificial foods. We have normalized using toxic chemicals on our skin, hair, and bodies, and eating foods with ingredients that we cannot pronounce. We take medications without a second thought. We sit indoors at desks all day. Return home to consume more unhealthy food alone, sitting in front of screens in our dark rooms. Our health is deteriorating. Our bodies are suffering. Our bodies are crying out for help. It is clear we cannot continue as before.

We need a revolution now! We are hurting ourselves in more ways than we know, all due to a lack of information and so much misinformation. We go to school for years on end, for what? To get a great education, a great job, a great house, a great life . . . but what happens to those dreams if we get sick? Will we be able to work well at our jobs? Will we be able to enjoy that house? Will we be able to enjoy vacations? Will we be able to enjoy life?

Without health, nothing else matters.

What do we learn in school? Math, science, reading, English . . . but what about learning about how we can live our lives to stay as healthy as possible? Sadly, they do not teach us that. All they do is teach us how the body works and let us figure the rest out on our own. Where are we supposed to learn how to keep our bodies healthy?

If not in school, then where? Our doctor? They are not taught anything about food or stress. What about our parents? They do not get taught that either. What about social media? Most people today are getting their information from online resources, but what is real and what is fake . . . who do we trust? It is a confusing world out there. We are getting conflicting information from everywhere.

Where is a teen to go for answers? This is why we wrote this book. To help you clear the confusion. No one was teaching us what to do, so we took matters into our own hands.

When the pandemic hit, the entire world was closed off, and we were worrying about our health, so we started our podcast. We interviewed health and wellness experts to help us understand how we can take care of our bodies and how we can thrive in today's world. We interviewed hundreds of *New York Times* best-selling authors, practitioners, physicians, White House journalists, and other experts to bring you the best information out there. We cut through the noise and went straight to world-renowned experts. We asked all the embarrassing questions, all the thought-provoking questions, and the questions that teens are asking daily. We asked the questions so you do not have to. You are welcome.

Navigating the Teen Health Revolution

Teens are on a path to discover who we really are, to discover who we are meant to become. As you continue on that path, we are here for you. We have compiled the information from hundreds of interviews, broken it down into simple, easy-to-follow steps that any teen can implement into their lives today.

The first part of the book starts off with the reality of our teen lives. What and why are we dealing with the surge of chronic health problems that are affecting our brains, bodies, and souls? We then introduce the teen health R-E-V-O-L-U-T-I-O-N framework, where each letter stands for a vital aspect of wellness:

> **R**—Revolutionize the Gut: The gut is the foundation of our physical, mental, and spiritual health. We will dive into why it is so important and how the standard American diet is causing our gut, the bacteria in the gut, and our health to suffer.
>
> **E**—Eat Real Food: Real food heals the body, mind, and soul. What is real food, and what should we be incorporating in our diet?

- **V**—Vanquish Toxins: Educating teens on reducing exposure to environmental toxins and helping our body to detoxify these toxins.
- **O**—Optimize Stress Management: Practical tips for managing our stress. No, this is not about how to sell your siblings.
- **L**—Love Nature: Connecting with nature to improve mental, physical, and spiritual well-being.
- **U**—Unite with Others: The significance of our friends and how to improve our relationships, even the difficult ones.
- **T**—Tech Limits: Setting boundaries for healthy technology use and digital detox strategies.
- **I**—Invest in Sleep: Highlighting the crucial role of sleep in physical, mental, and spiritual health.
- **O**—Open to Gratitude and Purpose: Practicing gratitude to enhance positivity, spirituality, purpose, and resilience.
- **N**—Navigate Your Decisions with Mindfulness: Learning the importance of making mindful choices by examining your emotions and building those life skills and habits to transition into successful, capable adults.

Part Two addresses "The Real-Life Revolution." With the help of our mother, we will dive into common teen physical and mental health challenges. We provide a lifestyle, holistic, and integrative approach that can be used to help aid your regular care with supplements, homeopathy, aromatherapy, and acupressure, addressing the root cause and improving your health.

We have included images and infographics (illustrated by Zain) that will help make complicated concepts easy to understand for all teen readers. We provide shopping lists and even include our home's favorite delicious recipes.

The Teen Health Revolution is not just a guidebook but a transformative tool for teens looking to improve their physical, mental, and emotional well-being. It is packed with actionable advice, practical tips, and resources. This book will equip teens with the knowledge and skills to lead healthier, happier lives in today's fast-paced world—cutting through all the confusion—getting straight to the point.

You Got This

Our goal in writing this book is to educate and empower teens from the inside out. We want teens and people of all ages to take control of their health and make good decisions for the rest of their lives. We are the future of our world. If most teens are stuck at home scrolling while eating a bag of processed chips, not sleeping, and stressed out, it will be hard to move on with taking care of the world if we cannot even take care of ourselves. We cannot do this alone. We need you! We need to do this together. We need a Teen Health Revolution. Time to choose your course.

We must challenge the norm, question the status quo. We need to wake up, start asking questions, research, learn, create change, and spark a revolution. We deserve better. Time to take charge. This book is a guide; we are here to inform and educate you. But the choice is yours. One of our favorite quotes, by the legendary Bruce Lee, is, "Absorb what is useful, discard what is not, and add what is uniquely your own."

We must warn you, no one said this was going to be easy. Read the book, take it one step at a time, one day at a time. Make it fun! Change is difficult. But change is necessary if we want to ride the waves. It will be hard to see your favorite foods, products, toxic friends, or social media time go away, but it will be worth it. Your body, brain, and soul will thank you. Every path is different. Every path comes with its ups and downs. When you are in the driver's seat of your own health, you become the captain your own ship. Will you be able to survive the waves?

PART ONE

TIME FOR A REVOLUTION!

It is time to wake up. There is another way, there is hope. This is NOT our new normal.

1

We Have an Emergency!

Every year more children are diagnosed with asthma, allergies, and eczema. Nut allergies are on the rise, and EpiPens are the new normal. This is our troubling new reality.

We Are Getting Sick

- Data from fourteen countries, which included thousands of children and adolescents in its analysis, found a ten-year increase in the prevalence of eczema.[1]
- One in six youth aged two to nineteen were overweight and one in five had obesity.[2]
- The incidence of diabetes is continuing to increase in children and young adults. It is estimated that US children diagnosed with diabetes at the age of ten years lose an average of nineteen years from their lifespans.[3]
- *JAMA Pediatrics* (a journal published by the American Medical Association) reported that one in three teens has prediabetes (the stage right before diabetes). The number of teens diagnosed with prediabetes has doubled in the past two decades.[4]

- One in five teens report experiencing depression or anxiety. The American Academy of Pediatrics, the American Academy of Child and Adolescent Psychiatry, and the Children's Hospital Association issued a joint declaration of a national emergency in child and adolescent mental health.[5] The CDC states that by the age of eighteen, 40 percent of all children will meet the criteria for having mental health disorders.[6]
- One in ten children have been diagnosed with ADHD.[7]
- Teen girls are experiencing record elevated levels of violence, sadness, and increased suicide risk. Three in five (57 percent) US teen girls felt persistently sad or hopeless, double that of boys.[8]
- Suicide is the leading cause of death for young adults ages ten to thirty-four and more than 20 percent of teens have seriously considered suicide.[9]

We need to wake up! These statistics are crazy, why isn't this a national emergency? We are spending more on healthcare, but we are getting sicker!

Dr. Will Cole, NYT best-selling author of *The Inflammation Spectrum*, emphasized to us that just because something is common does not mean it is normal. Just because something is there every day does not mean we need to settle for it. Common illnesses are affecting us more than our parents. We cannot settle for this.

Our Planet Is in Trouble!

It is not just us—the place we call home is also suffering. NASA reported, "There is unequivocal evidence that the Earth is warming at an unprecedented rate. Human activity is the principal cause."[10]

Global warming is happening at a rate not seen in the past 10,000 years. Global temperatures are increasing, the oceans are getting warmer, the ice sheets are shrinking, the sea level is rising, and extreme events are increasing in frequency.

Climate change can worsen air and water quality, increase the spread of diseases, threaten our food/water quality and diversity. Climate change may aggravate erosion, contribute to loss of soil biodiversity, desertification, and flooding.

In 1965, we used 46.3 million metric tons of fertilizer, and by 2021, this amount had increased to 195.38 million tons.[11]

All these chemicals and toxins we are dumping into the land and water have led to marine death and decreased biodiversity of the planet. Researchers predict that one-third of all animal and plant species on the planet could face extinction by 2070.[12] CBS News reported a plummet in the animal populations by nearly 70 percent in the last fifty years.[13] We have lost 75 percent of the pollinator species. The United Nations estimates we only have sixty years of topsoil left.[14]

The future will not be the same as it is now. Due to devastating wildfires and global warming, there will be fewer trees, food shortages, and coral reef depletion.

There Is Hope!

Minecraft, Roblox, Fortnite, Call of Duty . . . we are walking around with our heads down, video game controllers in our hands. When we are diagnosed with an illness—yet are told "this is your new normal" . . . and we continue to play video games and scroll social media.

It is time to wake up. This is where we need to start looking for answers . . . because this is NOT our new normal. When one has eczema, doctors give you medication. When you have allergies, doctors give you medication. If you have anxiety, doctors give you medication . . . conventional doctors have made us believe that we have no control over what we are dealing with. That the only thing we can do to optimize our health is to take medications. Are these conditions caused by a medication deficiency? This did not make any sense to us, so we went to the experts.

The experts helped us understand why children today are suffering. They gave us hope and an action plan. We cannot wait to share that knowledge with you. For that, let us start at the very beginning. Back to biology 101.

Your Body Is Amazing

The human body is one of life's greatest miracles. Every second, our body produces twenty-five million new cells. Our heart beats close to 100,000 times, and we breathe 22,000 times each without any instructions. The food you just ate is making its way down almost thirty feet of digestive tract, being digested into nutrients that are fueling our every cell, and the cells are the basic building blocks of our body.

The average human body contains around 37.2 trillion cells. Each cell is like a town of its own. A cell is defined as the smallest basic unit of life and is responsible for all of life's processes. The job of these cells is to provide structure and support to the body, convert nutrients from food into energy. Cells can repair themselves, replicate DNA, and communicate with one another. Cells are where a process called metabolism occurs and through this process cells create energy. For the cells to function at optimal levels, they need an optimal environment. For that, we need to eat the right foods and live a healthy lifestyle.

When the body is healthy, everything we eat gets broken down in our digestive tract, enters our blood stream, and is sent to the cell to create energy. Each cell has thousands of powerhouse organelles, called the mitochondria.

Dr. Molly Maloof, physician and author of *The Spark Factor*, stated that the mitochondria are much more than a powerhouse of the cell. The mitochondria are sensing and integrating the environment, like little quantum computers in every single cell. They are trying to take the signals from your sensory experiences and integrate them into action. Every single mitochondrion is always surveying the area and asking, "Am I safe, or am I unsafe?"

These organelles take in nutrients from the food we eat, breaking them down and then creating energy that is used to support everything our body does. Dr. Terry Wahls, internist and author of *The Wahls Protocol*, who herself recovered from an autoimmune disease (multiple sclerosis), describes the mitochondria's needs. The mitochondria need key elements, key building blocks to run chemistry in their organelle components. Dr. Wahls stressed that these mitochondria need a lot of healthy fats, vitamins, and minerals. If we have the building blocks, the mitochondria can make enough energy for the cell to do its job. The food we eat breaks down to glucose. Glucose is broken down within the cell then sent to the mitochondria which generates electrons. These electrons produce what is called adenosine triphosphate (ATP), and that is basically energy.

Our cells need the right environment to function the best they can. Dr. Maloof explains to us that when the nervous system gets dysregulated, through chronic threat or trauma, negative interactions with work, school, or family life, it can create conditions where the nervous system senses the world is unsafe, gets on guard. When the nervous system is on guard, it takes the energy made by the body and uses it to protect itself. Sometimes in trying to protect itself the body may over activate the immune system. The energy is no longer available to the cells to do all the things that are needed to keep us healthy.

Why Are We Getting Sick?

In 2020, we asked this question on our very first episode of The Holistic Kids' Show podcast to expert Beth Lambert, CEO of Epidemic Answers and Documenting Hope and author of *A Compromised Generation*. She said that there is something in the way we are living our lives that must be making kids sick.

Our bodies are protected by a series of defense systems working nonstop to keep our cells, organs, and every bodily activity functioning smoothly to keep us healthy. Maintaining and improving these defense systems are key to keeping our bodies in balance. Mitochondrial dysfunction leads to cells not working well and an improperly functioning immune system, and sickness. Our modern lifestyles and being disconnected from nature are the root of these problems (Figure 1.1).

What happens when these systems stop working correctly? The answer is: an epidemic. An epidemic of chronic disease, like mood disorders, autism spectrum disorder, diabetes, high blood pressure, fatty

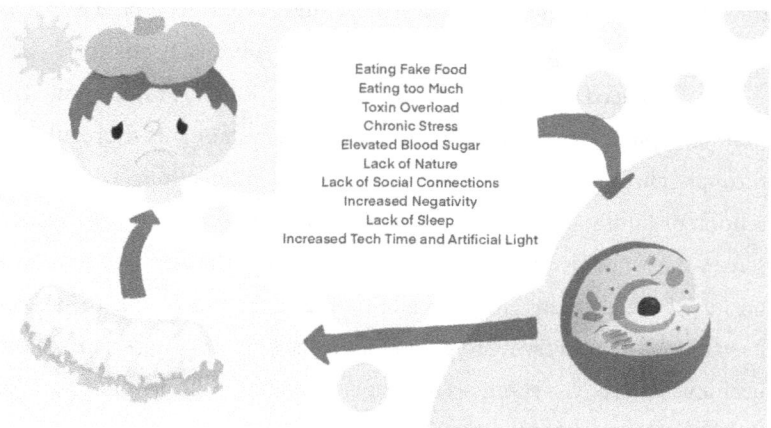

FIGURE 1.1 *Triggers of mitochondrial dysfunction, oxidative stress, and chronic inflammation. Illustration by Zain Ansari.*

liver disease, atopic dermatitis, ADHD, heart problems, and skin issues like acne and psoriasis.

When Emaad was dealing with terrible sinus issues, Zain and Qasim were dealing with eczema, and Abdullah was dealing with debilitating dizziness and inability to walk, our bodies were talking to us. Obviously, we know our cells cannot grow mouths and start talking to us, but through these symptoms our cells and our bodies were asking for help. Our bodies were telling us that we were out of balance. Our cells were begging us to provide it the nourishment and the environment it needed to thrive. We listened, we made lifestyle changes, and we began to thrive. It is the choices we make every day that can decide how we feel and function.

The Choices We Make Every Day Can Either Hurt Us or Help Us

A new day. A new you. A new life. Every day we wake up is a chance for change. We have so much control over our day-to-day lives. Do I wake up on the right side of the bed or the left? Do I want to wear jeans or shorts? Do I eat cereal or toast? We have control over our everyday tasks—what we eat, what we wear, how we move, and everything in between.

Our choices are powerful. Your everyday choices can either help you or hurt you. Dr. David Perlmutter, neurologist and *New York Times* best-selling author, stresses, "Our lifestyle choices every single day really determine how our brains are going to be when we get older."

We go about our lives thinking these daily choices really will not matter in the end . . . but that is where we are wrong. Dr. Terry Wahls explains, "The choices you are making are going to affect multiple generations forward. Your choices will affect your children, your grandchildren, and great grandchildren." Our choices have a massive impact on our future. How we choose to live, matters.

We can either live a balanced life or an imbalanced life. When we live a balanced life, our cells have everything they need to flourish, and everything works harmoniously—the building blocks of life are sturdy and keep us strong. When we live an imbalanced life, for example, we wake up angry, eat too much junk food filled with chemicals, don't eat enough of the good stuff, have lots of toxins surrounding us, suffer from stress, we are not spending time in nature, not sleeping, and are negative all the time—the fundamental blocks don't do their job well, the blocks are out of balance, this then creates a flame.

This flame gets bigger and bigger and leads to sickness.

Aaaaahhhh! We Are on Fire!!!

When we don't feel well, it is actually due to a wildfire inside of our body. This wildfire is called inflammation. Inflammation is a fire that burns you from the inside out. There are two forms of inflammation: acute and chronic. The good inflammation, acute inflammation, lasts for a brief time and is a good sign that the body and its defenses are working. But daily exposure to triggers like toxins, toxic food, allergens, and chronic stress can keep the immune system stuck in the "on" position—it can become chronic inflammation (wildfire) (Figure 1.2).

When everything is working the way it should, the body is able to keep everything under control. But when the triggers continue, day in and day out, the inflammatory molecules go out of control and destroy everything in its path.

This wildfire, or chronic inflammation, can lead to brain issues like depression, anxiety, autism, bipolar disorder, lung and immune issues like asthma, allergies, eczema, and even sinus issues. This wildfire starts out as a small flame even before the disease becomes noticeable, and when the wildfire gets out of control, it can destroy our body.

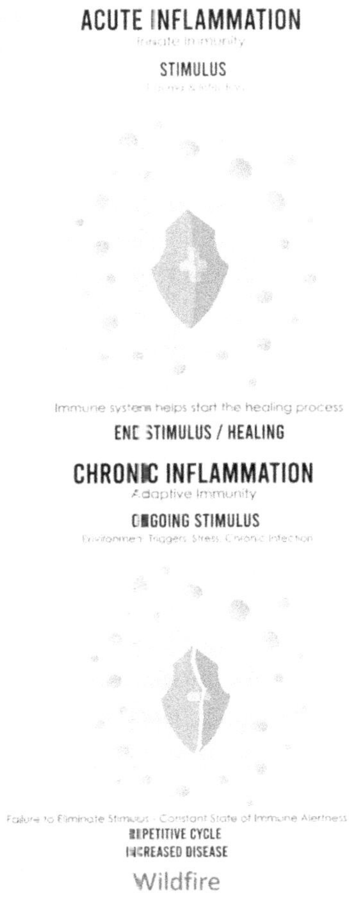

ACUTE INFLAMMATION
Innate Immunity

STIMULUS
Trauma & Infection

Immune system helps start the healing process
END STIMULUS / HEALING

CHRONIC INFLAMMATION
Adaptive Immunity

ONGOING STIMULUS
Environment Triggers, Stress, Chronic Infection

Failure to Eliminate Stimulus - Constant State of Immune Alertness
REPETITIVE CYCLE
INCREASED DISEASE

Wildfire

FIGURE 1.2 *Acute versus chronic inflammation. Illustration by Zain Ansari.*

Wildfires Affect Our Mitochondria

As we discussed above, the mitochondria are so important, and they are very sensitive to their environment. When cells are not working well, this can also cause the wildfires. The smoke from the fire or the oxidative stress reactions is not good. These are unpaired electrons that want to bind to things, which can lead to cell and mitochondrial dysfunction—and the cycle of sickness continues. Your mitochondria can remember a stressor for more than fifty generations!

Wildfires Mess with Our Genes

Genes house our DNA, the instruction manual that is found inside your cells. DNA is the blueprint that your body uses to make things and tells everything what to do. Your DNA is made up of 22,000 genes. Genes carry the information that determines your traits. If one of those genes has a mistake, the gene does not work well and makes us sick.

This may sound crazy, but we have control over our genes! Every experience and decision we make from when we wake up to when we go to sleep and even how we sleep can affect our genes.

Wildfires in our body can lead to smoke on our genes (dirty genes), which impairs the function of the gene. A large part of how we can clean these dirty genes, optimize mitochondrial function, and start to put out wildfires is with our lifestyle.

What do you call a fire that can float on water?
Flame-buoyant!

Is Your Body on Fire?

We know this all sounds scary. How do we know if our blocks are out of balance, and the wildfire is causing our cells to burn down?

If we are healthy, with almost no fire, then we also have little to no symptoms. We are not violent, we have lots of energy, we are able to control our emotions—our brain and body work great! If we do not have a fire in our body, then we can eat what we want and not have a reaction. When we go to the bathroom, our poop looks like snakes in the toilet. When we are healthy, we are also able to sleep right away.

If there is a wildfire in our body, we start seeing the smoke coming from the chimneys. The smoke is our symptoms. Symptoms like fever, congestion or sinus issues, inability to concentrate, headaches, allergies, weight issues, mood problems like depression and anxiety, skin issues

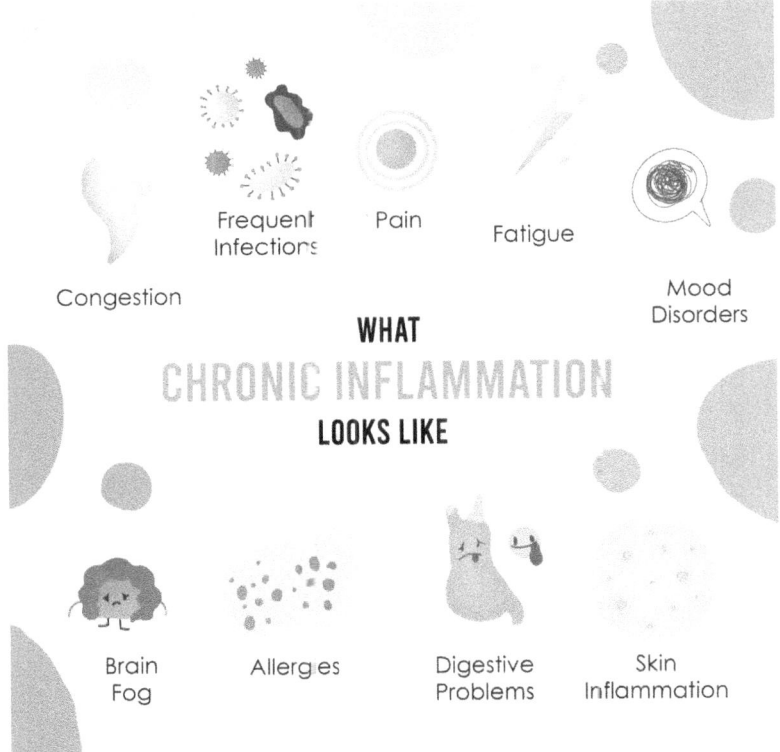

FIGURE 1.3 *What chronic inflammation looks like. Illustration by Zain Ansari.*

like acne or rashes, food allergies or sensitivities, digestive issues, autoimmune diseases, pain, fatigue, and so much more. It all depends on what part of the body has been affected by the fire (Figure 1.3).

Like we said before, our symptoms are our body talking to us and telling us to PAY ATTENTION! This is our body asking for HELP.

If you have any of these symptoms, you want to listen to your body. If we ignore what our body is telling us, then the blocks will fall, the flames ignite, and the wildfire will burn the city down.

Dr. Perlmutter emphasized to us that you want to fix the roof while the sun is shining. It is better to take care of your body now, before it starts sounding the alarm.

2

Our Lives Influence Our Bodies

We love cars. We love how they can allow us the freedom to travel the world. Cars need electricity or gas to work. What happens if we put soda in the car, if we do not give the car an oil change, and drive the car around 24/7? The car will break down and will malfunction.

The same is the case with our bodies. We need to give our body exactly what it needs to work. Our body cannot grow or function well if our cells are not given the proper environment. How do we give our cells what they need? Through our food, our sleep, our nervous system, nature, our environment—our lifestyle. And for most of us, our lifestyles are not giving our bodies and cells what they need to function.

What's Wrong with Our Lifestyle?

We Are Eating the Wrong Food

Let's face it—we can't live without food. We need food to run the trillions of biological processes that are occurring every second in our bodies. If we put all these unrecognizable ingredients or ultra-processed foods in our bodies, our bodies will work like junk. If we put real food in our bodies, our bodies will work the way that they should. Food goes into our digestive system. Our digestive system houses 70–80 percent of our immune system and trillions of gut bugs that decide our health.

With close to 70 percent of all kids' diets being from ultra-processed foods, how can our bodies work the way that they should? In a 2024 study, scientists reported that consuming ultra-processed foods was associated with thirty-two health problems, like heart disease, type 2 diabetes, and mental health problems.[1] These food-like substances cause blood sugar spikes that can lead to glycation (sugar sticking to things in the body, like protein, fat, and DNA), inflammation (wildfire), and oxidative stress (the soot or rust), which hurt our cells and our gut bugs, and destroy our immune system, leading to sickness and disease. These ultra-processed foods also lead to overeating of the fake food. Ultra-processed foods does not give our body what it needs to function, throwing our cells out of balance, leading to the wildfire and the flames.

We Are Not Eating Enough Real Food

Scientists estimate that there are at least 300,000 edible plant species on earth. Humans eat only two hundred species globally, less than 0.1 percent of the world's edible plants. With so many plants, only four plants (wheat, rice, sugarcane, corn) make up 75 percent of the world's calories! Most of these are turned into ultra-processed foods. This then leads to 90 percent of Americans that are deficient of key nutrients that are needed for our bodies to function. Nine out of ten children do not eat enough vegetables[2] . . . that is a problem.

Toxin Overload

The average person is exposed to more than 80,000 toxic chemicals a day.[3] Where are they found? Perfumes, makeup, plastic water bottles, cleaning products, air fresheners, carpets, water, food . . . almost everywhere. Our bodies are not meant to handle such a HUGE amount of toxins. These toxins make us sick.

Chronic Stress

Living in a world of constant stress, lack of exposure to nature, lack of exercise, constant negativity, our minds constantly on the go, an inability to sleep, and negative social relationships can lead to disease. Seventy-five percent of US high school students experience boredom, anger, sadness, fear, or stress while in school. On a 10-point scale, the average teen rates their stress at a 5.8, while adults rate their stress as a 3.8.[4] We spend 90 percent of our time indoors, leading to increased exposure to artificial lights at the wrong times, and limited sunlight exposure. We are also dealing with a lack of sleep crisis! According to the CDC, more than 70 percent of American teenagers do not get enough sleep.[5] Lack of sleep can contribute to unwise decision-making, addictive behaviors, negative emotions, imbalanced hormones, inflammation, and the inability to remove toxins and heal. We also move our bodies a lot less, as less than a quarter of children and teens are participating in sixty minutes of physical activity every day.[6] Sitting is more dangerous than smoking—we are killing ourselves just by sitting around all day.[7]

Lack of Social Connections

As of October 2023, 95 percent of US teens have access to a smartphone at home. Currently, more than half of US teens are spending an average of seven hours and twenty-two minutes of daily screen time, equivalent to a forty-hour work week! Teens are becoming addicted to the internet's mindless scrolling, disconnecting us from our higher brain functions. These phones are designed to be addictive. Twenty-five percent of teenagers say social media has a mostly negative effect on their lives.[8]

Excessive use of social media can lead to negative mental health effects like depression, anxiety, poor sleep, low self-esteem, eating disorders, and poor body image. According to the Mayo Clinic, using social media more than three times a day can predict poor mental health for teens[9] and those spending more than three hours a day on social media may be at increased risk for mental health problems.[10] Most teens are using over five hours of social media a day[11] and 41 percent of teens with the highest social media use rated their overall mental health as poor or very poor.[12]

Increased Negativity

Human beings have around 60,000 thoughts a day and about 90 percent of them are repetitive.[13] We live in a world where we are drowning in negativity. Teens are losing their sense of self and self-worth. Let's face it, people are 49 percent more likely to read something that is negative than positive.[14] Negative perspectives can lead to hopelessness and chronic stress.

Lack of Spiritual Connection and Purpose

Faith and spiritual connection play an important role in how teens think about their sense of purpose. Nearly 60 percent of young adults admit to a lack of purpose in their lives.[15] With everything already at our fingertips, what else is there to strive for? This lack of purpose leads to an increase in the likelihood of engaging in more risky behaviors, like substance abuse and violence, and has a negative impact on our overall mental health.[16] Spiritual health has a significant impact on our ability to bounce back after difficult situations (resilience).[17]

All of these imbalances have consequences.

Most of us know these things are not good for us, but we keep doing them. Why are we making terrible decisions? Why are we no longer mindful about the decisions we are making? Teens want control. Did you know your wants, needs, desires, and decisions are being hijacked? We are not in control.

We Are *Not* in Control!

Decisions are made in the brain. You think you want that bag of spicy red chips—you cannot just stop at one. You think you want to scroll reels/shorts—you cannot stop at one. Why are they so irresistible? Why do we want more?

You think all of these are your decisions . . . but are they really? Think again. That decision that you think you are making, despite the consequences, are not yours. You are being brainwashed.

Our Brains and Decisions Have Been Hijacked

You are what your brain is. What we wear in the morning, what we eat, the decisions we make and how we feel are dictated by our brains. Dr. David Perlmutter, neurologist and *New York Times* best-selling author of *Brain Wash* states, "We are the architect of our brain's destiny. The choices we made in childhood play a huge role in deciding how our brains are going to function when we are in our 20s, 30s and even much older in our sixties." The average brain is believed to generate tens of thousands of thoughts per day, with brain information traveling up to 350 mph.[18] There are two critical players that are involved in our decision-making skills, the prefrontal cortex and our amygdala.

The prefrontal cortex—according to Dr. David Perlmutter—is the adult in the room. The prefrontal cortex is the more developed part of the brain—it is responsible for rational decision-making skills; it examines the pros and the cons and helps us think through our actions after looking at the whole picture.

By contrast, Dr. Perlmutter explains, the amygdala is the child in the room. It wants what it wants. When we want to eat that cake, or want that toy right now, that is the amygdala talking. It is the reactive part of the brain; it is responsible for primitive, impulsive, fight-or-flight reactions, or decisions. To make a thought-out rational decision, we need to have both working together.

Unfortunately, because our lifestyles are out of balance, it makes the amygdala kick the adult out of the room, leading to poor decisions (Figure 2.1).

Our lifestyles determine our decisions, but what determines our lifestyles? Do we? Are we being fed this information from somewhere else, without our knowledge?

We want independence. We do not need our parents to tell us what to do. Reality check: You don't have any independence. There are organizations and corporations that are manipulating our wants, needs, and our decisions... Big Food and Big Tech companies are controlling us.

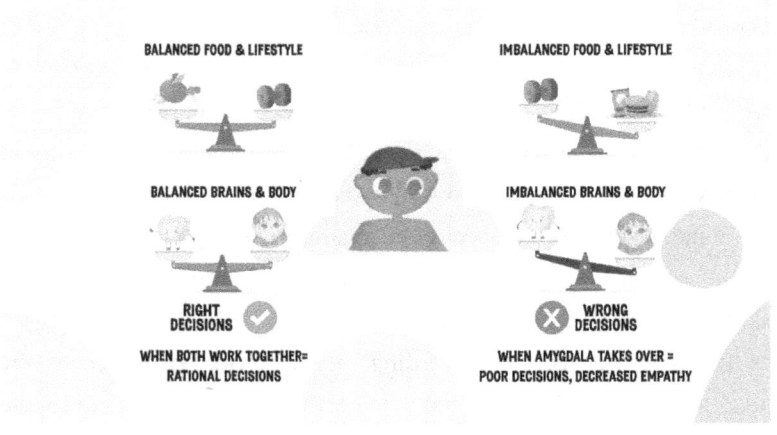

FIGURE 2.1 *Balanced life versus imbalanced life. Illustration by Zain Ansari.*

Running from Our Parents, Straight into the Hands of Corporations

Food/Tobacco Companies Control Us

Twelve percent of nearly seventy-three million children and adolescents in the United States today struggle with food addiction,[19] as fake food makes us crave it. Ultra-processed foods do not just get through the body quickly, but they also get to the brain quickly. In the world of addiction, there is this concept called the rate of delivery, the faster the drug hits your brain, the higher you get, and the more addictive the substance is.

For decades, massive food companies like Kraft and Kellogg's have made trillions through the manipulation of food science and food scientists and ultimately us. Their goal is much like tobacco companies: to do and say whatever they can to get us to buy their product repeatedly until it is no longer a want but a need.

Nowadays, we are eating flavorful, poisonous garbage. Big companies are adding chemicals that make us crave their food. The food industry uses the science of cravings to make their food more addictive. They study them, looking for the "bliss point" of pleasure, driving people to want more. Ultra-processed food companies are trying their best to get us hooked. Food companies don't care about our health; their only goal is to make money.

The delicious, fatty, salty, sweet foods that make up almost 70 percent of the American food supply have been brought to us by the nation's leading food manufacturers. They have spent millions of dollars on engineering food that tastes good and activates reward centers of the brain in ways that are similar to something like nicotine or alcohol. For decades, the tobacco industry hooked people on cigarettes by making their products irresistible addictions. Recent studies have shown that the tobacco companies have used those same strategies that worked for them to get us hooked on processed foods, as many of today's unhealthy foods are brought to us by big tobacco. In the 1980s, tobacco kings like R. J. Reynolds and Philip Morris acquired companies like General Foods, Nabisco, and Kraft. They developed an exceedingly high number of "hyperpalatable" foods, between 1988 and 2001, that then resulted in a substantial addiction-related influence on our US food system.

They applied the same tactics they used to make cigarettes addictive to food products. They pumped up and created food-like substances that were full of sugar, caffeine, fat, sodium, and carbs to create an artificially rewarding eating experience, overstimulating our taste buds but designed to never leave us feeling satisfied. Though the tobacco companies largely exited the food industry in the early 2000s, the shadow of big tobacco has remained.[20] These foods are designed to trick us into eating more than we want to eat, making us addicted.[21] Companies use all our senses to keep us hooked and addicted. Junk food addiction has all the same symptoms associated with other kinds of addiction, including withdrawal, binge eating, and cravings, as the chemicals hit your gut and signal pleasurable signals due to opioid and dopamine release.

When we talked to Ms. Vani Hari (the Food Babe), NYT bestselling author of *Feeding You Lies*, she taught us how these foods have been created to be hyperpalatable, and more addictive. So, your brain remembers the flavor, remembers the taste, and makes you eat more of that product than you should. Even everything from the texture of the product, how the product goes down, how you digest the product, how fast you can digest the product. If they make the product digest faster in your body, you will eat more of product, and they will make more money.

Big Food companies use commercials to make us want more. Highly processed foods make up 45.7 percent of food and beverage advertisements in the United States, which in turn manipulates our eating habits. Research suggests that food advertising can act as a cue that triggers physiological responses, such as increased heart rate and salivation, which can lead to overeating.[22]

In fact, the food industry has even paid "influencer" dieticians to shape our eating habits, paying them to post videos that promote sugar and artificial food.[23] The more junk food you eat, the more money they get.

Ms. Vani Hari emphasized that, "kids do not have enough significant warning on ultra processed foods to warn them that they are being designed to be highly addictive and designed to eat more of that product than you should. And unfortunately for teenagers, this has become a big issue. We need to hold these food companies accountable, as they have put profits over people."

Tech Companies Control You

If you have ever watched the Netflix documentary, *The Social Dilemma*, you will know what we are talking about. Big Tech and social media companies are manipulating our basic human needs of connection, to keep us hooked. We are inundated with likes, comments, shares, friend requests, notifications, pop-ups, and infinite scrolling abilities that all trigger our dopamine (which enhances pleasure). The constant life comparisons keep us hooked and stressed.

A famous quote from *The Social Dilemma* is, "When you aren't paying for the product, you are the product." This highlights how companies track, analyze, and manipulate people through their use of social media and the internet. Advertisers use this data to keep people hooked and make money for how long they spend on these devices.

The same goes with binge-watching (watching two or more TV episodes in one sitting). Binge-watching releases dopamine, resulting in a high like drugs. When we continue to binge-watch, our brain produces

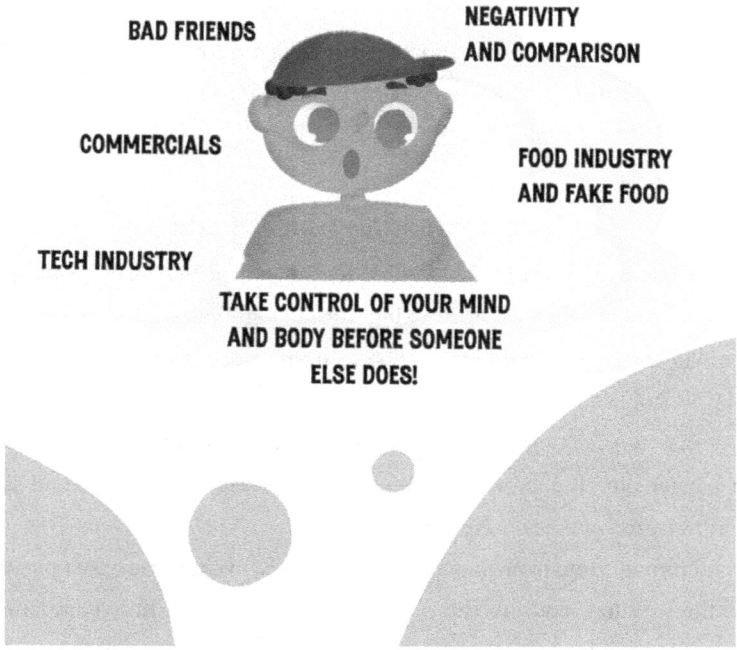

FIGURE 2.2 *Your body and mind are not yours! Illustration by Zain Ansari.*

dopamine, disrupts our sleep, and destroys our overall health. We are binge-watching our lives away. Who benefits? The companies! The more we stay on our device or on streaming platforms, the more money they make (Figure 2.2).

We Are the Product . . . Creating Consumers for Life!

As you can see, you are no longer in charge. We think we are making our own choices, but we are not. Now does that make you angry? It makes us angry and really worried about our future. Why isn't our government stepping in? Why aren't our doctors?

Some doctors are trying. In 2024, the US surgeon general Dr. Vivek Murthy did ask Congress to add warning labels on all social media platforms as a step to improving the ongoing mental health crisis in young people. Let's see how far that goes, but the sad reality is that sickness is profitable. Doctors don't get paid for how many people they heal; they get paid for how many people they see . . . so where is the incentive on getting people better?

Sad reality: the sicker we get, the more money doctors get, the more money drug companies get, the more money hospitals get, the more money insurance companies get. Hospitals and insurance companies profit from sick kids. Everyone makes money. We spoke to Mr. Calley Means, NYT best-selling author of *Good Energy*, who emphasized the need to ask questions and not just trust the experts. We need to make up our own minds.

> What has happened to our health is more of a spiritual problem, where we are losing our ability to operate efficiently and think clearly with our health. We are losing awe for the interconnection between our health and our environment, food, and soil.
>
> —Calley Means, NYT best-selling author of *Good Energy*

This is not a conspiracy . . . this *is* reality. We need to look up from our phones, wake up, and get back in the driver's seat of our health.

Wake up. Get back in charge of your decisions. If you don't take the wheel, someone else will. Are you ready to give that up?

We Need a R-E-V-O-L-U-T-I-O-N!

There is so much we can do every day to take back control of the health of our mind, body, and soul. All five of us live this way and it is so freeing. We are not addicted to anything. We are not addicted to food, to tech, to social media, to streaming platforms, to the pharmaceutical industry. We can breathe without sinus issues, we can walk and run, we have no pain, we no longer have rashes, we are comfortable, and we can control our emotions and our decisions. We are free—well, I guess we do still live with our parents, but otherwise we are free! It is the best feeling in the world!

We want you to be free too. Free of disease, full of energy, living in a body where your brain, your body, your soul work for your advantage, not anyone else's. To help you, we have taken the key steps to best health and freedom that are super easy to remember. Each letter from the R.E.V.O.L.U.T.I.O.N. describes a key piece of the puzzle to help us live more freely, with more energy and health, so we can do anything we put our minds to.

These are:

R—Revolutionize the Gut

E—Eat Real Food

V—Vanquish Toxins

O—Optimize Stress Management

L—Love Nature

U—Unite with Others

T—Tech Limits

I—Invest in Sleep

O—Open to Gratitude and Purpose

N—Navigate Your Decisions with Mindfulness

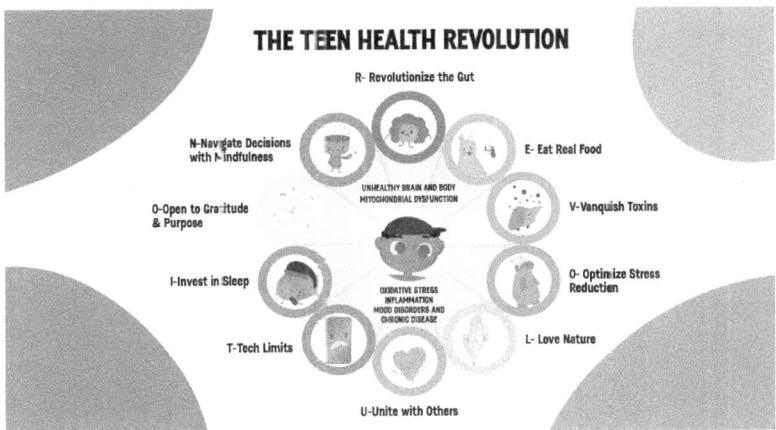

FIGURE 2.3 *The teen health revolution—Unhealthy brain and body. Illustration by Zain Ansari.*

By living a balanced life, we put the blocks back in line. We need to give the cells everything they need to do their job and thrive.

We all have to eat, we all have to sleep, we all need to learn to manage our stress, we all need to breathe, we all move, we all drink, so why not focus on the best way to do these things so it can benefit and optimize our mind, body, and soul.

When we are in balance, we can thrive, not just survive. Can you imagine if every teen were this empowered, this free, this healthy? If every teen's brain and body worked the best it could, can you imagine where our world could go, where we could take it?

This starts with you! Let us start with The Teen Health R.E.V.O.L.U.T.I.O.N!

PART TWO

THE R.E.V.O.L.U.T.I.O.N.

3

R—Revolutionize the Gut

When we were all sick, our podcast experts told us to look at our gut for healing. We were confused. We had never heard of that before. We had learned about the digestive system in school, but what did that have to do with our health?

In our discussions with Dr. Vincent Pedre, physician and author of *GutSmart*, we found that the digestive system was actually particularly important. He described the gut as a root system. He gave the example of a tree, which had branches, leaves, and roots. The roots were designed to absorb all the nutrients and bring them to the tree. If the tree became sick, we nourished the roots, and the tree got better. Unfortunately, conventional medicine is fixing the tree from the outside, like painting the browning leaf green. It does not solve the problem.

When you want to fix the body, you need to look at the root system or foundation: the gut. Your gut is the foundation of your health. Let's talk about the gut and its job in more detail.

The Gut Is More Than Our Poop Maker!

We all studied the digestive system in school. The digestive system processes the food we eat, absorbs nutrients, and regulates our metabolism. Being the gateway to our health, the gut is the first line of defense between you and the universe. Did you know that your gut houses about 70–80 percent of your immune system, just as it houses trillions of microorganisms that oversee your health and decisions? These bugs actually outnumber your human cells 10:1 . . . but let us not think about that . . . it is kind of creepy.

 Why was the small intestine always the life of the party?
Because it knew how to break things down!

In school, they taught us about the digestive system but did not teach us about the bugs that lived there. Our microbiome is a community of microorganisms (or bugs) that can be found living together in each habitat. Our skin, our respiratory tract, our urogenital tract all have their own microbiome (Figure 3.1).

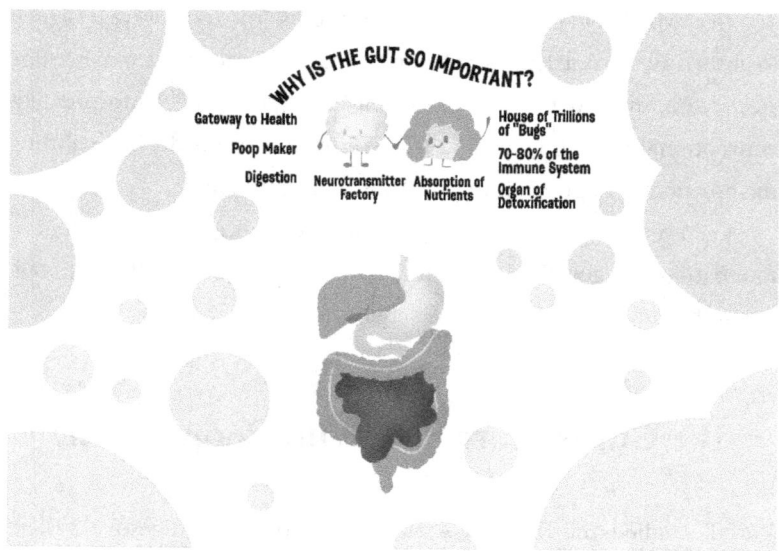

FIGURE 3.1 *Why is the gut so important? Illustration by Zain Ansari.*

What Do the Bugs Do?

Did you know that our gut bugs are critical for our health? They help shape our brain, mood, behaviors, and decisions. The microbiome is a critical player in most of our biological processes, like digestion, synthesizing hormones and vitamins, extracting energy, harvesting calories from undigested food, manufacturing neurotransmitters, and controlling blood sugar balance.

The microbiome has a key role in immunity, via the Gut Associated Lymphatic Tissue (GALT), and is the first line of defense between your internal and external world. Our gut is naturally permeable to allow vital nutrients—like proteins, starches, and digested fats—to pass through the tight junctions and enter the bloodstream. The intestines are covered by intestinal epithelium, a single layer of cells that separates our body from the food in the intestines. This means there is just one layer that will keep the harmful stuff away from us and the good stuff in.

Each cell has hundreds of fingerlike projections called villi that absorb the nutrients from the foods we eat. In between each cell is a "tight junction" that keeps the cells stuck together, preventing body-damaging substances from entering the body.

How Do These Gut Bugs Keep Us Healthy?

There are diverse groups of gut bugs. They are made of good bugs, neutral bugs, and bad bugs. We need the balance to be perfect to keep us healthy. When our gut bugs are not balanced or are sick, this can lead to an increase in immune cells. These then release cytokines that talk to other immune cells. Cytokines send messages to cells to help defend our body from disease and keep us healthy. The microbiome communicates with the brain and the immune system. When the microbiome is out of balance or disrupted, then the brain and body stop working, leading to inflammation like brain fog, anxiety, mood swings, and so much more.

How Does the Microbiome Affect Our Brain?

The health of gut bugs plays a significant role in our mental health. Did you know that our gut and our brain are connected? Think of your gut as your "second brain." The brain and the gut are directly connected by a superfast highway called the vagus nerve. When we spoke to neurologist Dr. David Perlmutter, he stated that the gut bacteria are making chemicals called neurotransmitters that control how the brain works, impacting mood changes, and influencing us at every moment. Most of the messages on this highway go from your gut to your brain, as your gut is the factory for 95 percent of our brain chemicals called neurotransmitters. Up to 95 percent of serotonin and more than 50 percent of dopamine (you know, the ones that make you feel happy) are made by your gut microbiome. There are a lot of neurotransmitters that are made by our gut bugs. Examples include dopamine (controls our movement and joy), serotonin (helps with mood, eating, and sleep), melatonin (supports our gut function, regulates our sleep and wake cycle, serves as an antioxidant), and others include acetylcholine, norepinephrine, and gamma-aminobutyric acid.

Your brain and body need these key neurotransmitters to function. A thriving microbiome helps with our memory, shaping the brain, decision-making, mood, learning, and behavior. An imbalanced microbiome can lead to many symptoms you may be dealing with like digestive issues, mood problems, allergies, sinus issues, diabetes, autoimmune diseases, behavioral issues, and even weight problems.

Imbalance of Gut Bugs = Sickness

We need a healthy balance of good bugs versus bad bugs. If that balance is disrupted, we suffer. There are a number of things that can disrupt the gut bug balance. But the most important are:

- Fake food and eating too much sugar
- Chronic stress and lack of play
- Environmental toxins, including glyphosate (a pesticide)
- Certain medications, especially nonsteroidal anti-inflammatory drugs, other pain killers, birth control pills, steroids, chemotherapy drugs, acid-blocking medications, opiates, and sleep medications can negatively affect the microbiome. The biggest contributor is antibiotics. Antibiotic resistance in children is becoming a big problem around the world.[1] Antibiotics destroy the gut microbiome, so always make sure you really need them before taking them.
- Other factors include overly strenuous exercise and exposure to infections that are never resolved (bacteria, viruses, fungi, or parasites, etc.)

Leaky Gut = Sickness and Disease

We talked about the balance of the gut bugs being super important for overall health. What happens if the imbalance of gut bugs goes on for a long time? The bad bugs and improperly digested proteins may activate the immune system, creating a fire in the gut as they trigger the immune cells, leading to inflammation. This then damages the gut wall and the junctions get "leaky," leading to "leaky gut syndrome." Dr. Pedre gives the analogy of a coffee filter. When the water pours through, you want to keep the coffee grains out of the cup. If there are little holes in the coffee filter, it lets things through that should not be getting through. The same thing can happen to your gut—it can become leaky (Figure 3.2).

When things get leaky, things that should not be passing through start to pass through the gut, like undigested food particles, bad bugs, and toxins that can trigger the immune system. Over time, the immune

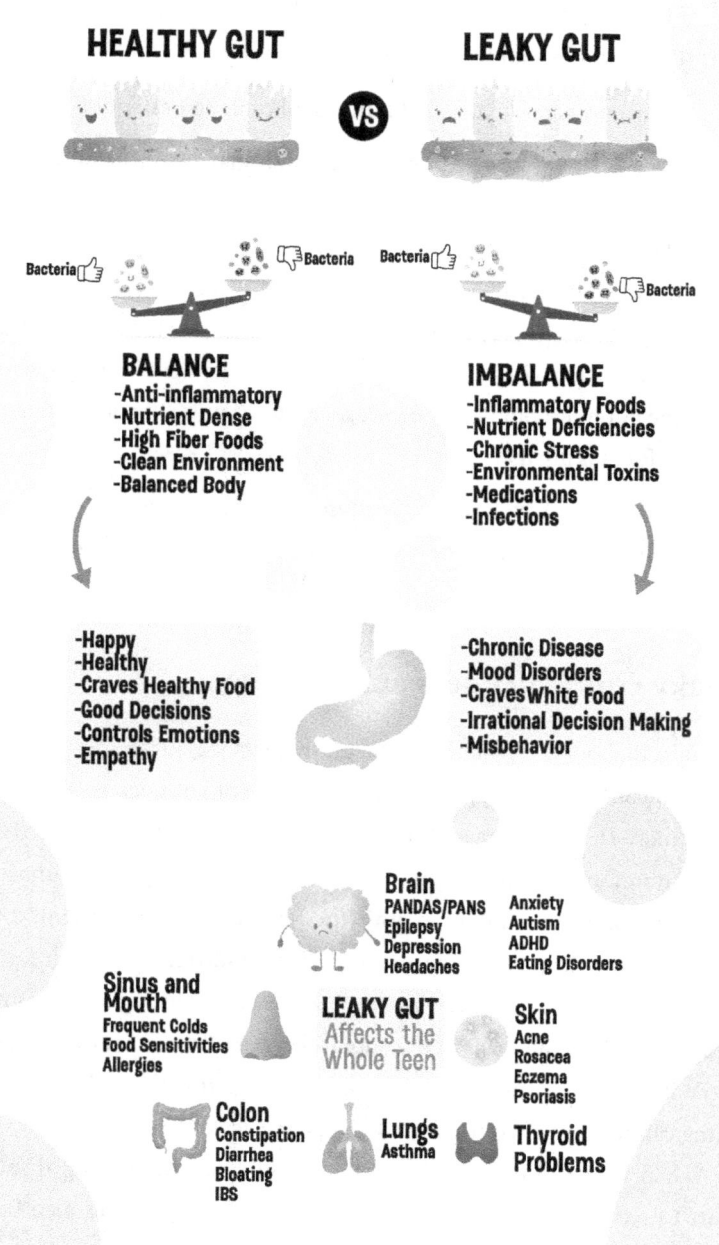

FIGURE 3.2 *Healthy gut versus leaky gut. Illustration by Zain Ansari.*

system becomes highly reactive, responding to anything that it would have previously ignored. This then activates the immune system further, releasing cytokines and inflammation throughout the whole body and brain. Leaky gut is connected with A LOT of chronic health conditions.[2] Leaky gut affects your mind, body, and soul (Figure 3.3).

 If you take care of your bugs, your bugs will take care of you.

A diverse microbiome is the key to overall health. Through diet and lifestyle, we can manipulate the environment in which these microbes exist, thereby making them work for us instead of against us. Dr. Elisa Song, pediatrician and author of *Healthy Kids, Happy Kids*, emphasizes, "The good news is that it's never too late to have a healthier, happier gut microbiome."

What Is an Easy Way of Checking How Your Gut Is Doing?

Here's a straightforward way to check how your gut is doing: Pooping! If your poop is like brown water or soft mushy mashed potatoes, you have diarrhea—your gut bugs are sad. If your poop looks like little rocks or is hard to poop, you are constipated—your gut bugs are sad. If your poop looks like a long twisty soft cucumber, then you did an excellent job with your poop. Give yourself a pat on the back, your gut bugs are happy.

Dr. Vincent states that if you have a gut issue, it can show up in another part of your body, creating symptoms like mental fog, allergies, sinus issues, skin rashes, migraines, or constant illness.

The bugs in our gut eat what we eat. When we are sitting at the table for a meal, they are sitting right along with us. The food we eat can

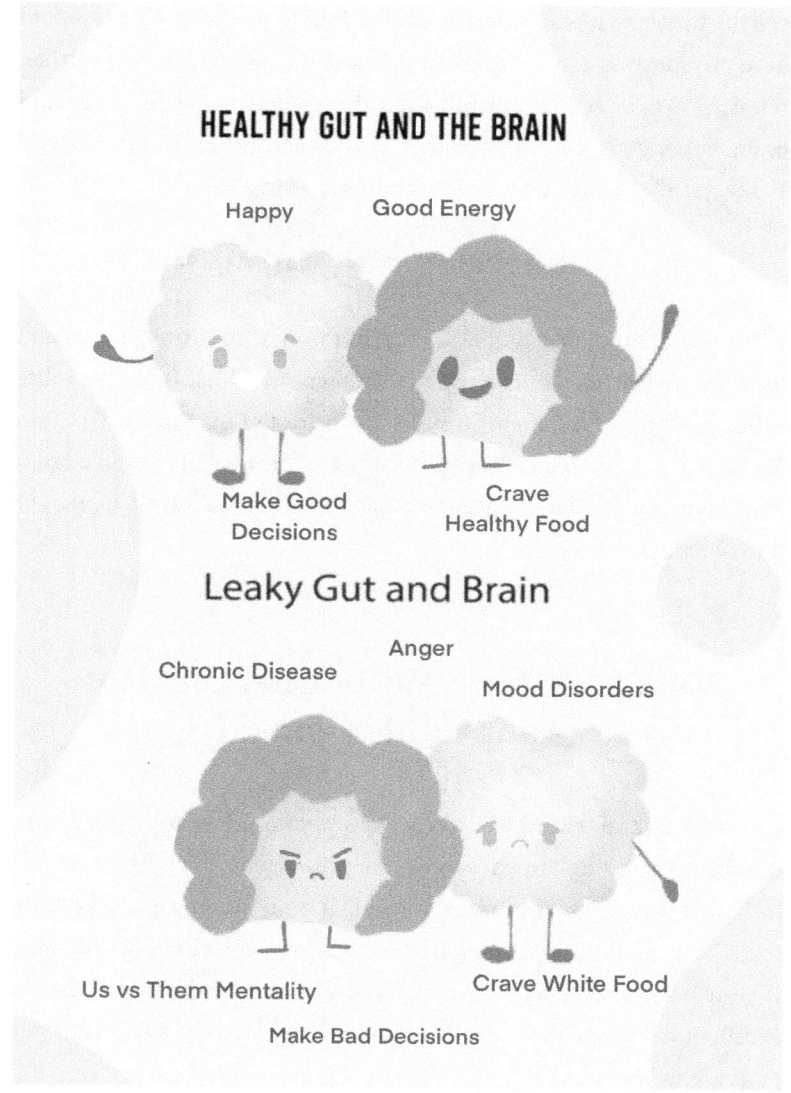

FIGURE 3.3 *The gut and the brain. Illustration by Zain Ansari.*

either hurt them or nourish them. The biggest factor in deciding how healthy our gut microbiome is by the food we eat. Let's talk about the "food-like substances," aka ultra-processed foods, which are destroying our microbiome, and thereby destroying our mind, body, and soul.

#1 Gut Disruptor—Ultra-Processed Foods

Americans love ultra-processed food. Ultra-processed foods are now 70 percent of what teens are eating.[3] But what are they? They are industrial ingredients that have been created through industrial techniques. That is where the ULTRA in ultra-processed food comes from.

Do you know those addictive snacks and treats that everybody loves? We are talking about stuff like white bread, cookies, cakes, candy, and the list goes on and on. The main feature of ultra-processed food that most people do not think about is that the processing is so extreme that we could not make it at home even if we tried. There is a show on Netflix called *Snack vs Chef*, where chefs try to recreate common favorites, but they are never fully able to. Almost every single time, whatever they made looked completely different from the original snack.

 Ultra-processed food is a science experiment, and they are experimenting on us.

The Science Experiment

The food we are eating now is completely different from the food our ancestors and our parents ate.

Just look at the back of a bag of US Nacho Cheese Doritos today:

whole corn, vegetable oil (corn, soybean, and/or sunflower oil), salt, cheddar cheese (milk, cheese cultures, salt, enzymes), maltodextrin, whey, monosodium glutamate, buttermilk solids, Romano cheese (part skim cow's milk, cheese cultures, salt, enzymes), whey protein concentrate, onion powder, partially hydrogenated soybean and cottonseed oil, corn flour, disodium phosphate, lactose, natural and artificial flavor, dextrose, tomato powder, spices, lactic acid, artificial color (including Yellow 6, Yellow 5, Red 40), citric acid, sugar, garlic powder, red and green bell pepper powder, sodium caseinate, disodium inosinate, disodium guanylate, nonfat milk solids, whey protein isolate, corn syrup solids.

Does this look like something that could be made in a kitchen, or does it look like it was made in a lab by scientists? When was the last time you were in the kitchen and made chips with twenty or more ingredients?

When did it start? Well, in the twentieth century, they started swapping out real food for chemically altered foods, or as we like to call it, "fake food." Nearly half of the foods marketed for kids and almost all the candies and fruity snacks contain artificial dyes and other junky stuff that is not meant for our bodies or gut bugs. The gut bugs eat what we eat and hate these fake foods. These fake foods kill off the good gut bugs, changing the composition of the gut bugs, leading to wildfires and disease.

Ultra-Processed Foods Are Destroying Us

Sadly, it is a global diet of doom, causing eleven million deaths yearly![4] What's even worse, all those additives and sugars can really mess up our gut bugs, causing that wildfire (inflammation), destroying our hormone balance, wrecking our blood sugar balance, and even leading to serious health issues in the future. Studies have shown that ultra-processed food can increase the risk of diabetes, heart disease, fatty liver disease, and even depression. Ultra-processed foods have been proven to be linked to over thirty-two different chronic health conditions. It can even cause harm like smoking and overeating.[5]

It does not stop there. Especially during the teenage years, fake food can mess with our brains, making it harder to think clearly, learn new things, and even control our impulses. Studies have shown that eating lots of junk food can increase our risk of feeling down or anxious. In fact, a study found that teens who eat a ton of junk food are almost 50 percent more likely to show signs of depression, have 10 percent smaller brains, and a lower IQ.[6] Ultra-processed foods are destroying our mind,[7] body, and soul, leading to an early death.[8] (Figure 3.4).

Most people have turned ultra-processed food from a want to a need, making it much harder to stop eating.

Take Back Control—Educate Ourselves on Fake Foods

The food world is confusing. Our food is becoming weaponized to confuse our bodies at a very high level. Over twenty-one million people in the United States depend on the food industry for jobs. What about the research? Did you know that ultra-processed food companies donate to large medical organizations such as the American Academy of Pediatrics and the American Diabetes Association? These are the same organizations that are making our recommendations!

Do your own research to find the truth in all the confusion and misinformation around food and food-like substances. You do not have to be enslaved to the food industry.

Let us catch you up on what we have learned about these deadly ingredients in more detail. This will help you make more mindful choices about what you want and do not want to put in your body.

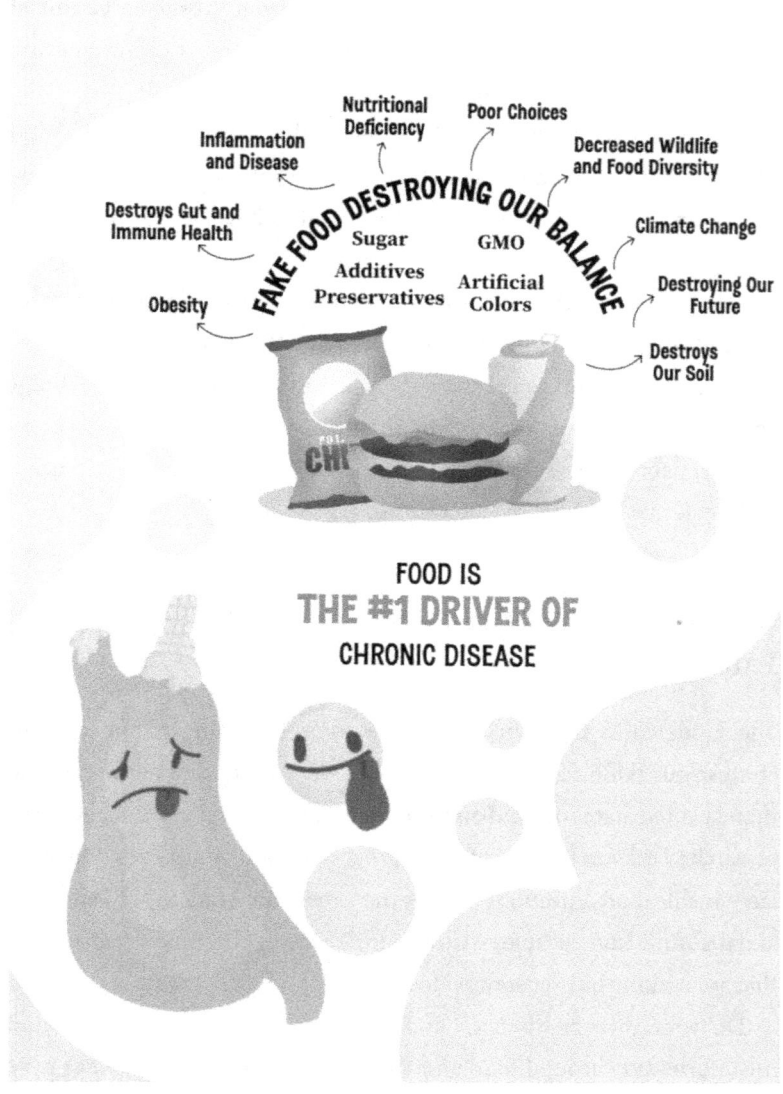

FIGURE 3.4 *Food is the number one driver of chronic disease. Illustration by Zain Ansari.*

Additives

Food additives are substances that are added to foods to serve a function like changing the color, consistency, texture, and taste, making it appealing to our every sense. Additives cause uncontrollable hunger and binge eating. They can also be added to prevent mold growth and prolong the shelf life. Additives can be natural or synthetic. They can be one chemical or a mixture of many chemicals.

The responsibility of regulating our food falls mostly in the laps of the Food and Drug Administration (FDA). They regulate 80 percent of the American food supply. A new food additive or chemical can get introduced into our food system by petitioning the FDA, and they have to consider the evidence about that substance. There must be a consensus in the scientific community that it is safe. GRAS substances are food additives that are generally recognized as safe (GRAS). But the problem is that in 1997, the FDA loosened the protocol, allowing companies themselves to declare substances as GRAS without notifying the FDA. This created a new loophole that allowed companies to greenlight thousands of substances that have entered the food supply. The FDA can always go back and say something is not GRAS, but with so many new substances and the FDA's resources, it is impossible to go through them all. Since the year 2000, 99 percent of the new chemicals that have entered our food supply have done so through the GRAS loophole and have avoided FDA scrutiny. There are approximately 10,000 approved food chemicals, only half of which have been approved. The European Union has approved only 411 additives and has no GRAS equivalent. Sadly, the number of additives on the market continues to increase. Science has now shown the harmful effects of additives. The global food additive market in 2024 is $310.9 billion and is forecasted to reach $551.4 billion by 2034.[9] Many additives are banned for use in different countries because of their effects, as they have been found to directly harm the gut microbiome and lead to disease.[13] Oh, and did we mention that the FDA is funded by the pharmaceutical industry? This is why we need to educate ourselves! Mr. Calley Means, NYT best-selling author of *Good Energy*, stresses that every day there are new chemicals added to our food. The FDA does not know of all the chemicals that are in our food. The FDA has been asleep at the wheel, as the FDA has a nonprofit sector that accepts funding from the food industry.

Food Additives Are Everywhere

Types of food additives are anticaking agents, antioxidants, artificial sweeteners, emulsifiers, food acids, humectants, flavors, flavor enhancers, mineral salts, preservatives, thickeners, vegetable gums, stabilizers and firming agents, flour treatments, glazing agents, gelling agents, propellants, raising agents, and bulking agents. Get the picture? There are so many different things that can be added to our food. Let us go through some:

Preservatives—Preservatives are substances that are artificially made to keep food from becoming old. For example, preservatives would keep a piece of bread fresh for weeks. If you have ever heard that McDonald's food lasts a long time, this is why.

Color Additives—Coloring additives are everywhere. These are extremely common in food, snacks, beverages, and medications. These additives are most commonly used to make the food more appealing but are associated with everything from cancer to hyperactivity in kids. These are present in all our favorite-colored candies, like Skittles, Jell-O, cake mixes, Takis, Cheetos, Doritos, and even in Costco cakes! Some common artificial color additives (made from petroleum) include:

- Yellow 5 and 6: A yellow dye found in a variety of foodstuffs and drinks like gummy candy, soft drinks, and puddings or custards. It can cause allergic reactions such as asthma, urticaria, hives, itching, coughing, and vomiting and can cause adrenal tumors.

- Red 40: A coloring agent known as red dye that is a constituent of beverages, desserts, snacks, and ultra-processed food items. It can cause brain toxic effects, irritability, ADHD, aggressive behavior, depression, hyperactivity, skin irritation, migraines, watery eyes, or sneezing; accelerates the appearance of tumors and more. Found to be contaminated by cancer-causing agents. Red #3 has recently been banned from our food thirty-five years after it was banned in cosmetics.
- Blue 1: A blue dye that is used in candies, desserts, and drinks. It can cause hyperactivity, increased risk of kidney tumors, skin rashes, hives, nasal congestion, and more.
- Caramel color: brown food coloring linked to cancer.

Other Additives

- Aluminum additives: toxic to brain cells.
- Butylated hydroxytoluene (BHT): proved to cause cancer in animal tests; can cause liver, thyroid, and kidney problems and affects lung functions and blood clotting. Butylated hydroxyanisole (BHA) is listed as a cancer-causing agent.
- Calcium propionate: found in all commercial bread produces a toxin that harms the brain and contributes to autism and sleep disturbances.
- Carrageenan: leads to inflammation, leaky gut and is a possible cancer-causing agent.
- High fructose corn syrup: your liver must work harder to break it down, increases the risk of fatty liver disease and diabetes, obesity, and heart disease.
- Monosodium glutamate: damages brain cells, leading to headaches, allergies and damages the gut. This is what increases

food cravings and irresistibility. MSG can be disguised as autolyzed protein, yeast extract, calcium caseinate, gelatin, glutamate, glutamic acid, hydrolyzed plant protein, maltodextrin, modified corn starch, modified food starch, monopotassium glutamate, natural flavor, protein isolate, seasonings, soy sauce, sodium caseinate, textured protein, yeast extract, yeast food, and yeast nutrient.

- Nitrates and nitrites: found in processed meats, probable cancer-causing agents.
- Potassium bromates: a dough conditioner, causes cancer in animals and "possibly carcinogenic" for humans.
- Sodium benzoate or potassium benzoate: synthetic preservatives that when combined with vitamin C produce benzene which is a known carcinogen.
- Tartaric acid: an emulsifier to make bread fluffier, destroys gut lining that leads to digestive disease.
- Tert-butyl hydroquinone (TBHQ): a synthetic preservative found in packaged fried foods and commercial seed oils linked to stimulating the immune system, behavioral problems, stomach cancer, liver enlargement, vision issues, and negatively affects T cells and promotes allergies.
- There are so many others like titanium dioxide, propylparaben and brominated vegetable oil, sulfite, propyl gallate (carcinogen) . . . read the label and if you can't pronounce it and don't know what it is—DON'T EAT IT!

Natural Flavors?

Natural flavors are anything but natural! They are a mixtures of chemicals derived from anything in nature. Flavors may have up to one hundred ingredients, including synthetic chemicals, additives, propylene glycol as a solvent, and the preservative BHA, as well as GMO derived ingredients, and MSG. Organic natural flavors are likely better.

Artificial Sweeteners

Artificial sweeteners are substitutes for sugar that add sweetness to food and drinks without increasing calories or impacting blood sugar levels. They are anywhere from 200–500 times sweeter than sugar. Artificial sweeteners like aspartame and sucralose are synthetic chemicals which are linked to causing hunger, gas, bloating, have a detrimental effect on gut bacteria, lead to headaches, increase anxiety, sleep issues, weight gain, obesity and contribute to type 2 diabetes and cancer. Others are saccharin (linked to bladder cancer) and acesulfame potassium (Ace K). Stay far away from these fake sweeteners!

Bad Oils

Vegetable oils can often be found lurking in things like baked goods. Just because they have the word vegetable in its name does not mean it is healthy. Think of corn oil, soybean oil, canola oil, and others. These oils are hydrogenated, which means they have trans fats.

These oils are loaded with omega-6 fats, which can cause inflammation in our bodies and mess with our gut health, leading to leaky gut syndrome. They can also mess with our immune system and cell metabolism, upping our risk for heart disease, obesity, diabetes, and even cancer.[11]

#2 Gut Disruptor—Sugar

We all love our lattes, donuts, cookies, and cakes. Refined sugar has now infiltrated our lives; it is found in 74 percent of packaged foods, even foods that we would never expect to have so much sugar. Findings by the National Health and Nutrition Survey show that the average teenager consumes 28.3 teaspoons per day![12] That is three times more than the new recommendations.

Ultra-processed sugar has been designed specifically to make money and even hurt us. The question is how? Ultra-processed sugar can cause fatty liver, cell aging, and it can interfere with your brain's functioning to regulate how much to eat, and that is what makes it so much more toxic. With so many adults and children suffering from being overweight and obese, it is time to change before it gets worse.

The Food Industry Has Us Hooked on Sugar

The food industry has been increasing how much sugar there is in products for the last thirty years. Sugar is how they are making money. The question is, who is going to stop them?

Our bodies can only manage a little bit of sugar, meaning that a little is okay but a lot is not. Sugar is being slipped into all our food without us knowing. When we looked at the ingredients of a ketchup bottle and found out that there was over a teaspoon of sugar in it we thought "why in the world would there be sugar in ketchup or tomato sauce?" Sugar is everywhere from baked beans to mayonnaise. Take a look in your pantry and you will be surprised about how much sugar is in what you're eating. You have probably eaten a lot of sugar without even thinking about it. Even your pumpkin swirl frozen coffee has 185 g of sugar in one drink! That is forty-six teaspoons of sugar or fourteen glazed donuts. Get this: in the ingredient list there are twelve mentions of sugar or high fructose corn syrup and not even any pumpkin in it!!! Only artificial flavors!

Get sugar out of your system and beware of all its other code names like bran sugar, dextrose, glucose, dextran, fructose, agave, barley malt, brown rice syrup, high fructose corn syrup (HFCS), hydrogenated starch, maltodextrin, maltose, lactose, disaccharides, monosaccharides, sorghum, sucrose and xylose. Sugar is hidden in everything.

Sugar Is Poison!

We are going to say it like it is—sugar is poison, and we know that might make you mad when you hear that but that is just the reality. If you still do not believe us, then do your own research. Ultra-processed sugar is killing us, and we do not even know it. Overeating sugar is damaging our bodies. Ultra-processed sugar has been engineered to make us addicted, meaning it is not entirely our fault.

> You're not supposed to eat so much sugar at one time and then your body can't handle it properly. Over time that can cause issues with some of your organs like your liver and pancreas.
>
> —Dr. Joel Warsh, pediatrician, author of
> *Parenting at Your Own Pace*

Abdullah was sitting in class waiting for the bell for class to end one day, when the teacher announced that the school administration was considering banning certain sugar-packed candy like Skittles and Oreos. That is when the entire class erupted saying things like, "they can't do that" and "I need my candy and cookies!"

Abdullah looked over to his classmate and just casually said, "I mean, it is not the end of the world. Don't you know what that stuff does to your body?"

His classmate shrugged and said, "No I just like the taste of Oreos."

Abdullah said, "Well sugar actually changes how our brain works which affects us physically, emotionally and psychologically."

He looked at Abdullah, confused, and said, "Wow! I did not know that!"

So let us tell you what sugar does.

Sugar harms our brain. Studies show that teens who ate too much sugar were at high risk for cognitive problems, obesity and hyperactivity as adults.[13] Sugar can even affect our behavior.

When we eat a lot of sugar it shrinks the brain. People who have a high sugar diet have smaller brains than people who eat low sugar diets and this is based on MRI scans done in adults. I rest my case.

—Dr. Ana Maria Temple, pediatrician, author of
Healthy Kids in an Unhealthy World

Sugar negatively influences our immune system. Thirty minutes after eating simple sugar, immune cells that eat up the bad guys decrease by 50 percent! This lasts up to five hours.[14]

Sugar feeds the bad bugs in the gut, leading to gut dysbiosis and inflammation.[15] Sugar can also lead to an elevation of glucose, leading to insulin resistance and blood sugar imbalances.

Sugar leads to weight gain and chronic disease.[16] Diets excessive in added sugars were related to continual diseases which include type 2 diabetes, coronary heart disorder, and metabolic syndrome.

You think, "I'm stressed, I just need sugar . . . it helps me feel better." But did you know that sugar does not help your body during times of stress? It makes it worse, as sugar before a stressful event can make that stress seem worse than it actually is.[17]

Sugar in Drinks

"Don't drink soda, it is just poison," says Dr. Molly Maloof. "It is like pouring water in a car's gas tank."

Sugary drinks are now a huge part of our diets. We might not realize this but even a small can of Coca Cola will have more than five teaspoons! In one bottle of Coca Cola there is around five days' worth of the recommended intake of sugar. If someone's diet is high in sugary drinks it can lead to problems in every part of their body, especially their teeth. One can of soda a day can increase the risk for type two diabetes by 26 percent.[18] These drinks have been linked to weight gain, obesity, type 2 diabetes, heart disease, kidney disease, and nonalcoholic fatty liver disease. There are diseases that were never seen in kids before but now are on the rise. When you drink a sugary drink, it has been linked to increased risk of premature death. Beverage companies spend billions on marketing sugary drinks. Oh, and alcohol is just sugar too. Stay away from it, it destroys your brain, liver, and gut. Also avoid fruit juices, as they have a lot of sugar.

#3 Gut Disruptor—GMOs

What really are GMOs? It means Genetically Modified Organisms. GMOs are created through biotechnology. GMOs are organisms where the DNA has been changed in a lab, from plants, animals, viruses, or bacteria to produce foreign compounds that cannot occur in nature. GMOs were designed to withstand the exposure of herbicide/pesticide like glyphosate (the main ingredient of Roundup) and/or to produce an insecticide.

> As a science-based physician, I believe that GMOs and pesticides are affecting kids' health.
>
> —Dr. Michelle Perro, physician, co-author of *What's Making Our Children Sick?*

Glyphosate is a pesticide used on GMO plants and used to dry crops after harvest, like wheat, chickpeas, and legumes. The news has been talking all about glyphosate and cancer. This stuff was made to be an antibiotic by Monsanto, but today it is used in weed killers. As an antibiotic, it destroys the bugs in the soil, leading to soil that does not have the nutrients that it once had. It also destroys the gut bugs, as it kills beneficial probiotic bacteria while not touching the harmful ones.[19]

Glyphosate exposure has also been connected to things like more cases of cancer, allergies, and issues with our digestive health and immune systems. It hurts the brain because it destroys the gut. It damages our liver. Even a little bit of exposure can cause damage to cells in unborn babies and affect how our genes work. It can even mess with our hormones and potentially mess up our chances of having healthy kids in the future, as glyphosate exposure can lead to ADHD, autism, and emotional problems in your future children.[20] As little as three weeks of roundup can dramatically decrease the diversity of your microbiome.

The FDA, which is supposed to make sure our food is safe, didn't even do their own tests on these foods before saying they were okay.[21] That means the only tests done were by the companies making the GMO seeds and chemicals which means there's probably some bias.

All of us are different about how much glyphosate we can tolerate, so it is best to avoid it altogether. What foods are we talking about here? Things like soy, canola, corn, cornstarch, soybean oil, cottonseed oil, corn syrup, corn oil, sugar, and even some fruits and veggies like potatoes, summer squash, apples, rainbow papayas, and pink pineapples. Even meat and dairy, as the animals eat 95 percent GMO feed. Despite what we are told, there is no solid evidence that genetically modified foods help us grow more food or solve world hunger. It is something we need to think about when we are making choices about what we eat, so it is best to eat organic when possible.

Take Care of Your Microbiome

Kiran Krishnan, microbiologist and gut expert, recommends eating real food. The more diverse food you eat, the more diverse your gut bugs are, the healthier you are. Go outside in nature. Avoid toxic personal care products, as many of them have a negative impact on your gut bugs. Do not over-sanitize your home. He also recommended fasting to improve your microbiome diversity. Remember, our gut microbiome starts in our mouths. Dr. Mark Burhenne, world-renowned dentist, explained to us that the best way to take care of the oral microbiome is to leave it alone and to let it do its job. The good bugs need fiber and prebiotics, and do not over disinfect it. Dr. Elisa Song, pediatrician and author of *Healthy Kids, Happy Kids*, breaks down the five things every kid needs to do to create "microbiome magic" every day. She emphasized to keep our microbiome healthy we need to nourish ourselves well, breathe, move, drink, and sleep. We will go through these in the chapters to come.

Your gut is important. It is the gateway to your health. Remember, small changes over time create a profound effect on your health. Are you looking at your lunch right now and confused whether you should eat it or not?

Now that we talk about all the food we should avoid, let us talk about the foods we should concentrate on. We must tell you; we LOVE talking about this next topic! Yes, we talk about it at school, at home . . . you know why? We love real food!!!

What Do the Holistic Kids Do?

We take our gut health seriously, so we eat real food and never eat fake food. Yes, you heard that right. We will never put these artificial ingredients in our bodies. Knowing this information gives us power, because we do not want to be tricked into doing something we know is not good for us. In our house, we call them "food-like substances" or chemicals. At school, everyone eats pizza, and yes it smells great, but we know that it just looks like food, but it is not, so it does not even look appetizing to us anymore. We do not crave it. We do not want it. We know you may think we are lying, but honestly, when you have learned as much as we have, and have tried real food, we cannot stand the sight of fake food. When Abdullah was ten years old, Emaad made a gingerbread house with all the artificially colored candies on it. Emaad brought it home, but Abdullah could not stand looking at it, to him it just looked like poison. When Zain was seven, he got candy from school, he came home and threw it out, saying why would I give poison to someone else? It is all poisonous chemicals. So, does poison ever look appetizing? NO!

In the next chapter, we will provide you with more information about what you *can* eat and give you some sample meal ideas!

Revolution Recap: Revolution the Gut

- Get rid of fake food, sugar, and GMOs.
- Eat more vegetables and fiber.
- Eat more fermented foods.
- Drink more water.
- Get out in nature and exercise.

4

E—Eat Real Food

Food is power. Food is information.
Food makes up every cell of our body.
We are made up of food.
Food can either help us or hurt us.
Choose wisely.

Good nutrition is important for everybody but it's even more important for kids, because kids are still growing and they're still developing their brains, their bones, their muscles, and tissues.
—Chris Kresser, author of *Unconventional Medicine*

Foods to Optimize Our Brains, Body, and Soul!

There is nothing like the smell of freshly baked chocolate chip cookies, the taste of a homemade pizza, the satisfying crunch of crispy fried chicken, the vibrance of a colorful salad, the sizzle of a steak on the grill, or the warmth of a hearty chicken soup on a cold day . . . ahhhh! The joys of food! Food is not just enjoyable, but every cell of our body is made from food. We are made from food. Real food contains biological instructions that promote health, lower inflammation, balance hormones, optimize brain function, improve the gut microbiome, and even optimize gene expression.

Real foods can reverse climate change, build our soils, thereby increasing nutrients, biodiversity, restoring the ecosystem, and protecting our water. These real foods contain 25,000 or more phytochemicals in the plant kingdom and are critical for overall health. These foods influence all the thirty-seven billion chemical reactions that occur in our bodies every second. We are made from nature. We need nature's food to connect us all and increase our spirituality and faith.

Now that we have learned what to avoid, what do we eat? I do not know about you, but we LOVE to eat. Whenever we eat, we make sure we eat food that:

1. Keeps our gut happy, healthy, and diverse.
2. Regulates our glucose levels, decreases insulin resistance, and balances hormones.
3. Is super nutrient-dense.

What are these foods? Two words: REAL FOOD! We focus on real foods to improve our mind, body, and soul.

Whenever we are hungry, go down the list:

1. Veggies
2. Clean protein
3. Healthy fats
4. Healthy carbohydrates (like fruit)
5. Hydration

Figure 4.1 is what a healing plate should look like.

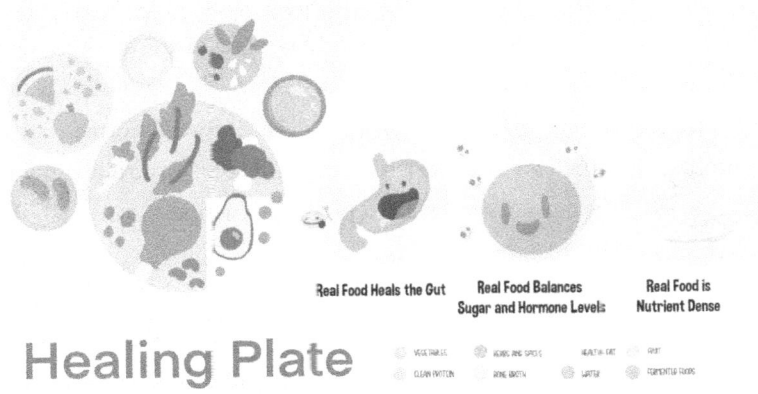

FIGURE 4.1 *The healing plate. Illustration by Zain Ansari.*

Nutrition is the study of food and how it works in our body. Why is nutrition so important for teens? Can't we wait until we are older to focus on our health? Teens can eat whatever they want whenever they want, right?

WRONG! Our bodies are growing and changing every day. If we do not take enough calories and nutrients, then we can experience health complications like stunted growth, delayed puberty, and menstrual irregularities, which can negatively affect our mood, energy levels, and even athletic and academic performances. We talked about how food affects our gut health and microbiome, but food even affects our hormones and blood sugar balance.

Food Affects Our Blood Sugar and Hormones

Hormone imbalances are on the rise. More teens today are becoming prediabetic (the stage before diabetes) and insulin resistant. Insulin resistance is stealing our future.

Before we dive into what insulin resistance is, let's first start to talk about what happens when we eat food. We are made of cells. Our cells need glucose for energy. Glucose can't enter the cell unless it has a key called insulin. Insulin is a protein and fat storage hormone that is produced by the pancreas, which is responsible for controlling blood sugar levels. This key opens the cell door and allows the glucose into the cell from your bloodstream.

Over time, the flood of increased blood sugar, stress, or inflammation starts to wear down this key because it keeps on using it repeatedly. When the key wears down, the body has more difficulty listening to the insulin, so the body pushes more insulin out until the key stops working completely and the body stops responding to insulin. When this happens, the body is unable to absorb glucose adequately, leading to diabetes (Figure 4.2).

Insulin manages our glucose levels. For years, we may not notice insulin resistance, as the body is working harder by pumping extra insulin, forcing the glucose into the cells. During this time, the blood sugar may be normal. But over time, the cells get overwhelmed and are filled with fat and mitochondria that do not work well—this is when you will see a rise in blood sugar. This leads to blood sugar problems like prediabetes and diabetes that affect almost 30 percent of children! Studies have shown that children with the highest levels of insulin are thirty-six times more likely to become obese as adults.[1] This state of rising blood sugar leads to hormonal imbalances, overeating, chronic inflammation, and weight gain—this is a problem when currently 93 percent of US adults have some sort of metabolic dysfunction.[2] Kids with metabolic dysfunction (when the body is unable to process food into energy) are at higher risk for infections.[3]

Insulin resistance is the root of many of the common chronic diseases, but symptoms can start long before. Insulin resistance affects our brains, bodies, and behavior. Symptoms of insulin resistance are

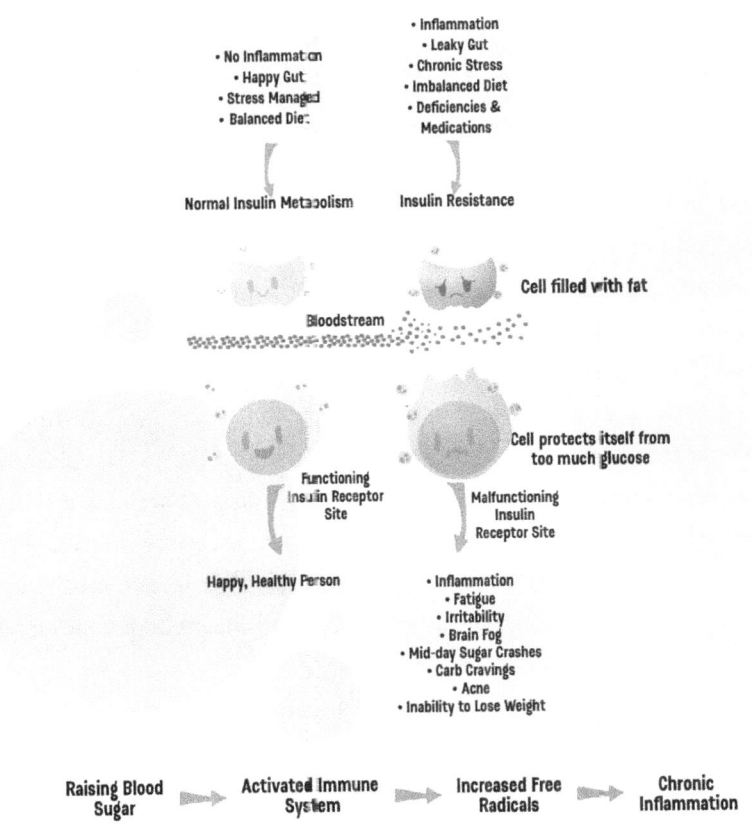

FIGURE 4.2 *Our cells and insulin. Illustration by Zain Ansari.*

fatigue, irritability, brain fog, memory or concentration issues, weight gain around the midsection, sugar crashes in the middle of the day, and the inability to lose weight. Someone may be addicted to carbohydrates, yet still have hypoglycemic attacks. Other symptoms are acne, irregular periods, premature puberty, skin around the folds and creases that can become dark and thick (acanthosis nigricans), infertility, cysts, polycystic ovarian syndrome, and increased hair growth. Fatty liver may also occur, which has now become prevalent in teens. This occurs when metabolic dysfunction leads to liver cells filling up with fat and worsening insulin resistance.

What Is Causing Insulin Resistance?

Our blood sugar imbalances are directly related to our diets full of fake foods. Look at this chart of the glycemic load of common foods. The glycemic load (GL) is a measure of how much a food or meal raises blood sugar levels. Fake foods raise your blood sugar higher than eating real food (Figure 4.3).

A lack of fiber can lead to increased visceral fat, while artificial sweeteners have been linked to weight gain and diabetes. Stress, leaky gut, or dysbiosis, pesticides, toxins in the environment are now making the cells numb to insulin. Sleep deprivation, a sedentary lifestyle, and stress can influence hormones, which can then alter insulin sensitivity. Nutrient deficiencies (especially vitamin D and magnesium deficiency) are leading to insulin resistance in teens.

Sadly, food companies have also mastered the science of glucose spikes to make foods more addictive, as cravings can happen after a blood sugar spike followed by a sugar crash. Diets rich in ultra-processed foods make us eat more. Also, let's not forget leptin. Leptin is a hormone that regulates appetite, it tells us when we are full. Just like insulin resistance,

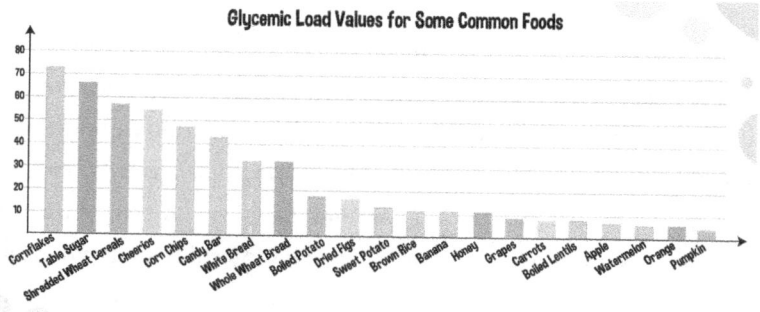

FIGURE 4.3 *Glycemic load values for some common foods. Illustration by Zain Ansari.*

when we eat ultra-processed foods, it can lead to leptin resistance, which can make us overeat and is associated with obesity in teens.

The Solution—Eat Real Food!

The food we eat can either help or hurt our health. We talked a lot about food that hurts us in the last chapter, but what about food that helps us, that nourishes us, that heals us and the planet—one bite at a time? Choose real food for all its benefits. Remember, vegetables, clean protein, and healthy fats. Eat the real food rainbow.

Vegetables

Half of your plate should be vegetables. A vegetable is the edible part of a plant, vegetables usually come in all diverse types of shapes, sizes, colors, and flavors. Now, I know what you are thinking: "But veggies are boring!" Hear me out—there's a whole rainbow of veggies out there, many more colors than just green, and they're cooler than you think. We are talking about a veggie party and everyone is invited!

Rainbow Foods

When it comes to food, the more real color foods we have in our diet, the better. Let's start with the rainbow color vegetables because believe it or not, vegetables aren't just green. Dr. Deanna Minich, author of *The Rainbow Diet*, recommends the importance of eating the rainbow, meaning we select plants from each of those colors (Figure 4.4).

Red foods like tomatoes, peppers, beets, and carrots lower inflammation.

Orange foods (carrots, pumpkins, sweet potatoes, orange bell peppers, and squash varieties) are great for eye and reproductive health.

FIGURE 4.4 *Eat the real food rainbow. Illustration by Zain Ansari.*

Yellow foods like yellow corn, peppers, carrots, squash are great for your digestion as they contain fiber.

Green foods (greens, collards, broccoli, bok choy, cabbage, kale, arugula, watercress, mustard, fennel, broccoli sprouts, etc.) are packed with sulforaphane, which raises glutathione (a super antioxidant of the body) that may help to prevent cancer and contribute to detoxification.

Sea vegetables like seaweed or edible algae are rich sources of iodine and strengthen the immune system. We love seaweed and broccoli sprouts!

Blue-purple foods like purple potatoes, red cabbage, and eggplants are great for brain health and detoxification. We love our coleslaw! Emaad always says he is eating his glucoraphanin when he eats red cabbage. Glucoraphanin supports sulforaphane that increases glutathione!

Brown foods like mushrooms and dark chocolate can enhance immune function.

White foods (garlic, onions, cauliflower) have powerful antimicrobial, immune-boosting, anticancer and anti-tumor properties.

The world of color is so good for you!

Importance of Fiber

Most of these vegetables have fiber that is important as it feeds healthy bacteria, helps us feel full, stabilizes blood sugar, and helps fight chronic disease by lowering inflammation. Ninety-five percent of Americans are fiber deficient. One should aim for about 25–30 g per day for a teen girl or 30–38 g per day if you are a teen boy. We love making apple sauce at home— it has fiber specifically from pectin that keeps the gut bugs very happy.

Foods that are rich in fiber per cup (approximate)

- Split peas, cooked: 16 g
- Lentils, cooked: 15 g
- Black beans, cooked: 15 g
- Chickpeas, cooked: 12.5 g
- Kidney beans, cooked: 11 g
- Avocado: up to 10 g
- Chia seeds: 2 tablespoons: 10 g
- Artichoke: medium: 10 g
- Raspberries: 8 g
- Edamame, cooked: 8 g

How can you start incorporating fiber into your diet? Add it to your favorite foods. We love to use lentil pasta, packed with vegetables that can be added to the meat sauce. We love chia pudding, topped with berries, nuts, and seeds. We love to add fresh guacamole to everything, and we also have prebiotic fiber powders that we can add to our smoothies!

Eat Your Ps: Prebiotics, Probiotics, and Postbiotics

Prebiotics are "food" for probiotics. They nourish and stimulate the growth of "good" bacteria while reducing disease-causing bacteria and lowering inflammation. Prebiotics can be found in green leafy vegetables and other high-fiber foods, like asparagus, carrots, garlic, leeks, raw onions, radishes, tomatoes, apples, flaxseeds, garlic, Jerusalem artichoke, konjac root, seaweed, carrots, pear, chicory root, cocoa, dandelion greens, flax seeds, and burdock root.

Probiotics are beneficial bugs that live in our gut, found in fermented foods such as unpasteurized natural sauerkraut, yogurt, and kefir. Probiotics support your gut and its functions, lowering the amount of harmful bugs. Think of these probiotic foods as your "extra-special probiotic pals." Dr. Tom O'Bryan, author of *Autoimmune Fix* and *You Can Fix Your Brain*, emphasizes that eating a little bit of fermented vegetables every day can make us run faster, think faster, be stronger, and react quicker.

Postbiotics, like butyrate, are the waste left behind after your body digests the prebiotics and probiotics. Healthy postbiotics can slow down the growth of harmful bacteria and lower inflammation. We can get more postbiotics by eating the rainbow, eating more prebiotics, high-fiber foods, and eating more foods rich in butyrate like ghee and fermented foods.

Clean Protein

Protein is not only used for getting bigger muscles; it also helps us grow, thrive, heal, control our appetite, and balance our hormones. When it comes to protein, quality is important over quantity.

We should always choose grass-fed, pasture-raised, organic protein because they are much higher in omega-3 fatty acids which are great for fighting disease. Sardines, clams, oysters, and salmon are great options if packed in olive oil. Dr. Terry Wahls recommends having organ meats once a week. That can be difficult, so we add organ meat supplements or spices.

Foods with the highest protein per ounce:

- Chicken: 9 g
- Lean beef: 7 g
- Salmon: 5.6 g
- Tuna: 8 g
- Tofu: 2 g
- Lentils: 2.3 g
- Raw Beans: 6.1 g
- Peanuts: 7 g

Healthy Fats

Healthy fats are our brain and body's best friend. They help our body absorb important nutrients, help cells grow, and support our immune system, hormone health, and metabolism. Healthy fats help us function properly.

What are sources of healthy fats? Ever heard of olive oil? It is so good for you and is great for cooking or drizzling on salads. We also love to eat olives as a snack. Grass-fed butter and ghee not only taste delicious but also have anticancer properties and can help heal your gut. Don't forget about avocados and coconut oil! Nuts and seeds are our favorites.

Next time you're thinking about snacks, reach for something with healthy fats. They will keep you satisfied! Remember to avoid processed oils and processed fats and try to go for organic options whenever you can (Figure 4.5).

FIBER
FEED HEALTHY BACTERIA

LOWER BLOOD PRESSURE

SUPPRESS APPETITE

REMOVE TOXINS

FIGHT CHRONIC DISEASE

CONTROL CRAVINGS

DECREASE INFLAMMATION

STABILIZES BLOOD SUGAR AFTER A MEAL

HEALTHY FATS
AIDS IN THE BODY'S IMPORTANT HORMONAL AND METABOLIC FUNCTIONS

REQUIRED TO MAKE CHOLESTEROL

BALANCING MOOD

NEEDED FOR CELL STRUCTURE

IMMUNE SYSTEM FUNCTIONING

REQUIRED TO MAKE HORMONES

AIDING IN DEMENTIA PREVENTION

AS OUR BRAINS ARE MORE THAN HALF FAT

CLEAN PROTEIN

OPTIMIZE IMMUNE SYSTEM

ABILITY TO BURN CALORIES

BUILD MATERIALS FOR ENZYMES

CONTROL APPETITE

SYNTHESIZE MUSCLE

INCREASE METABOLIC FIRE

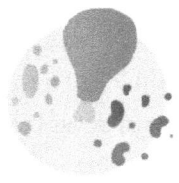

FIGURE 4.5 *The importance of fiber, healthy fats, and clean protein at every meal. Illustration by Zain Ansari.*

Hydration

Drinking water is so important to stay healthy, as we are made of 75 percent water. The sad thing is many people don't drink the recommended amount of water a day (including us). Water forms blood, digestive juices, urine, and is contained in muscle, fat, and bones. Our brain is made of 80 percent water, leading to headaches when you are dehydrated. Water can regulate body temperature, which is important for detoxification and improving brain function. Your age, gender, height, and how active you are dictate how much water you need a day. We recommend sticking to half your body weight in ounces. Remember that people with obesity are ten times as likely to be dehydrated as others that are leaner. Even one additional glass of water per day lowers a child's risk of becoming overweight by 30 percent.[4]

How to Drink More Water

We know water can be boring or bland, but it can also be fun.

- Add some lemon with a sweetener like honey or stevia
- Add some flavor with fruit
- Add electrolytes (find your favorite brand without artificial ingredients or natural flavors)
- Sparkling water
- Drink herbal teas packed with so many antioxidants!

Another way to remember to drink water is by filling up a huge water bottle and keeping it with you—that is what works for us. We also love steel straws. Do not use paper or plastic straws. When we drink more water, it makes a huge difference; we feel so much better!

Bone Broth

We also love to drink bone broth. Bone broth contains nutrients that can easily be absorbed, like calcium, magnesium, phosphorus, and sulfur. It helps heal and seal the gut lining, which is very important for your gut. It also promotes the growth of good bacteria, reduces inflammation and food sensitivities. A warm bone broth soup feels like a warm hug from the inside out.

Other Drinks

Around 83 percent of teens drink caffeinated beverages. Coffee may have some benefits but should be avoided by those who have diabetes, prediabetes, high stress levels, mood disorders, or difficulty sleeping. This is because coffee can increase insulin production and cortisol (as it can stress the adrenal out more). Some teens can tolerate coffee (black or with coconut/nut milk). The American Academy of Pediatrics recommends that kids between twelve to eighteen should limit their caffeine intake to less than 100 mg per day, which is about one small cup. Remember, teens are more sensitive to caffeine. There was a study that showed consuming energy drinks was linked to poor mental health and substance use due to the caffeine.[5]

Teens should stay away from alcohol. Alcohol is just another form of sugar that spikes the blood sugar levels, provokes a leaky gut, impairs the liver, and messes with impulse control.

Nature's Candy: Fruit

 Every color of the real food rainbow provides its own healing powers.

Fruits don't just taste good; they have many different health benefits. They are packed with antioxidants, minerals, and vitamins that lower inflammation and improve detoxification. They lower the risk of diseases, including diabetes and cancer. As we said previously, each color of fruit has its own benefits to the body. Did you know stone fruits like peaches, plums, nectarines, apricots, cherries, lychee, and mango have anticancer properties and protect our DNA from being damaged? So cool . . . but there is more.

Pomegranates are also powerful fruits. Research has now shown that they can help prevent and treat lots of chronic conditions such as high blood pressure, oxidative stress, and even cancer through lowering overall inflammation. There is a bacterium in the gut called *Akkermansia muciniphila*, which makes up 1–3 percent of all bacteria in the gut. This specific strain can help improve glucose metabolism, decrease inflammation, and combat obesity. This is the power of food as medicine. Pomegranates and cranberries can increase these gut bacteria! Isn't that cool? If you can't tell . . . we love our fruit!

How to Eat More Fruit

Look for local, organic, and seasonal fruits in moderation, and if you think you are diabetic, overweight, or insulin resistant, then you should choose low glycemic fruits like oranges, pears, plums, peaches, watermelon, cantaloupe, apples, and nectarine, to be taken in less than a cup per day.

Widen your palate. Eat fruits you would normally not eat like amla (Indian gooseberry) or rambutan. Combine fruit with a protein and fat source. Some simple ways that you can incorporate more fruit into your life are by having them for snacks or adding them to smoothies, salads, and even by using them as natural sweeteners for certain recipes.

Is Organic Food Just Hype?

Is organic important? We need to decrease the toxic load that we are carrying. The best way to do that is by going organic. In agriculture, "organic" refers to a method of farming and food production that does not use any pesticides. Organic normally refers to foods or substances that have not been sprayed with pesticides or are not artificially made. If people do not eat organic, they are not having the same benefits as if they ate organic. Studies have shown that those who ate organic had less urinary pesticide.[6]

Organic food in packages usually has a label on it saying it is organic. If it's organic, it is already non-GMO. If it has a label calling it non-GMO, it's good but it's not the best. If you are on a budget, then check the Environmental Working Group's clean 15 (don't need to eat organic) and dirty dozen lists (eat organic). Remember, if you cannot afford any organic produce, that's okay—just buy the nonorganic versions.

What About Apeel? Apeel is made up of purified monoglycerides and diglycerides that leaves an ultrathin protective coating that slows the rate by which the produce spoils. There is not enough safety information on Apeel produce, so it is best to avoid. When doing our research, it looks safe, until you look at the ingredients list. Other ingredients, which are not named, make up 99.34 percent of the product! That is a big red flag! Unfortunately, they are starting to put it on organic fruit as well. Call the store to see if they use these products.

 What's a vampire's favorite fruit?
A blood orange!

Herbs and Spices

For the last centuries, humans have been eating with different herbs and spices. America has moved away from these herbs and spices and started putting artificial flavors in food. Adding herbs and spices to our meals is a powerful way to add rainbow foods to our diet. Herbs lower inflammation, improve brain function, regulate blood sugar levels, boost the immune system, fight infections, and boost metabolism. Try adding different spices like turmeric, ginger, cinnamon, garlic, rosemary, oregano, basil, cardamom, and even black seeds to your food. Experiment with spices from different countries. The more variety the better.

 Why don't skeletons like spicy food?
Because they don't have the stomach for it!

Sweets

We all love sweets. We talked about why sugar was bad for us in the last chapter, but what are healthy alternatives? Natural sweeteners are good for you and taste delicious! They are less processed, have antioxidants and minerals and help your body detoxify and heal. Try coconut sugar, maple syrup or sugar and raw honey. We also love organic raw stevia as an occasional treat. Stevia does not raise your blood sugar. We grew it in our house and the leaves were so delicious!

We use honey in our cakes and cookies, use maple syrup for our pancakes and stevia for our lemonade. We make cheesecake with maple sugar and have shared it at parties, no one can tell we didn't use sugar!

Salt

Salt is an essential element of our food. The type of salt is important. Lots of types of salts contain chemical ingredients like anticaking agents. Table salt is different from sea salt. Table salt is toxic and can make us sick.

Sea salt, Celtic salt, and Himalayan salt are more natural and unprocessed. These are full of trace minerals like magnesium and calcium, and so many more that are all needed for the body.

Whole Grains

Grains are the edible seeds of grass-like plants. As you learned from food pyramids in first grade, grains are important parts of our diets, especially whole grains. Whole grains are great sources of energy, and provide other nutritious elements such as fiber, vitamins, and minerals. Fiber keeps our tummy happy and our digestion running smoothly. It also helps us feel full.

Common Grains:

- Wheat
- Rice
- Oats
- Barley
- Corn
- Quinoa
- Buckwheat

The problem is that grains are complicated. Grains have been a major part of human diets for 14,000 years, but today we are eating more ultra-processed bread and grains leading us down the road to sickness.

The Shift to Ultra-Processed Grains

Bread used to be made from three ingredients—water, yeast, and flour, but today our breads can contain up to twenty ingredients, including salt, sugar, fats, a cocktail of chemicals like dough conditioners, ascorbic acid, bleach, and more. During the 1800s and 1900s people have changed up many grains to become processed and the nutritious food that people had been eating for centuries became detrimental to our health. Most of the commercial whole grain products have dealt with processing methods that have stripped away some of their nutritional value. We cannot stress enough about reading labels and choosing whole grain products with minimal processing and added ingredients. For most teens, unprocessed whole grains are okay to incorporate into our diets. If you are dealing with insulin resistance, prediabetes, or a chronic health condition, be more careful, as they do raise your blood sugar. Gluten is one of the more problematic grains.

The Problem with Gluten

Some teens may have problems with wheat. Wheat contains gluten, which is a protein found in grains like wheat, barley, rye, kamut, and spelled.

In the 1880s, we saw the industrialization of bread by producing mechanically milled the flour into fine flour. Then they added chemicals, and other ingredients, to increase the shelf life of bread. In the late 1800s, they invented commercial yeast that can last for weeks. In the 1930s, mass produced loaves made up a large part of the American's diet. Then we started to see the effects of eating bread that had all the nutrients removed from it, like pellagra, rickets, iron deficiency, and birth defects, so they started to fortify breads with nutrients. The white bread you see today adds chlorine dioxide gas to the flour before it reaches the manufacturing plant, bleaching the bread. Breads can contain azodicarbonamide that can be found in vinyl flooring and yoga mats, and a biproduct that can be cancerous. In the last fifty years, in order to increase its production, modern wheat has been hybridized (different varieties or species are intentionally crossed to create offspring with specific desired traits) and manipulated to contain a "super starch" that raises blood sugar higher than any other starches, leading to insulin resistance.

Unfortunately, the average human body reacts badly to today's gluten, prompting an immune response, leading to inflammation, including mental illnesses like depression and schizophrenia, autism, dementia, obesity, heart disease, and even cancer.

How is that possible if we do not feel sick when we eat it? We interviewed Dr. Tom O'Bryan, author of *Autoimmune Fix* and *You Can Fix Your Brain* who explained to us that the science shows that for every one person that gets a stomach problem when they eat a food that is not good for them, there are eight people that don't get stomach problems when they eat a food that is not good for them. Those people may not have stomach problems, but they can get brain, skin, joint problems, insomnia, or fatigue. That is why it is difficult for them to know what foods are bothering them and which are not.

Why is wheat causing a problem? The reason we get sick from wheat is because our immune system gets confused. Dr. Tom explains that at the first part of the intestine, there is a sentry that stands guard, to attack anything that does not belong. When we eat food with a bad bacteria, the sentry tries to fight the bad bug by activating the immune bullets, inflammation, and leaky gut to try to kill the bug. The problem is that the way the sentry recognizes the bug is by looking at the surface, by looking at the protein. Wheat has the same protein that is on the bad bacteria. Dr. Tom explains that every time anyone eats wheat, it looks like bad bacteria and the immune system attacks it every time we eat it. The crazy thing is that it affects everyone, even if we feel it or not.

The problem today is that because there is a lot more in our food, like GMOs, pesticides, and insecticides our gut is more irritated than ever. Our body is able to tolerate a little bit of gluten in our food, but if we keep on eating it, our immune system starts to fight it and then we get symptoms and start to make antibodies to the wheat. Wheat has always been an irritant, but because there are so many more irritations in our food, wheat is more of a problem now more than ever.

From all the experts we talked to, we concluded that it is best to avoid it all together (if possible), especially if you are dealing with any chronic condition. If you want to incorporate a little bit into your diet, we recommend leaving it as a treat with sourdough bread and barley. Listen to your body, as every diet is personalized.

Choose organic, less processed, and sprouted grains (rice, corn, oats, ancient grains). Sprouting the grains can increase the content of some nutrients and fiber that improves digestion, the immune system, and metabolism. Remember, if you do stop eating gluten, you may have withdrawal symptoms, as gluten binds to the opioid receptors in the gut, the same receptors that morphine and heroin bind to. This makes the body crave it.

We know that gluten free products may sound appetizing, but Dr. Tom says they are not healthy for you—they are just not bad for you. The problem is that a lot of gluten free products don't have fiber (that can make your gut suffer) and are made up of rice, tapioca, or a corn flour that raises your blood sugar levels. We choose gluten free products that are made with almond, coconut, or cassava flour as treats.

 What do you call cheese that is not yours?
Nacho cheese!

Dairy

A dairy product is a product that comes from the milk of an animal. They are a significant part of the human diet unless the body is lactose intolerant or sensitive to dairy.

Dairy products are packed with magnesium, calcium, vitamins A, B6, B12, added vitamin D, zinc, selenium, and A2 milk boosts glutathione and so much more. About 70 percent of the world's population have milk related digestive issues.[7]

What's Wrong with Today's Dairy?

The cows of today aren't the same cows our grandparents or great-grandparents had. People have been drinking the processed, more toxic form of dairy for too long. Dairy from these genetically improved cows triggers an inflammatory response in the body and has been linked to disease. In kids, cow's milk is a common cause of food sensitivity/allergy, which can also be associated with recurrent ear infections, congestion and sinus problems, acne, schizophrenia, ADHD, autism, autoimmunity, and diabetes. Drink organic A2 or raw milk when possible, and try sheep, goat, and camel's milk. Listen to your body and do what works best for you.

Finding a Diet for You: It Is Very Personalized

Everyone is different. Food affects everyone differently. Find a diet that is best for you. Listen to your body. Finding the right diet for you might be a challenge and based on trial and error.

You will also need to know if you have a food allergy or sensitivities to certain foods. If you have allergies, you know. Sensitivities are less severe. A sensitivity could cause symptoms that show up days after. Taking certain foods out and then adding them back in can help to know what you are sensitive to. Start with either a blood test or just start experimenting with different foods you think might be causing the problem. For many people dairy and wheat can cause them problems, so you can start with those first. If you know you are allergic or sensitive to something, stay away from it. Also start experimenting with different common diets.

Most Common Diets

Vegetarian and Vegan Diets

Vegetarians eat tons of veggies and stay away from any meat but eat dairy and eggs. Vegans eat anything that does not involve an animal, including honey.

Mediterranean Diet

This diet is rich in fruits, vegetables, whole grains, fish, nuts, and olive oil.

Paleo Diet

This is a diet that stays away from man-made foods or processed food and eats real food like veggies, fruits, meat, nuts, and more. Most paleo diets don't include grains.

Keto Diet

A diet that is high in protein and low in carbs.

Low Lectin Diet

Lectins are a class of proteins that bind to carbohydrates. We interviewed Dr. Steven Gundry, NYT best-selling author of the *Plant Paradox*, who discussed how we are eating more lectins than ever before. Lectins are found in tomato seeds, peels, and grains. Processes like fermentation and pressure cooking the food can break down the lectins.

Intermittent Fasting

Long intermittent fasting is not really recommended for teens because it deprives them of nutrition. Time restricted eating is better for kids. Have a meal, then give your stomach a break. We are not eating while we are sleeping, so that is a minimal period of a ten-hour fast which can be beneficial for the body.

Raw Food Diet

This diet does not mean you just take a bite of red steak; it means that you limit or eliminate eating cooked foods. This diet is filled with fruits, veggies, nuts, and seeds.

The Teen Health Revolution Food Pyramid

After carefully examining all the diets and talking to all the experts on our podcast, here is The Teen Health Revolution Food Pyramid to help you summarize the foods we should eat.

Everything is built from food. Due to the way we grow our crops, there are fewer nutrients in our foods. A fruit or vegetable today has up to 40 percent fewer nutrients than the same food would have had seventy years ago.[8]

Where can we get our vitamins and minerals from?

- Vitamin A—liver, fish, eggs, and dairy products
- Vitamin B12—organ meats.
- Vitamin C—citrus fruits, berries, potatoes, tomatoes, peppers, cabbage, Brussels sprouts, broccoli, and spinach
- Vitamin D—salmon, mackerel, sardines, mushrooms
- Zinc—oysters and red meat
- Iron—nuts and seeds, dried fruit
- Potassium—apricots and dried fruit
- Magnesium—greens, nuts, seeds

Eating for the Earth

With climate change being a big problem, did you know we can save the planet with every bite we take? How? We talked about eating for you, but how do we eat for the planet? Most experts believe that we need to eat more plants. It is all about regenerative agriculture. The fake food and the resulting carbon emissions that impact the environment because of industrial food manufacturing are what cause a lot of issues. If we want to save the planet, we should eat real food and cut down on food waste. Forty percent of the entire US food supply goes to waste (120 billion pounds) every year![9] Meal planning is key. Freeze what you feel will be wasted. That way you can save the planet by using your freezer.

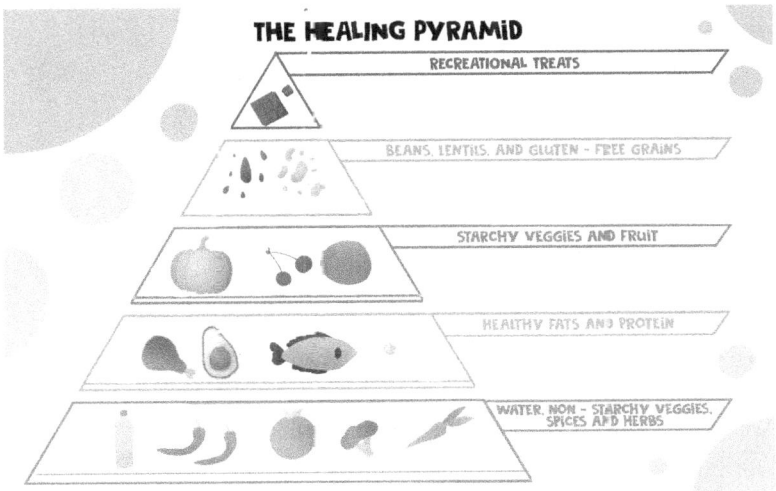

FIGURE 4.6 *The effects of real whole foods. Illustration by Zain Ansari.*

To save yourself and the planet . . . eat real food! Say goodbye to fake food snacks and say hello to a world of delicious, nutrient-dense foods that nourish your body from the inside out. Try out different fruits and vegetables. Try healthy alternatives to your favorite fun foods. Embrace the journey and explore the world of fun real food (Figure 4.6)!

What the Heck Should We Eat?

We get you. We go to a public school; we deal with all the same crazy questions and looks you get. What do we do? When someone told Emaad, "Why is your food so weird?" He said, "At least I am not eating pipe cleaner glyphosate!" Stand your ground and educate others. Most teens don't know any different.

When you are hungry, focus on the most nutrient-dense foods that will heal your mind, body, and soul.

Go down the list:

1. Rainbow vegetables with tons of fiber
2. Clean protein
3. Healthy fats
4. Hydration and fruit

Healthy Meal Examples

We keep it simple. We focus on the most nutrient-dense real foods that will improve digestive health, support glucose, and balance hormones. Focus on what you can eat, not what you cannot eat. Here are our favorites that work best for us.

Breakfast

- Fruit with nuts (we love dates or banana with nut butter)
- Pancakes (eggs, pb, and banana or eggs, pumpkin, and banana, we also love cassava flour pancakes)
- Waffles (almond flour, coconut flour, or cassava flour)
- Muffins, banana bread/zucchini bread (almond, coconut flour, cassava flour)
- Eggs/quiche
- Kabobs
- No-grain cereal in almond milk with fresh or frozen berries
- Chia seed pudding with berries, seeds, and nuts
- Smoothies, green, fruit, and/or nut butter
- Fresh fruit

- Sautéed greens
- Veggie/protein hash

The options are endless.

School Lunch

Abdullah has to be on the bus by 6:30 a.m., so we need something that can be put together with limited stress. We pack our lunch in little glass storage containers and stainless steel thermoses. Zain has been making everyone's lunch on his own since he was nine years old.

Following the same list, these are our school lunch favorites:

- Egg or chicken or salmon/sardine salad
- Meat roll ups with veggies
- Soup/chili (made with tons of diverse kinds of veggies and beans/lentils in bone broth)
- Zucchini pasta with meat sauce
- Unwich (lettuce wraps)
- Stir fry with meat and veggies
- Kabobs, burger patties, meatballs
- Unwrapped egg roll in a bowl
- Fajitas
- Tacos served with lettuce to make wraps or in cassava flour taco shells
- Barbeque leftovers
- Soups
- Falafels

- Fish
- Lentils or bean salad
- Yellow chicken
- Fried fish
- Lentil pasta
- Veggies (carrots, broccoli, sweet peppers, cucumbers, cauliflower, etc.) with avocado oil dressing or guacamole
- Olives, nuts, and seeds or baked goods that have been made with it (usually left over from breakfast), no-grain crackers and no-grain chips
- Dark chocolate

Then we always have a piece of fruit, and we love our almond flour, cassava flour, or tigernut flour sweet treats.

Snacks for Home

- Fruit or veggies with nut butter
- Nuts with dairy-free dark chocolate, goji berries, or raisins
- Sugar snap peas with hummus
- Jerky
- No-grain bars
- No-grain granola
- Ants on a log
- Olives and other vegetables

The options are endless!

Lunch and Dinner

- Grilled salmon with cauliflower rice and sweet potato fries
- Cassava flour fried fish with coleslaw
- Curries with cauliflower rice, no-grain wraps, or chickpea naan
- Chili/Soup
- Lentil pasta with grass-fed beef and hidden veggies (like cauliflower, mushrooms, and broccoli sprouts—we promise you cannot taste it)
- Cassava flour tacos or burritos
- Burgers—we love lettuce wraps or almond flour bread as buns
- Chicken wings, yum!!!
- Dessert—Fruit or baked goods made from cassava, tigernut, almond, or coconut flour

We have our favorite recipes at the end of the book.

Eating Out: We only eat out at organic restaurants or those certified as non-GMO restaurants. If not, we ask for the protein and veggies to be cooked in only olive oil, sea salt, and pepper. Yum!

Where Do We Begin?

1. Read Labels

In today's world, the first step to eating better is to be mindful of what you are eating. Ms. Vani Hari recommended that we read labels. Know what we are putting in our bodies. Avoid artificial ingredients (Figure 4.7).

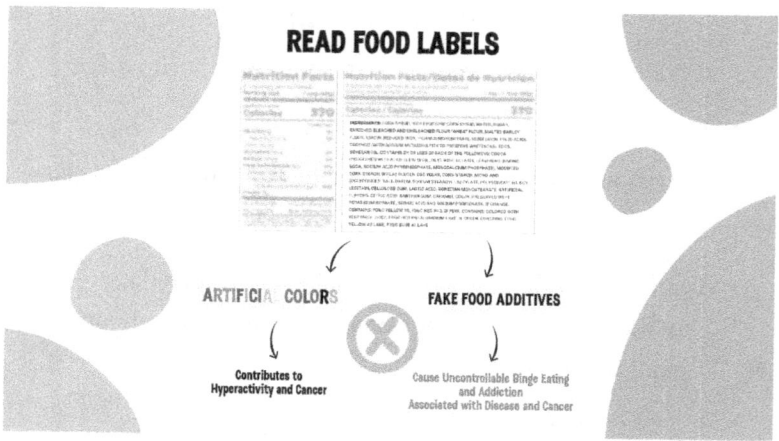

FIGURE 4.7 *Read food labels. Illustration by Zain Ansari.*

Parts of the Label:

Serving Size: The serving size is how much the entire food label is talking about (twenty-six crackers per serving).

Calories: This shows the number of calories in one serving of the food.

Nutrients % Daily Value (%DV): This is the amount of nutrients in one serving.

Ingredients List: This list is extremely important, the ingredients that are the first are the ingredients that the food has the most of. If the top is an artificial product or unhealthy, it's better to stay away, but if the ingredient list is filled with foods you can pronounce and the first ingredient is something better, that food is most likely very good (the best foods are the foods that are organic but non-GMO is the second best).

- If you see the word artificial, put it back.
- If you cannot pronounce the ingredients, put it back.

- Find the foods that are non-GMO and organic (if it's organic, it's non-GMO).

Allergen Information: Some labels will specifically call out common allergens like nuts, soy, wheat, dairy, or more.

Additional Information: Depending on the product, you might find other information like recommended uses, preparation instructions, or health claims. Be cautious of any health claims.

Swap Out Fake Food for Real Food

2. Now that you know how to read ingredients, find a better replacement for your favorite foods. Look at these two products and tell me which is better for you.

Skittles

Ingredients: sugar, corn syrup, hydrogenated palm kernel oil; less than 2 percent of: citric acid, tapioca dextrin, modified corn starch, natural and artificial flavors, colors (red 40 lake, yellow 5 lake, blue 2 lake, yellow 6 lake, titanium dioxide, blue 1 lake, yellow 6, red 40, yellow 5, blue 1), sodium citrate, carnauba wax

Or

YumEarth Giggles

Ingredients: Organic cane sugar, organic rice syrup, organic palm oil, citric acid, organic flavors, turmeric (color), sodium citrate, organic sunflower lecithin, malic acid, (radish, sweet potato, carrot, blackcurrant) color, organic carnauba wax, spirulina (color), pectin.

You get the picture. You can still eat your favorite foods, just find replacements that are high-quality foods.

Make a list of your favorites and then look for a healthier choice to make a swap.

Here is a list that works for us:

Fake Food to Real Food Alternatives

- Punch/Roohafza/energy drinks/juice → Fruit-infused water
- Lattes and specialty coffee → Make at home with organic creamers and honey
- Soda → Sparkling water or Olipop
- Takis/Doritos/Hot Cheetos/Chips—Siete (they have been bought by PepsiCo, so keep an eye on the ingredients), Lesser Evil, organic/non-GMO popcorn
- McDonalds, Subway, Pizza Hut, Taco Bell → Chipotle
- Chicken 65, artificially colored biryani → BBQ chicken, use turmeric and saffron to color biryani
- Hot dogs and lunch meat → Organic hot dogs and lunch meat without nitrates
- Pita bread, naans, and bread → Organic bread, Base Culture Bread, Unbun
- Bagel → Organic bagels, Unbun
- Canola oil → Organic olive oil, ghee, coconut or avocado oil
- Sugar/High Fructose Corn Syrup → Dates, honey, maple syrup
- Oreos/Chips Ahoy → Simple Mills, Siete Cookies
- Artificial food dyes → All-natural food color, turmeric, saffron, beet, spirulina, and so on.
- Artificially colored candy → Organic candy or fruit
- Cake boxes → Organic cake boxes

- Fake ice creams → Frozen, Cosmic Bliss ice cream, Ice Cream for Bears, Alden's or Alec's
- Donuts and baked goods → Make at home with organic flours Fake colored cereal → Organic cereal, Lovebird and Seven Sundays Artificial Chocolate → Organic chocolate bars with date or coconut sugar (Hu or Navitas)
- Fake fruit yogurt → Cocojune, Forager Project, or organic grass-fed yogurt

Let's save our world and our mind, body, and soul with every bite we take.

What Do the Holistic Kids Do?

We Make Every Bite Count!

We ONLY eat real food. Yes All. The. Time. We go down the list. We like to add foods that are packed with nutrients like broccoli sprouts and microgreens into pasta sauces, sandwiches, and even on salads, as just a little is super packed with nutrition. We also love to use spices that are packed with phytonutrients. Dr. Jeffrey Bland, the founder of functional medicine, even recommends Himalayan Tartary buckwheat flour and sprout powder that are packed with polyphenols. We mix it into pancakes, muffins, cakes, and even chocolate chip cookies! We love to eat sauerkraut daily. We have a rainbow of different fermented foods, and we try to get different colors. We are gluten free and limit dairy and grains. We find that if we eat grains, we do not eat our vegetables. Most of the time we do not even need to eat grains, because after having our veggies, clean protein and healthy fat, and drink water . . . we are already full . . . and we stay full for a while. We do have gluten a couple times a year and organic basmati rice and corn once a month or once every other month (depending upon our symptoms)—we save dairy and grains for special occasions and treats. Occasionally, as a treat we love our raw homemade fermented yogurt topped with frozen organic wild blueberries. We have one drawer of veggies in the fridge and one drawer of fruit. Our pantry is stocked for success. Our mom only stocks the house up with all the food we can eat. It is awesome!

When we go out, we look for the cleanest restaurant—we turn it into a game! We do the same with parties. We do bring our own food everywhere we go . . . our mom loves to cook, and we help her. In our house, real food is fun food!

Revolution Recap: Eat Real Food

- Read food labels.
- Swap out fake food for real food.
- Every time you are hungry, go down the list—veggies, clean protein, and healthy fats, and then make sure to have some fruit.
- No naked carbs.
- Fiber, prebiotics, and probiotics.
- Hydrate.
- Experiment with spices.
- Eat non-GMO/organic.

5

V—Vanquish Toxins

The next step in the teen health R-E-V-O-L-U-T-I-O-N is V for vanquishing toxins. Vanquish—we feel like we are in a superhero movie, ready to vanquish toxins!!! Isn't that fun? Fun and confusing because where are the toxins?

Hidden toxins are all around us. The couch you are sitting on, toxic. The food you are eating, toxic. The makeup on your face, toxic. The carpet you walk on, toxic. Clorox you clean with, toxic. Your shampoo and soap, toxic. We are swimming in a toxic soup right now. Everything around us, the air we breathe and the food we eat to the water we drink, contains toxins, and we are more exposed today than ever before.

Currently the US imports about forty-five million pounds of synthetic chemicals daily,[1] about one thousand new chemicals are put into use every year, and only five chemicals have ever been banned in the United States. The United Nations projected that by 2030, global chemical production is expected to double, reaching more than a trillion pounds per year![2] Approximately 90,000 compounds are currently approved for commercial use, but only a handful have been evaluated for toxicity![3]

Dr. Aly Cohen, rheumatologist and author of *Non-Toxic*, emphasized that the environment plays a key role in human health and has been associated and correlated with short-term and long-term chronic conditions like autoimmune diseases, asthma, obesity, diabetes, and cancer.

What Is a Toxin?

Toxins are substances created that are poisonous (toxic) to humans, as they are foreign to our body. The body can get rid of these toxins from our skin, urine, poop, lymphatics, and liver. The liver, an organ found in the belly, is important for detoxifying the body, shipping all the stuff that does not belong, like toxins, old blood cells, spent hormones, and shipping them off to the kidney to get rid of them from the body. If there is an excessive amount of toxins, it can overwhelm the body. We can also think about it like this: if there is a lot of junk in the computer, then a game we are playing will lag and glitch out, not allowing us to play the game properly. The same can happen to the liver. With an overload of toxins, your liver gets glitchy, unable to do the work it needs.

Toxins don't just affect you, they also affect your children and your grandchildren. Toxins can affect the proteins that control gene expression as well as other mechanisms involved in controlling gene function. Because of a glitchy liver, toxins accumulate in the body, damaging the mitochondria, affecting our epigenetics, our hormones, inflaming the gut, and worsening chronic inflammation.

 There is a lot we cannot control, but there is so much we CAN control!

If we limit the amount of toxins we are exposed to, we can lower our toxic load and improve our overall health.

Common Toxins

What toxins are we talking about? There are so many all around us.

Heavy Metals

Heavy metals like mercury, lead, and arsenic are common in our lives. Mercury is a common element and can be a huge issue in the world. Mercury can be found in mercury fillings, tattoos, and fluorescent light bulbs, but 80 percent of it comes from fish. Most mercury can be stored in our organs, in muscle and fat. Mercury in our body causes diseases including Alzheimer's, irregular heartbeat, and even certain cancers. In older children, mercury can lead to a delay in the transmission of auditory brain signals.

Lead is a common toxin that is found in packaging and in things we use in our everyday lives. Vaping has been linked to toxic lead and uranium exposure, which can harm brain and organ development. Those that vaped had urine levels 40 percent higher in lead than occasional users.[4] E-cigarettes during teen years may increase the likelihood of metal exposure. According to the World Health Organization, "Almost 1 million people die every year due to lead poisoning with more children suffering long-term health effects."[5]

Arsenic can be found in our drinking water, rice, leafy green vegetables, and conventionally raised chicken. It can lead to diabetes, cancer and autoimmune issues.

Uranium is a heavy metal that can lead to oxidative stress, genetic damage, inflammation, and metabolic disorders. It can deposit in the kidneys, where it can cause kidney damage, fibrosis, and tumors in lung tissue.[6]

Cadmium is a toxic heavy metal that can be found in food like potatoes, seeds, cereal grains, leafy greens, tobacco, water, air, and soil. Recently, Consumer Reports found that a third of chocolate products were found to have heavy metals, as they can enter the cocoa plant from the soil! Increased cadmium can increase the risk of cancer.

Heavy metals are the most dangerous for kids,[7] even at low concentrations. This poisoning does not happen overnight and takes time to build up in the blood. Asymptomatic heavy metal poisoning causes nonspecific symptoms such as behavioral disorders, aggression, and difficulty in learning.[8]

 Why did the beet start a detox program?
It wanted to "beet" the toxins!

Endocrine-Disrupting Chemicals

These are substances that, once absorbed, can send mixed messages to the endocrine system (collection of glands and organs responsible for our hormones), thus disrupting the hormones' natural actions. They can mimic the effects of estrogen and human hormones, build up in fatty tissues, and lead to increased inflammation. These chemicals can be linked to early puberty, period problems, male infertility, low sex drive, obesity, and cancer. They are found in meds, UV filters, food preservatives, personal care products, plastics, coolants, plasticizers, and pesticides.

Microplastics and nanoplastics are becoming an increasing concern and can be found everywhere around the globe.[9] Kids are more exposed to microplastics than adults. They affect the body by stimulating the release of endocrine disruptors, heavy metals, and organic pollutants during absorption. Microplastics have been found in brains, hearts, lungs, breast milk, placenta, and human penises. We ingest/inhale credit card size of microplastics weekly.[10]

This is just the beginning when it comes to toxins. We need to protect ourselves by learning where they are hiding. To find these toxins, we need to look at our water, air, homes, mouths, and our food (Figure 5.1).

Toxins in Our Water

Most of us take our clean water for granted, but studies have shown that drinking water sources may hold a variety of contaminants like

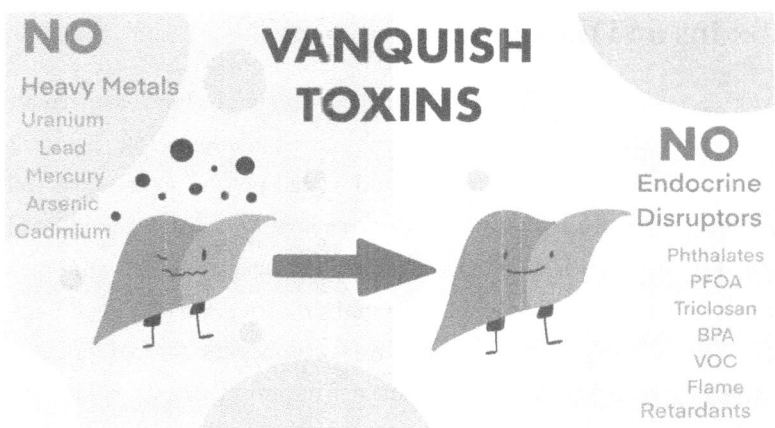

FIGURE 5.1 *Vanquish toxins. Illustration by Zain Ansari.*

microorganisms, heavy metals, glyphosate, atrazine, and even chloroform and forever chemicals.[11]

Toxins in Our Air

Air pollution is a big concern, as the air can have carbon monoxide, sulfur dioxide, and nitrogen oxides, leading to respiratory problems such as asthma, bronchitis, and even lung cancer.

Tobacco smoke has tons of toxic chemicals. Even if you do not smoke yourself, secondhand smoke exposure can still pose serious health risks. It increases the likelihood of developing respiratory infections, asthma, and other respiratory conditions, increasing the risk of heart disease and lung cancer. Vaping is not better, it exposes us to thousands of heavy metals and chemicals that can lead to cancer, lung damage, organ damage, and the chemicals in vapes are known as volatile organic compounds that can cause health issues.[12] In our homes, we bathe in toxins daily. Common household cleaning toxins include ammonia, a chemical used to clean windows and bathrooms, which can agitate skin and make it more difficult to breathe.

Toxins on Our Body

Most personal care products, like makeup, body products, and female sanitary products, hold toxins. The average woman puts 168 chemicals on her body every day![13] Toxins found in nail polish can cause several health problems, such as cancer, reproductive harm, and neurological damage. Triclosan is a chemical that is an antibacterial and antifungal commonly used in soaps and hand sanitizers. Triclosan kills good bugs, can disrupt hormones like reproductive hormones and thyroid function. Most detergents hold toxic chemicals such as phosphates, formaldehyde, and synthetic fragrances, which can irritate the skin and respiratory system and release chemicals into the environment.

Electromagnetic Fields (EMFs)

Electronics and EMFs constantly surround us. They are produced by electrical devices, like the phones and appliances. Three to ten percent of the world's population is sensitive to EMFs. These EMFs can cause heat production to tissues, causing a level of interference to normal signaling in the body, which hurts the mitochondria, leading to fatigue, brain fog, sleeplessness, DNA damage, psychological and cell membrane damage, and oxidative stress.

Toxic Food

Today's produce is packed with pesticides, insecticides, fungicides, and herbicides. Antibiotics and hormones administered to livestock to promote growth and prevent disease result in residues that can disrupt human endocrine systems and contribute to antibiotic resistance. Exposure to pesticides has been linked to various health problems, including cancer, neurological disorders, hormone disruption, and increased adolescent depression.[14] Nonstick cookware having PFOA or

PFOS (aka forever chemicals) should be avoided, as they release toxic fumes when heated. They are cancer-causing, cause reproductive/developmental issues and liver damage.

Mindful around Toxins

Toxins are everywhere. Limit toxins around you by being mindful of your surroundings and what you use on a regular daily basis.

Educate Yourself. Learn where the toxins are (as we discussed above) and how to avoid them. Do research on the products you use. When we buy detergents, soaps, lotions, and cleaning supplies, we read the ingredients and find healthier alternatives . . . because what you put on your skin should be as clean as what you put in your mouth. Here are the specific areas we focus on to lower our toxic load.

 Why did the lemon go on a detox cleanse?
It wanted to zestify its Life!

Organic/Natural Body and Cleaning Products

Organic sanitary products, makeup, nail polishes, shampoo, conditioner, and lotions are available. Look for ones made without these harmful products. Check out the Environmental Working Group to find out what they rate the products. This way you are making a more informed decision about what you are putting on or in your body. You can reduce the risk of exposure by using nontoxic detergents and soaps while avoiding and boycotting cleansers with toxic chemicals, artificial additives, and fragrances. It is better to use organic detergents and essential oils for perfumes.

Filter Your Water

Ask your parents to invest in a reverse osmosis filter with a high-efficacy charcoal filter. Inexpensive water filters are effective at reducing some impurities but not bacteria, harmful chemicals, and heavy metals.

Limit Plastic Use

Plastics, microplastics and, nanoplastics have toxins like BPA, heavy metals, and phthalates. Do not store food in plastic containers. To avoid this, store food in stainless steel, glass, ceramic, and tons more. Instead of plastic bags, use paper bags. Get rid of your plastic cutting board for an organic wood one. Limit the use of plastic clothes, all polyester, and stick to cotton clothes. Spending a little more on higher-quality clothes can save you and the planet. Quality over quantity.

Ventilate

Indoor spaces are like prisons that do not let toxins out. In our house, we use an air purifier that we have in every room. Do not use perfumes or spray air fragrances, they are bad for you. Use essential oils instead.

Limit EMF Exposure

This can be difficult, but even a little goes a long way. Turn off the TV router at night. Never carry a cell phone on your body. Use speakers or headsets when on your phone. Switch to airplane mode anytime you can (especially at night). Make sure to unplug all electrical devices that you are not using and keep them far away from you. Getting out in nature, getting good sleep, grounding daily, eating a diet packed with antioxidants and lowering stress can help to protect the body against EMFs.

Oral Health

Our mouth is where the health of our body starts. Our gut microbiome starts in your mouth, so do not forget to give it the attention and respect that it deserves. Choose toothpaste, floss, and mouthwash without fluoride and toxic ingredients. We use wood toothbrushes to limit the plastic exposure in our mouths. When you go to the dentist, say no to fluoride as recent studies show it may lower our IQ.[15] Find a dentist that collaborates with you—we go to a holistic or biologic dentist. Say no to mercury fillings.

> Make sure you are using the right oral health care products; there are some that have some kind of yucky ingredients in them that can damage our healthy microbiome so making sure that your parents are reading or helping you read the ingredients on your toothpaste is super important.
>
> —Dr. Anastacia Staci Whitman, DDS,
> board certified dentist

Detoxify Daily

We are living in a toxic soup but there are things we can do to support our own detoxification pathways to help lower the toxic load.

Poop, Pee, and Perspire!

When toxins come in, they must leave the body though our skin, poop, and pee. Make sure every day you are pooping, peeing, and perspiring! Drink filtered water, eat real food, and heal the gut to keep the poop perfect and your fluids flowing! Get outside, run, exercise, use an Epsom salt bath

(1/2 cup of Epsom salt in the bath water for twenty minutes) to detox through your skin! Using a dry brush, brush your body before getting into the shower, and a hot and cold shower can help with detoxification.

Cook, Eat, and Drink to Detox

To limit toxins, it is best to cook your food at home, because you know exactly what is going on in your food. Your pots and pans should be either cast iron, ceramic, or stainless steel. Increase foods with glutathione like cruciferous vegetables, broccoli sprouts, brazil nuts, and fish. Glutathione is the most important antioxidant produced by the body and is found in every cell in the body, but its highest concentration is in the liver. Eating real foods can help to improve glutathione levels, especially cruciferous vegetables. Glutathione gives protection against oxidative stress, toxins, and infections. Keeping good levels of glutathione through a healthy diet, supplementation, and lifestyle choices is important for being healthy and preventing disease. We love broccoli sprouts as they are rich in sulforaphane (a compound found in cruciferous vegetables) that boosts glutathione production in the body. We put it on everything!

> You can clean your genes by taking glutathione. You can clean your genes by eating broccoli which supports sulforaphane which also makes sulforaphane which also makes glutathione.
>
> —Dr. Ben Lynch, author of *Dirty Genes*

Meditation, yoga, and other stress management techniques can also boost your glutathione. Dr. Ben Lynch gave us an amazing analogy. He emphasized that if you walk by cars on your way to school and you had broccoli the night before, you've got some glutathione in your body and your body can process the car exhaust better, compared to someone who only eats junk food. Fiber is also important for our bodies to detoxify (Figure 5.2).

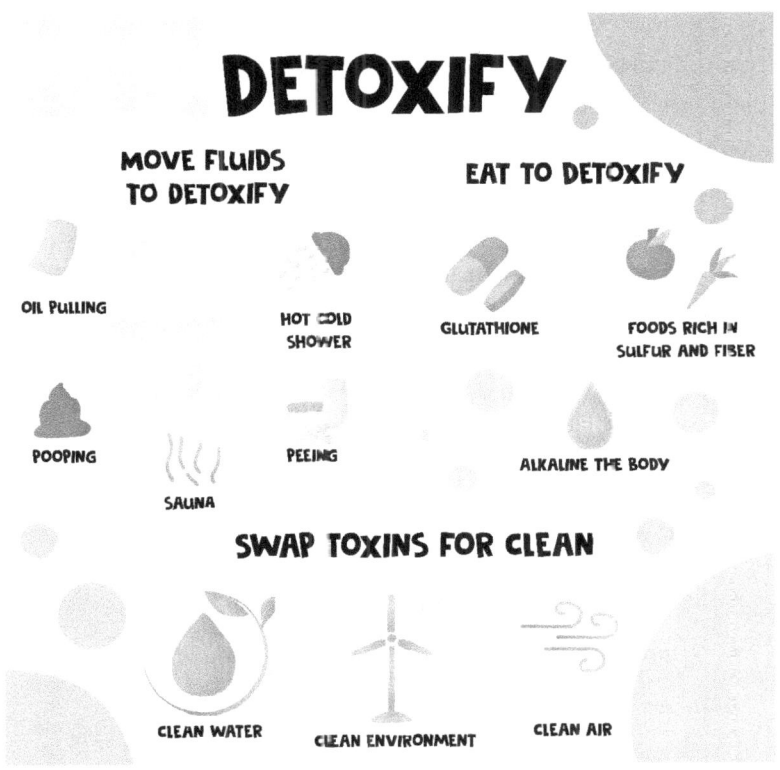

FIGURE 5.2 *Detoxify. Illustration by Zain Ansari.*

How Do the Holistic Kids Detoxify?

We know that it is overwhelming, but if we are mindful of our everyday choices, we can lower environmental toxins. We prioritize our water intake, make sure we are pooping, peeing, and sweating daily. We also like to do Epsom salt baths at least once a week. We support our detoxification pathways in our body by taking glutathione supplements (our mom puts them in our smoothies). All our products are organic and natural. We eat the real food rainbow, and for school lunches, we take our food in glass containers or stainless steel. We cook our food in ceramic or cast iron cookware. We drink filtered water. Before we get into the shower, we dry brush, as it stimulates the lymphatic system to remove many toxins, and we try to do a hot and cold shower in the bath. We love nature and prioritize our sleep.

Knowledge is power. Read the ingredients of all your products, find natural, nontoxic replacements, eat real food, drink filtered water, and clean your air. We need to deal with all the toxicity in our lives. We are swimming in a toxic soup all day long, with the water level continuing to rise. If we do not prioritize our detoxification, before we know it, we will drown. Vanquishing toxins can improve our mind, body, and soul from the inside and out!

Revolution Recap: Vanquish Toxins

- Replace the toxic products for the cleaner products.
- Nature, exercise, sweating, peeing, and pooping.
- Increase glutathione.
- Epsom salt baths a couple times a week.

6

O—Optimize Stress Management

Two hundred more emails, one thousand more notifications, twenty different apps, breaking news notifications, flooding, murder, suicide, war . . . a tidal wave of stress the moment we open our eyes. We are trapped in a circle of constant stress, glued to screens, drowning in a world of negativity.

Stress was meant to protect us. When there is a lion chasing us, good stress keeps us aware of what is happening and protects us. There is also bad or chronic stress when our body feels like there is a lion chasing us all the time, but there is no lion. We talked to Dr. Romie, a neurologist and author of *The Busy Brain Cure*, which describes the two states that exist in our body: the sympathetic state when our body is in fight-or-flight mode and the parasympathetic state, where our body is resting and digesting.

The vagus nerve is the main part of the parasympathetic state and is the communication system between the brain and the rest of the body, including the heart, lungs, and stomach. It controls the heart rate, controls the muscles in our lungs, helps our stomach produce digestive juices, and keeps food moving through our digestive system. Most importantly, it activates the parasympathetic nervous system, helps the body enter a state of rest, helps with digestion, and regulates the immune response. The vagus nerve helps us manage stress.

Stress Makes Us Sick

Stress worsens almost any chronic illness, causing more than 80 percent of complaints that are presented to doctors.[1] When we are stressed and have no way to get rid of our stress, then our mind, body, and soul fall apart. Our body releases a hormone called cortisol. When these chemicals get out of control, stress shuts off the part of the brain that helps us make decisions. Chronic stress makes it difficult to concentrate, weakens the immune system, negatively affects the gut microbiome, increases cravings, raises blood sugar, and causes memory issues, hormone imbalances, and weight gain.

The problem is that most of us were never taught how to manage stress and pain. We manage stress by falling into unhealthy habits of eating fake food and sugar, grabbing our gadgets, drugs, and other addictions. They do not solve the problem. They lead to more chronic stress and inflammation (that wildfire)—influencing our internal and external world.

Stressors

What is stressing us out? A stressor is anything that causes stress. What stresses one person out may not stress the other person out. Our experiences, thoughts, emotions, environments, illnesses, situations, relationships, life changes, deaths, divorces, extreme schoolwork load, overbooked schedules, or even money issues can all lead to stress. Look at your life, what is stressing you out? Any trauma? What are your personal challenges? Is the issue relating to emotions, unrealistic expectations, low self-esteem, fear, or guilt? Your thoughts or emotions?

Dr. Caroline Leaf, a clinical neuroscientist and author of *How to Help Your Child Clean Up Their Mental Mess*, discusses the importance of our thoughts and experiences. She explains that a thought is what is growing in our head at any moment. Every experience is the roots, we grow branches with how we think. Everyone's branches look different. A toxic experience will grow into an unhealthy tree. The good ones help us function fine, but the bad ones can leave us feeling stressed. Stress makes us view the world in a negative way and can affect our thoughts. We all react to stressors differently.

Managing Stress

If you are like us, you are busy. Incorporating a stress management technique into our everyday routine is important. But guess what? We can de-stress with something we are already doing without thinking. . . . It is called breathing. Humans breathe all day, but unfortunately, we are not breathing the right way.

Breathing

Dr. Chris Willard, psychologist, faculty at Harvard Medical School, and best-selling author of books on mindfulness and meditation like *Alphabreaths*, says that the way we are breathing changes how we feel. He says that our breath is like a remote control. It can turn the volume down on the alarm system for the big emotions overwhelming our brain or turn the volume up on the happy emotions of our brain, helping us calm down. When we are stressed, we breathe shallow, and it tells our body to dial 911 and go into panic mode. When we are relaxed, then we breathe more deeply. The reset button is at the bottom of our lungs. Just by mindfully breathing, we can stimulate our vagus nerve, helping our body to relax.

 Combine belly breaths with an activity we are doing every day.

Focusing on our breath is the easiest, fastest, and most powerful way to de-stress immediately. Find an activity you do every day and remember to breathe during that time. For example, we pray five times a day, so we have connected that with deep breaths before and after our prayers. We can also connect it with talking to someone or breathe deeply when we are doing our homework.

There are several types of breathing exercises; find ones that work best for you.

- The 4-7-8 breathing technique will help you when you are really stressed and will at once soothe our nervous system. Empty our lungs of air, breathe in for four seconds, hold for seven seconds, and then exhale out of our mouth for eight seconds. Do this four times.

- Box breathing: inhale for four seconds, hold for four seconds, exhale for four seconds, and hold for four seconds. Repeat this for five minutes.

- Dr. Willard taught us the "hot chocolate breath" to pretend like we are holding a hot cup of cocoa or holding a candle and gently blow to cool down the hot chocolate (or a candle) or ninja breathing, making our breath more silent. When Dr. Romie gets stressed, she loves to do the lion's breath. She inhales, exhales, and then crosses her eye, sticks out her tongue, and breathes out. It makes us all smile and laugh.

You can learn to turn our vagus nerve on and turn it off. Dr. Navaz Habib, author of *Activate Our Vagus Nerve* and *Upgrade Your Vagus Nerve*, gave us the analogy of the Hulk. He says, there was a moment in the movie when Hulk was controlling his heart rate to make sure he did not turn into Hulk, and he was controlling his heart rate with his breathing. We can do the same. We can control our vagus nerve through our breath.

Mindfulness

Mindfulness is knowing what we are doing when we are doing it. Mindfulness is paying attention to what is going on right now and how one feels in THIS moment, internally and externally, without judgment. Mindfulness trains us to be calm and present in the moment. It will help to bring our nervous system back into balance and decrease stress. Mindfulness helps us be the absolute best version of ourselves.

We all get worried. Some worries are normal. Mindfulness can help us think less about the future and more about the present. Dr. Willard recommended finding more awareness and mindfulness around the things we do every day. Do you notice the color of the food you are eating? Think about how the food tastes, smells, and feels in our mouth. Be mindful and eat with all our senses. Incorporate baby steps into our life every day. Go outside. Breathe. Think about what you are listening to, how you feel, what you hear, what you smell and taste. Stare at a fire in the fireplace, a fish tank, the clouds. Bring mindfulness into every activity.

Meditation

The practice of daily meditation and positivity intensifies calmness, cultivating optimal physical, mental, and spiritual health. Meditation helps us be more resilient, no matter what the environment we live in.

> Meditation . . It helps us to handle trauma or stress. It is giving your body very deep rest.
> —Emily Fletcher, author of *Stress Less, Accomplish More*

This is just a superpower to help you become a superhero. Meditation is going to make us better at what we love and better at life. Ms. Emily recommends not starting meditation when things are hard. She recommends three steps in meditation: mindfulness, meditation, and manifesting.

- Mindfulness (as discussed above): Focus on our breathing, what you hear, see, smell, feel, taste, and then combining all the senses.
- Meditation: Concentrate on a mantra or a word. If we start to have thoughts, slowly bring them back to the mantra or word.
- Manifesting: Is your dream for the future. Consciously creating the life you love. Get intentional about what you want our life to look like? Manifesting is putting our attention into our dreams.

Gratitude, Love, and Faith

Gratitude will change our heart rhythm in a healthy way. Heart rate variability (HRV) is how the heart varies beat to beat. We want a nice pattern that will tell us we are happy, peaceful, and calm, but if that pattern gets all jagged, it tells us we are stressed. We know that love and gratitude is the best thing we can do to improve our HRV and improve our mind, body, and soul.

When we spoke to Dr. Jill Carnahan, a physician and author of *Unexpected*, she discussed her primary way of managing stress was believing in a higher power. For her, that was where faith came in. She has a deep connection with God, and she will pray, pause, and focus on all the things she is thankful for. Refocusing on the good can help us manage our stress.

Laughter

Laughing can lower stress (now you know why we have jokes throughout the book). Laughter allows us to run away from the stress of the world. Dr. David Friedman, author of *Funny Bones*, discussed the benefits of laughter. It improves brain health, heart health, mental and social health as it releases dopamine and serotonin, improving mood, lowering stress hormones, activating immune cells, and strengthening the immune system to fight off infections.[2] Friedman emphasized, "We get smarter when we laugh."

Time Management

Many teens are overwhelmed by the amount of work they must do. We must manage our time. Figure out what you need to do first. Put away the phone, to limit distractions and then set realistic goals and a to-do list.

Nature

Spending some time in nature can relieve stress and lower inflammation (wildfire). Forest bathing, the simple method of being calm and quiet among the trees, observing nature around us while breathing deeply, can help youth de-stress and boost health and well-being. Try to spend at least thirty minutes a week, if not more, in open nature. We all need our vitamin N.

Play

Go play outside, climb a tree, do things outside. Play releases "miracle grow" for the brain. Play improves our mind, body, and soul. Play is powerful for our nervous system.

Harmonious Sounds

Music and other harmonic sounds can help us de-stress and calm down. We can stimulate our vagus nerve by reciting, chanting, religious practices, and even humming like a bee at the bottom of our throat. Listen to the sounds around you. Be mindful.

Spend Time with Family

Spending time with those you love—family meals and pets are powerful ways to de-stress.

Manage Toxic Thoughts

Dr. Leaf has a five-step scientific mind-management system that helps us prevent toxic thoughts and memories from affecting our mental health. She describes this as learning to fly a plane. First, we need to prepare our mind. Breathing and meditation will help to bring us back in balance. Then the steps are gathering awareness, how we feel in our body, how the thoughts we are having affect our behavior, how the thoughts affect the way we look at life. That will pull us into the conscious mind. The healthier our minds are, the healthier our body and brain.

Good Stresses: Temperature

This is where we are going to talk about something called hormesis. Hormesis is a short amount of stress on our body that does the body good. Like taking cold showers, plunging into ice baths, heat therapy, and high intensity interval training. These mild stresses keep our body resilient to future challenges.

An easy thing to do is take hot and cold showers. Take a shower as you normally do, but at the end of the shower, do cycles of hot and cold water. Thirty seconds of a cold shower, then switch back to thirty seconds of hot shower, doing this cycle about three to seven times and working up to a total of one minute of hot and then one minute of cold. Start with five or ten seconds working up to thirty seconds each. We turn it into a game.

Try Apps or Programs

We love technology. If you have a phone, try to incorporate some apps, or attend a program online. There are even apps on Netflix by Calm and Headspace. We also recommend zivaKIDS, an online meditation program. New apps and programs come out all the time, so check them out and see what works best for you.

Exercise

> One of the best things you can do is exercise.
> —Dr. Molly Maloof, physician and author of *The Spark Factor*

We need to move our bodies. We need to run around. When we move our bodies, we create more mitochondria, our body needs energy to grow. Lots of teens these days do not think of exercise as necessary; they just look at exercise to get big muscles or abdominal muscles, but it is necessary. When we are feeling overwhelmed by school, work, or just life, a good workout can be our escape from the real world. Exercise is our stress-crushing superhero! Exercise can increase our happiness while helping our body get rid of calories and toxins. If we need a break from life, just go on a walk, jog, or play a fun sport of our choice.

Benefits of Exercise

- Reduces stress and anxiety
- Improves cardiovascular health
- Enhances sleep quality
- Boosts concentration and academic performance
- Strengthens the immune system
- BDNF (brain derived neurotrophic factor), a "miracle grow" for the brain. It stimulates the brain to grow new brain cells, and takes care of existing brain cells, allowing us to learn better.

Goals

- Add it to your daily routine and make time for it. There is so much more to exercise, and if we think of exercise as a chore, it will become a chore. Think of it as a chance to improve yourself

- Be consistent. It is recommended to do a minimum of thirty to sixty minutes a day. You can start off by doing it two to three times a week.

- Make it fun and be active! Play sports, dance, bike, play games, play outdoors, hike, swim, kayak, rock climb. Play sports with friends, and schedule it on the calendar. When you have fun, you can stick with it.

- Social media is filled with unrealistic expectations of how our body should look. Keep goals real and not just some crazy expectation. If you can only do one push-up, do one, then try to do two. Keep trying to get better every day. Practice and increase the time of exercise. Just remember nobody is perfect and there is no perfect body standard; just take care of your body.

Make Stress Management a Part of Our Lifestyle

Lifestyle is a big part of avoiding stress. With a terrible lifestyle, it is a lot easier for chronic stress to affect us. We had a detailed discussion with the NYT best-selling author of *Adrenal Transformation Protocol*, Dr. Izabella Wentz. She emphasized the importance of incorporating stress management techniques into our daily routine. Along with what we talked about above, she recommended that we look at the mirror and say five things we are proud of about ourselves. We can start by saying "I love you" by looking at our eyes in front of the mirror. If we do this regularly, we will see a difference as we will start seeing the person we want to be. We just need to believe that we are worthy of goodness.

What we eat affects our vagus nerve. Our vagus nerve likes stable blood sugar and when we eat enough protein, fat, and fiber at every meal.

FIGURE 6.1 *De-Stress. Illustration by Zain Ansari.*

Dr. Wentz emphasized the importance of sleep, staying away from blue light after sunset, and the importance of hugging our siblings, friends, and parents—she even recommended a good big butterfly hug to help us. She stressed the importance of replenishing the nutrients, fish oil, probiotics, B vitamins, magnesium, zinc, and electrolytes can help manage stress. Epsom salt baths can help to tell our body to unwind. Revitalize ourselves by taking time to do things we love (Figure 6.1).

How Do the Holistic Kids Manage Stress?

We manage stress as a whole-life approach. For us, we prioritize gratitude, prayer, exercise, breathing, and nature. We have found our higher purpose. We connect deeply to a higher power and incorporate our meditation, mindfulness, and breathing with our five daily prayers.

This is what we do:

1. Sit up in a spot, eyes closed, back supported.
2. Breathe/belly breathing: in through our nose and out through our mouth—2/4, 3/6, 4/8 (seconds in/seconds out).
3. Mindfulness: we ask ourselves what we are hearing, what are we seeing, what are we feeling . . . and then putting it all together.
4. Mantra: concentrate on a word.
5. End with gratitude (we love our gratitude) and a prayer for our future.

Stress makes us sick, stupid, and slow. When we learn to manage stress, we can bounce back faster from whatever life throws our way.

Revolution Recap: Optimize Stress Management

- Take some deep breaths.
- Go outside, play and exercise.
- Find time for mindfulness.

7

L—Love Nature

School, home, sleep, school, home, sleep. With our terribly busy schedules, there is little time to spend in nature. When we are outside, we are mostly viewing the world through our phones. The world has provided humans with everything we need to stay balanced, including nature. Unfortunately, time spent outdoors has been declining and is at its lowest rate since 2006.

With the projections that over 70 percent of us will move to large cities by 2050, moving away from nature is coming with consequences.[1] When one loses connection with the environment, one starts to lose connection with themselves, facing a global environmental crisis. Human beings have been entrusted with this world, but how can we care for it well if we are completely disconnected from it?

Nature Heals Us

Spending time in nature can improve physical, mental, social, and even spiritual health. Getting out in nature can relieve stress and lower inflammation. Being close to nature's creations can boost the immune system, boost serotonin leading to a better mood, improve the ability to focus, improve sleep, lower blood pressure, pulse, and heart rate variability, increase mindfulness, the ability to cope with stress, lower cortisol, and increase energy. Trees, especially palms, pines, and cedars, release an essential oil called phytoncide which interacts with your immune system to fight off cancer. Negative ions accumulate in places like beaches and waterfalls, which boost immune system function, reduce stress, kills microbes, and improve sleep. Spending unplugged time in nature has been shown to regulate our nervous system. Even simply looking at a picture of nature has benefits.[2] Getting at least fifteen to thirty minutes of "forest bathing," like a meditative nature walk, has been shown to create a beneficial shift in the microbiome of the kids.[3]

Grounding

The human body and the earth are both electric, and this balance of electrical charges plays a critical role in our health. Electrical charges in humans can become imbalanced due to modern living. By placing our feet on the ground (known as grounding or earthing), we can discharge and neutralize this buildup of positive electrical charges which can help to reduce free radical damage, improve various immune-related health conditions, improve sleep, lower inflammation and cortisol levels, and regulate immune function.[4] Dr. Will Cole recommended that we find a small piece of land and a tree, take our shoes off, and sit underneath the tree. The more nature you have the better.

Nature Connects Us Spiritually

Nature helps us experience awe and gratitude, helping us focus on something bigger than ourselves. Nature can support a sense of purpose and spirituality. Studies have shown that children who played outside five to ten hours a week expressed feelings of peace, happiness, and a sense of belonging.⁵ They also felt a high level of curiosity, imagination, and creativity. By escaping, observing, contemplating, and reflecting about nature, the body is given time to reconnect with its roots, thus increasing the sense of calm, mindfulness, and helping us reset our lives and feel intimately connected to our higher purpose, grounding us in our existence.

Loving Nature in Real Life

 Teens are obsessed with screen time, but now we need to incorporate "green time" into our everyday routine.

We get it, life gets busy. We love to go out in our backyard that is packed with trees and play soccer or basketball. Here is how we like to prioritize getting "green time" into our lives.

Get Early Morning Sun

Wake up to natural sunlight, spend some time outdoors when you wake up, and play outdoors when possible. Morning sunlight regulates our body's natural clock, helps to balance hormones like melatonin which helps us fall asleep, regulates stress, triggers serotonin to improve mood, boosts cognition, and improves our metabolism. It is best to get sun exposure in the first thirty to sixty minutes after waking. Sunrise and sunset light are the best times to be out.

Be Mindful in Nature

Go outside without your phone. Use this time to have a little digital detox to refresh your mind. Have trees around you, breathe, and be mindful of the world around you. Take in nature with all your senses. What color are the trees, what animals are around, what are the different sounds, how do you feel outside?

Hug a Tree

Yes, you read that right. People who hug trees feel calmer, more relaxed, and it has been shown to increase oxytocin.[6]

Get Your Hands Dirty and Compost

We are one with the earth. Dr. Maya Shetreat, pediatric neurologist and author of *The Dirt Cure*, recommended building a garden and growing your own food. Getting our hands dirty with soil and eating freshly picked produce can increase gut microbiome diversity.

Just two square centimeters of soil will have more microbial diversity than anything in the universe and eliminates the need for chemicals. As we discussed earlier, we are losing our soils. When we interviewed Rob Herring, the director of *The Need to Grow*, he emphasized that our land can be regenerated. Nature returns when soil returns. He recommends that, instead of throwing away food scraps, composting is important to help regenerate the earth. You can compost in a controlled environment. The food scraps will decompose into new soil, and you can use that in your garden. In our house, we compost as much as food as we can.

Other ways to take care of the planet are to shop at farmers markets, eat the rainbow of real food, and prioritize organic if possible. Collaborate with your school to get a school or community garden going or start a seed library at school. Start a composting bin at home and at school. Kids can regenerate the soil and save the planet.

Bring Nature Inside

Decorate your home with plants. We have indoor plants in every room. Take whatever planter you like, find seeds, and stick them in the soil. Water and watch it grow. Start with something simple and powerful like broccoli sprouts. You only need seeds, water, and a glass jar! It cannot be easier than that! We love the nutrient benefits of sprouts. Here is how you can get started. You can get special sprouting kits on Amazon, but all you really need is:

- Wide-mouth quart mason jar with a lid
- Wide-mouth mesh sprouting jar lid
- Sprouting rack or anything that can keep the sprouts jar at a 45-degree angle to drain liquid.
- Organic sprouting seeds
- Water

Directions:

1. Soak two tablespoons of seeds overnight at room temperature for about eight hours, filling the jar halfway with water. This is the only time you will let the sprouts sit in water.
2. After eight hours, dump the water out.
3. Rinse out the seeds twice, two times a day.
4. Place it facing down in a large bowl at a 45-degree angle in a dark area.
5. Everyday rinse twice, two times a day until sprouts fill the jar.

That is it!! After three to five days of rinsing and draining your sprouts, they should be ready to eat! It is that easy! Now you have home grown sulforaphane packed sprouts that will heal your mind, body, and soul from the inside out!

Schedule Vitamin Nature

Nature can be easy to get if we build it into our schedule and add it to our calendars. Trying to get your family to incorporate at least thirty minutes or more of nature a week. Build a garden or a fort, hug a tree, and go on a hike. Encourage your friends to go with you. There are apps you can download to help you identify what kinds of plants and animals are in your area.

Make it fun! Try rope courses, zip lining, snorkeling, climbing a mountain, skiing, wilderness adventure, rafting, kayaking, and camping. If you are creative, try to make it a fun inspiration for your artwork. Take your paint supplies and a sketchbook, documenting as you go (Zain loves to do this on all our trips) (Figure 7.1).

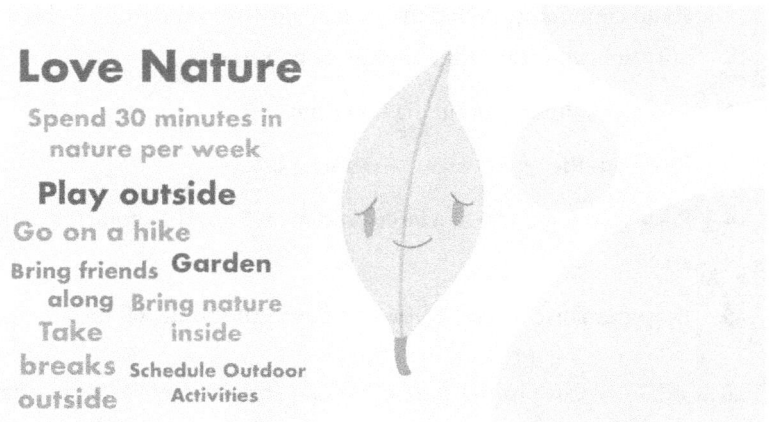

FIGURE 7.1 *Love nature. Illustration by Zain Ansari.*

What Do the Holistic Kids Do?

We love nature and spend a couple of hours a week in nature when we can. We must admit, sometimes we do not want to leave the house, but we schedule nature hikes into our daily routine. When we go on our hikes, we all love to climb and explore new trails, some dangerous . . . our mom has to drag us out. We love ziplining, kayaking, and we absolutely love snorkeling, we can do that for hours! We love checking out new parks, new trails, new ponds, lakes, seeing the unexpected is so much fun!

We prioritize early morning sunlight. Abdullah likes to go straight outside to shoot some hoops right when he wakes up. Emaad and Qasim love to garden and pick fruits and vegetables. Zain loves to drink his water outside. We have lots of indoor plants . . . even too many. We live in Illinois, so we do not have beautiful weather all the time, but in the summertime, we love to garden and have lots of fruit trees. We do not waste food. Composting is amazing!

This earth is a home we all share; we need to take care of it the best we know how. When we start taking care of it, it will take care of us.

Revolution Recap: Love Nature

- Spend least thirty minutes in nature a week.
- Schedule outdoor activities.
- Garden.
- Bring nature inside.
- Be mindful outdoors.
- Go on a hike.
- Bring friends along.

8

U—Unite with Others

Snapchat, TikTok, Facebook, Instagram, YouTube . . . we are more social but lonelier than ever. Humans are social creatures by nature. We need each other to survive. If you go into a perfume shop, you come out smelling good. If you go into a smoke shop, you smell like smoke. It is the same with real life. If you spend time with bad influences, your body starts to subconsciously acquire their habits. Surrounding yourself with loving relationships is powerful medicine. We are the average of the five people we spend the most time with—including our friends, who can dictate our behavior and influence our decisions.

Love Heals

Love really does heal. Love and social connection can buffer our fight-or-flight response. Kindness increases oxytocin and serotonin, lowers stress, improves the immune system, increases self-esteem and heart rate variability. When we show kindness, everyone around us benefits from the same immune effects. When a person sees someone showing an act of kindness, that person's immune system improves. Giving and receiving love from positive, loving relationships with friends, family, even pets inspire healing—physically, emotionally, and spiritually. Being connected can lower your mortality (death) risk by 45 percent![1] Positive company can increase a teen's sense of belonging and purpose, boost happiness, reduce stress, improve self-confidence and self-worth, and help a teen cope with any traumas. Friends can change your life forever—for better or worse.

Studies have shown that negative relationships and loneliness can lead to premature death, increase cortisol levels, weaken the immune system, and cause long-term problems such as stress, anxiety, and depression. Loneliness is found to have the same mortality (death) risk as someone who smokes fifteen cigarettes a day.[2] Studies have shown that isolation can make one more prone to illnesses. If you have a toxic friend, it might be time to let them go.

Revolutionize Your Relationships

You are wired to need friendships and to need an intimate partner when you grow up. Those are as important as food and safety. When you build a community of friends that nourishes you, it is as important as what you eat.

—Dave Asprey, NYT best-selling author and father of biohacking

When we spoke to Mr. Dave Asprey, he emphasized that if he could go back in time, he would have started studying relationships, as it would have saved him from a lot of suffering.

Let's face it, we need our peers. Our teenage years are a time we get to learn what makes a good partner or friend. Learn what builds a community. Learn how to behave in a relationship and learn to build trust.

What Others Think of You Is None of Your Business

Eighty percent of teens care about what others think of them.[3] We try to mold ourselves to fit in with those around us. Mr. Asprey gave us some amazing life advice. Someone that is popular has the greatest number of positive micro interactions. When they walk down the hallway, they are connecting with people—letting them know they are seen. People want to be seen.

You have your morals and code of ethics. To find friends that best fit your needs, you need to start with yourself. Work on being healthy, so your brain and body work. Then learn the steps it takes to connect with people. Mr. Asprey recommended we start reading books like *Influence: The Psychology of Persuasion*, all about how people manipulate others, and *The 48 Laws of Power* that share stories in history on how people become rich, famous, and powerful, and how they stay that way.

To revolutionize your relationship, Mr. Asprey recommended that we increase our positive connections, help people be seen, then pick the very best people and spend more time with them. Look for friends who:

1. Lift you up and make you a better version of yourself. Not all relationships are lasting or truly fulfilling. Remember, if we are constantly trying to make our friends happy, their happiness is always dependent on someone else—that is not a healthy relationship. At the end of the day, we manage our own happiness. You should not feel put down, unsafe, or like you are walking on eggshells. Not everyone needs to be our best friend, and it is okay to stop hanging out with those that do not value you.

2. Someone on whom you can rely. If something is going wrong in your life, your friends are the ones who have your back no matter what. You want to be able to trust them, respect them, and they

will want to empathize with you. They own it when they screw up and do not blame others.

3. Look for people that are minimal maintenance. We are busy, we are studying, building our lives, so find a friend that does not need your constant attention but is there for you when you need them. And of course, you are there for them when they need you. Effective communication is key.

4. Find friends that have similar goals. Relationships change, we get busy. Friends should grow and change together. This may mean meeting new challenges, going through life changes, and encouraging each other's personal growth.

 Know your boundaries. Protect your peace.

Mr. Asprey emphasizes that peace is the hardest thing for most humans to have. When you take care of your body, you have energy, you can feel peace. . . . That makes you the most powerful person in the room. If you fail a test or pass a test, you are peaceful. If you get rejected by a friend or invited by a friend, you are at peace. When you are at peace, you are able to interact with those around you better. You can attract friends that respect you and that you love spending time with. Be conscious of your boundaries and protect your peace.

Peer Pressure

The pressures of the real world can be a lot! There is good pressure and bad. Bad peer pressure can decrease self-confidence and lead to poor academic performance.

Trust your gut and be mindful. If something does not feel right, just say NO.

Deep breaths, mindfulness, and positive affirmations can help you feel more in control. If the pressure gets too much, take a break from it. Remember, you do not have to do this alone, there are always people here to help you, talk to an adult you trust. Being a teen is not easy.

Revolutionize Your Romantic Relationships

Teenage years are all about discovering ourselves. Who are we today? Who are we truly meant to be in the world? We are living in a world where we are becoming adults younger. We get our hearts broken so many times, especially when we think we have found "the one."

How do we really find "the one"? How do we stop wasting our time? How can we lower emotional and physical stress? We have asked the experts for you. You may not like what they had to say—but it is the cold hard truth.

There are a lot of people in the world that are not looking for any real connections and only looking to get their joy from taking it from others. To know whether the person is worth sticking around for, it is best to hold off on any intimacy.

Abstinence can have many benefits, including allowing couples to build strong foundations for their relationships and prevent unwanted physical and emotional consequences. Physical intimacy can stunt a friendship's learning process. Love and intense feelings can affect decision-making. Intimacy before commitment clouds the water of what the other person is really looking for from the relationship.

This is the true test to find "the one." If the other person really wants to be with you and genuinely loves you for your heart, they will respect your decision and wait for physical intimacy until there is a real commitment.

Abstinence until commitment will test to make sure they:

1. Have self-control. If a person has had that self-control before marriage, they are likely to have it after marriage. That is the person you want to be with. Someone you can trust, through the hurdles of life.
2. Really love and respect you. They see a future with you. When they choose to wait, and are still with you, boy do they love your whole self and not just your parts. They honor your decisions.
3. Are ready for commitment. When your significant other respects your decision to wait, they are committed to you. With more teens being afraid of romantic commitments more than earlier generations, this is a quality you want to really find "the one."

These are the qualities you want to find in the one that will be your child's mother or father. They will be there with you through thick and thin. They have a higher likelihood of being there with you till death do you part.

You are a gem and deserve someone who will kiss the ground you walk on. You deserve someone who really loves you for you, all of you, not just your parts. Holding off any intimacy can help you find the right person for you, who will support you, love you, and treat you like the king or queen that you are. Positive relationships are ones that challenge you, help you learn more about yourself and support your values and your goals.

Find Real Healthy Relationships

Some of us are great at finding friends, and some of us are not. It is important to find friends and relationships that will pick you up, not drag you down. Where is a teen supposed to find that?

Common Interest Gatherings

If you love playing chess, go take classes for chess, because the kids in that class also love to play chess. If you love to work out, go to the gym and attend teen classes. Combine physical activity with social connection and put it on the calendar.

Volunteer

Science has shown that volunteering can decrease depression, help one stay mentally and physically active, reduce stress, and help us live longer.[4] Volunteering increases our sense of purpose. Find places to volunteer, like hospitals, food banks, nonprofit organizations, and places of worship.

Join Groups

Joining support groups in the mosque, church, and other religious places of worship, taking a class at a local gym or community venue, and traveling groups helps us find people with similar interests.

Random Acts of Kindness and Generosity

We all love when someone unexpectedly opens a door for us or helps us with something. Ask yourself: do one of my friends need extra loving support? Keep an eye out for that. Does someone in your neighborhood need help? Does an elderly neighbor need someone to help them shovel or cut the grass? Give them a call, let them know you are here for them. The simplest, most powerful thing someone can do to improve themselves and others is to smile.

Talk Not Text. Yes, Even with Your Parents

Researchers measured the oxytocin and cortisol levels of teenagers who were talking to their parents in person or on the phone. They found a reduction in cortisol and an increase in oxytocin.[5] Do not let go of real-life connections for the digital life.

Dealing with Bullies

Bullying is an abuse of power. It is defined as aggressive behavior or intentional harm by peers that is carried out repeatedly and involves an imbalance of power. Bullying can take many forms. It takes the form of verbal bullying, physical bullying, psychological or social bullying, even cyber bullying.

Bullying is a major risk factor for poor physical and mental health, self-harm, depression, sleep problems, and even suicide in teens. It has lingering effects into adulthood like mental health issues, suicidality, anxiety, smoking, less income, poor performance in school and managing finances and poor relationships. Bullying alters brain structure. Researchers have found that adolescents being bullied by their peers are at greater risk of the initial stages of psychotic episodes and in turn experience lower levels of a key neurotransmitter in a part of the brain involved in regulating emotions.

Tips to Taking Down Bullies

Let us be realistic—real life is filled with bullies. Do not take bullying personally, as the bully is more inflamed and "out of balance" and does not know how to treat someone any differently. A bully lacks empathy, desires to be in control, feels frustrated, angry, and/or depressed. A bully lacks social skills.

Be strong, stand tall, and keep firm on what you are saying. Sometimes kindness is the best weapon. A bully wants your attention, so do not give them that. Simply walk away, unbothered. If it gets too much, do not be afraid to talk to your friends, family, or a trusted adult for backup.

FIGURE 8.1 *Unite with others. Illustration by Zain Ansari.*

Be Mindful

Look at the friends you have in your life now. Ask yourself: How many are supportive or comforting? How many of them live within a 50-mile radius? How many of them are real friends? How many give you joy? Do you have a ride or die? Is your family supportive and loving? Or toxic and packed with problems? Then ask yourself, "What are the skills I am lacking on how to connect with other people? How do I become the best in the world at being a good friend?" When your relationships are strong and safe, they can add years to your life (Figure 8.1).

What Do the Holistic Kids Do?

We keep people around that will lift us up. We recognize those that are hurting us, and we move away from them. Zain had a friend that threatened to kill him . . . let us say Zain stopped talking to him and is no longer his friend. We find friends that like to do the same things we like to do. Our cousins are also our best friends. We do spend a lot of time in our places of worship, go to the gym, play at the park, and go on hikes with friends. We even have a friend that likes to podcast with us and help us with editing. We value friends that value us.

Remember, each time you smile, each time you connect with someone, every joyful interaction will keep you healthy and will help you live longer. We love you!

Revolution Recap: Unite with Others

- Work on yourself, find your peace.
- Show others that you see them.
- Have friends that pull you up, not drag you down.

9

T—Tech Limits

Ninety-one percent of teens own a smartphone by the age of fourteen.[1] We have the entire universe of information in our pockets—and that comes with huge temptations and challenges.

Boys are mostly playing video games and playing with each other, while girls are more likely to be on social media platforms. Social media comes with benefits but also a substantial number of problems. Context, hand gestures, tone of voice, and facial expressions are all lost.

Dr. Will Cole, NYT best-selling author, describes technology as a double-edged sword. Treat social media and digital connections like sugar. We see those shows where the animal sticks its head in the dirt to hide away and not deal with the situation? We are now that animal. Most of us teens are hiding away from the pains, unease, and questions of life by submerging ourselves in our phones.

We are now living with a leash. Three out of four Americans confess to using their phones on the toilet, with 96 percent of Gen Zs saying they cannot go to the bathroom without their phones.[2] This phone-based life has pulled us downward. It has changed the way we think, live our lives, and even the way we look upon others. We no longer think for ourselves; we are physically leashed.

Tech Affects Us

Teens are at a crucial stage of development where our bodies are going through incredible changes in our personality, cognition, and biology. Our brain is vulnerable to the internet and consuming media. Tech companies have gotten us hooked, and we are dealing with the consequences. Teens are falling into a tundra of deceptive darkness, lack of authentic relationships, unhealthy distractions, lack of purpose, and wasting our time from what really matters in life.

Tech and Our Physical Health

With our necks bent forward all day long, and our thumbs and fingers in positions that were not meant for humans, we are suffering. Now add in all the blue and artificial light we are consuming daily, and the dopamine hits that are keeping us addicted and hurting our health.[3] We are suffering from back pain, neck pain, and eye strain, not to mention the ongoing insomnia that is then leading to further physical symptoms. Social media has been linked to poor physical health among college students, where those who used excessive social media were found to have higher levels of CRP, a blood marker of inflammation that predicts chronic diseases like heart disease, diabetes, cardiovascular disease, and stroke. The more social media that was used, the more likely were headaches, chest and back pain, and more frequent visits to doctors for treatment of illness.[4]

Tech and Our Mental Health

Social media is really affecting our mental health.[5] Social media can be both a source of connection and a cause of stress. Teens can feel more disconnected from the world. Social media often presents a curated version of reality, leading to feelings of inadequacy and FOMO (Fear of Missing Out).

Tom Kersting, author of *Raising Healthy Teenagers*, talked to us about the harms of social media on our subconscious. He said that thought comes from experiences. Our brain can reshape itself. All the information is downloading into our subconscious mind and affects every part of our health. When you spend so much time on the phone, you miss play, nature, and even thinking. It also leads to shorter attention spans. You are an amazing human being, but you cannot know yourself if you are never present. Sadly, most teens do not know who they are.

Social media can sometimes breed negativity and cyberbullying. Cyberbullying can be even worse than physical bullying, as it is more humiliating, happening in front of the world and not just at school. Take cyberbullying seriously.

Tech and Our Spiritual Health

As described in the NYT best-selling book, *The Anxious Generation*, staring at our phones all day can affect our spirituality. Most spiritual practices involve getting together as a whole, using stillness and silence, have us focus on forgiveness and less judgment, have awe in nature, and self-transcendence Social media keeps us from all of these. It keeps us so preoccupied with loneliness, with the clicks, alerts, likes, it is taking us away from connecting with a higher power. When people come together to practice together, move together, share a meal together, it increases trust and unity, reducing loneliness. Social media binds us tightly to our egos, which goes against spirituality. Social media is adding to our growing spiritual crisis.

Being Media Safe

Social media is an open door to predators. Your safety and privacy online should always be a top priority. Be mindful of the information you share.

Avoid posting sensitive personal details and use privacy settings to control who can see your content. Beware of strangers, and be cautious when interacting with people you do not know in real life. If something feels off, trust your instincts and report any suspicious activity.

Mindful Use Is Powerful

Social media has the power to create positive changes in the world. Mindless scrolling offers little to no benefit. Go on social media with a purpose and be mindful of your usage. Ask yourself: Why am I picking up this phone? Am I bored, sad, upset, or stressed? Find a better way to deal with those emotions.

Be mindful of who is in control. Dr. Will Cole recommends asking yourself, is tech controlling you or do you control it? You will know intuitively. He recommends uninstalling apps that do not serve you well and are time consuming, put down time limits on your phone, and put your phone in airplane mode while you are in school.

Whatever time you are using on your phone or video games, explore what less time on your phone can look like. What are you going to do with your time when you are not on it? Focus on activities that you love like getting out in nature, getting a hobby, reading a book, playing a board game. Be mindful about how it is affecting you and if you find yourself getting addicted, then do something about it right away before you get too deep into the addiction.

In our interview with *The Anxious Generation* researcher Zach Rausch, he recommended we protect ourselves in the online world, by:

1. No smartphones before high school.
2. No social media before sixteen.
3. Phone-free schools (it improves mental health and socialization).

4. Far more unsupervised play and childhood independence. Kids need to be given the chance to play. We need more recess. Find a group of friends and go out for an adventure.

Consciously Keep Your Subconscious Positive

Do not compare your behind-the-scenes with someone else's highlight reel. Remember, what you see online is only part of the story. Everyone experiences highs and lows, successes, and failures. Embrace your uniqueness and celebrate your journey. We need to consciously train our subconscious to be positive, by prioritizing gratitude. Do not let likes and followers dictate to yourself. Remember, you are more than your online persona.

Prioritize Self Care

It is critical to have a routine that is without your phones or devices. Phones should never be in the bedroom; this leads to sleep issues. A tired teen is a nonfunctional teen, so set ground rules. A drawer in the kitchen with all the chargers can be used to plug your phone in at night and keep it out of sight and out of mind. Stop using your phone at least one hour before bed and keep it at least six feet away from you.

Create a morning routine without your phone. An example is waking up, doing a gratitude practice and prayer, going to the bathroom, brushing your teeth, meditating, sunshine, eating a nourishing meal, and setting your goals for the day, all without your phone. Know your values, morals, ethics, and goals before you jump on social media.

Dr. Will Cole recommends finding time to do a digital detox. Creating new habits away from your phone will be uncomfortable at first because we are so used to constantly checking our devices. He stresses, "when

Put a screen time limit on your phone
Commit to a digital detox
Mindful consumption
Create a phone-less routine
Make time for play
Increase time in nature
No social media before 16
Phone free schools

Limiting Tech

FIGURE 9.1 *Limiting tech. Illustration by Zain Ansari.*

this technology doesn't make you feel the way you want to be feeling, you need to do something different."

Social media is a tool that comes with great responsibility. Every post, like, comment, and share leaves behind your digital footprint. Think before you post anything, and make sure the digital foodprint you leave behind reflects who you really are. You are smarter than your phone (Figure 9.1).

What Do the Holistic Kids Do?

We live by these principles. Zain, fourteen years old, does not have a phone; we have no iPad, no electronic devices except our computer that we do play an hour of video games on, but we have our limits. Abdullah just got a basic phone in the middle of tenth grade but still has no social media. Emaad and Qasim do not have social media or phones. We live by what we preach, and we are free . . . we want you to be the same! Are you hesitant because you think you will be bored without screens? We always find things to do, which is so much more fun. Boredom leads to creativity; we are using our minds without it using us. Zain loves to draw; he has even illustrated our mom's children's book called *Adam's Healing Adventures: Real Food vs Fake Food*. Abdullah loves to create speeches and speak in public. Emaad loves solving the Rubik's Cube and learning magic tricks, and Qasim loves to make new recipes! We can only do all of this because we are not on screens all day. A world free of addictions can help us make all our dreams come true. We use the internet to spread a positive message—our podcasts, reels, shorts, are all managed by our mother.

Revolution Recap: Tech Limits

- Create a morning and evening routine without your phone.
- Put a screen time limit on your phone.
- Commit to a digital detox.
- Make time for play.
- Increase time in nature.
- No social media before sixteen.
- Phone-free schools.
- No cell phones before high school.
- Mindful consumption—tech with purpose.

10

I—Invest in Sleep

BEDTIME!!! ... Don't you hate it when your parents scream at the top of their lungs? Does it make you sad that you must stop what you are doing and just sleep?

Most teens and adults alike tell themselves that now it is time to go to sleep, but then they think to themselves, "You know ... now that everyone thinks I am sleeping, I can quickly enjoy scrolling through social media for ten minutes."

Then you open social media and BOOM there goes one, two, or three hours of your time. But you tell yourself, "It's fine ... sleep is not that important."

Is Sleep Really That Important?

I know you do not want to hear this, but sleep is super important for adults, teens, and children. Sleep allows our body to recharge for the next day. But unfortunately, according to the CDC, six in ten middle schoolers and seven in ten high schoolers are not getting enough sleep.[1] According to Johns Hopkins pediatricians, teens need 9 to 9½ hours of sleep per night—that's an hour or so *more* than they needed at age ten.[2]

Why Aren't We Sleeping?

A major cause of decreased sleep is the increased use of blue light. And where is blue light most commonly found? Yup, you guessed it . . . electronic screens! Looking at your phone before bed is a . . . BAD IDEA!

—Dr. Michael Breus, PhD, Clinical Psychologist, Sleep Medicine Expert, NYT best-selling author of *The Sleep Doctor's Diet Plan* and *Good Night*

Why Is Blue Light Not Good for Us?

Each teen has a sleep cycle and a wake cycle that is known as the circadian rhythm. Our circadian rhythm is important for most of our biological processes. What makes artificial blue light different from natural blue light? When blue light hits our eyes, it tells our brain to not secrete melatonin (our sleepy hormone), which causes us to sleep. When we start using our phone right before we go to sleep, it prevents us from feeling drowsy.

When our body gets sunlight, it prepares our body to wake up. At night, our body starts preparing to go to sleep. The problem with blue light is that it tricks our brain into thinking it is morning, worsening the quality of sleep. Teens and adults do not realize the effect of scrolling on social media before bed. Half of all children use screens the hour before bed,[3] leading to lower expression of BDNF and an increase in mood disorders.

Tips to Stop the Scroll

When we interviewed Ms. Kim West, aka the Sleep Lady, author of the best-selling book *The Sleep Lady's Good Night, Sleep Tight*, she gave us some amazing tips.

1. Do not have your phone right next to your bed, limiting the temptation to scroll.
2. Put a timer on how long you are going to scroll.

Dr. Breus recommends stopping electronics ninety minutes before bed.

Why Is Sleep So Good for Us?

Kids need more sleep than adults.

—Dr. Michael Breus

Our brains are developing really fast, at a rate of 800 synapses per second (which is fast). One synapse is like a lightning-fast network connection when we've texted someone; now imagine 800 of those at once. That is how fast our brain processes information. On our podcast episode, Ms. Kim talked about three important things that happen when we sleep.

1. Sleep helps your body produce proteins and cells that fight infection and disease and improve your immune system. If we are sleep deprived, we are more likely to get sick.
2. During sleep, our brain is working on our memory retention, storage, and organization. If we get a good night's sleep, our memory and recall will be better. For example, we will do better on a test.
3. During sleep, our body produces and secretes growth hormones and other hormones. We need these hormones to keep us growing, healing, and repairing our body.

When we are well rested, we tend to make better eating choices, less carb cravings, we have better coordination, perform better in sports.

—Kim West

Sleep is important to prevent type 2 diabetes, obesity, poor mental health, injuries, attention or behavior problems, and emotional and social disfunction, which all affect everyday life and schoolwork. How can we properly focus on our test or assignment if we cannot focus at all?

Good sleep is just too important to ignore. Even Albert Einstein always made sure to have ten hours of sleep.[4] A recent study found that 48 percent of kids who did sleep enough had a 44 percent higher likelihood of showing curiosity in learning new information and skills. They were also 33 percent more likely to complete all their homework and 28 percent more likely to care about doing well in school.[5]

What Happens If We Do Not Sleep?

What do you call a Himalayan cow that does not sleep?
An insomnia-yak!

What do you call kids that do not sleep?
A BIG Problem!

All jokes aside, a lack of sleep can lead to major problems! Kids who experience poor sleep during preschool and early school age years are at an increased risk of developing cognitive and behavioral problems in mid-childhood.

Sleep restrictions were also found to increase irritability, acting out, restlessness, lead to depression, increase challenging behaviors, hyperactivity, reduced academic performance, substance abuse, suicide, and other behavioral challenges.

The Best Thing You Can Do

> Look at sleep as the best thing you can do for your brain. Sleep is a superpower for your brain.
>
> —Dr. Austin Perlmutter, NYT best-selling author of *Brain Wash*

We have a confession. We also struggled balancing sleep, school, and family, especially on the weekends when we just wanted to enjoy our break. But after we heard so many podcast guests talk about the importance of sleep, we now prioritize our sleep. To be the best we can be, we do our best to invest in sleep and we really feel the difference. What do we do? A sleep routine helps us sleep better!

Optimizing Sleep

A sleep routine is important and no, it is not just for babies. There are various stages of sleep. Stage 1 is when you are just starting to sleep, and dozing off, stage 2 your body is preparing for deep sleep. Stage 3 is deep sleep that is usually at the beginning of the night and your body releases human growth factors that can repair cells, your brain also starts its cleaning process through the brain's lymphatic system. Stage 4 is REM sleep, this is where we dream, processing information and connecting memories, we need this stage of sleep for better concentration.

> When you have more consistency, your body knows what to do. It helps with our circadian rhythm. Having a routine cannot only help you fall asleep but stay asleep much longer.
>
> —Dr. Breus

Dr. Breus recommends relaxation activities before you go to bed. Remember your sleep routine starts the moment you wake up.

1. Wake up with gratitude.
2. Eat real food.
3. Stay away from things that can disrupt your sleep (stress, too much artificial light, fake food, sugar, and caffeine).
4. Start winding down two hours before bedtime. We love to take Epsom salt baths.
5. Write down your worries.
6. Decrease EMF exposure by turning off Wi-Fi routers.
7. Do not eat right before you go to sleep, if you want to eat something eat a meal that is high in fat and lower in carbohydrates.
8. Make your bedroom cool and dark. Organize your room, get rid of the mess.
9. Put a houseplant in your room to help clean the air.
10. Limit bright artificial light between 10:00 p.m. and 4:00 a.m., that can improve your overall health and wellness.

 The way we live during the day, can help you get your best sleep.

Live for a Successful Snooze

Wake up with gratitude and prayer. Get natural light exposure for the first one to three hours of the day. This is easy for us, because we usually get on the bus for school early in the morning. On the weekends, we drink our water outside in the sun. Also, if you are drinking coffee, do not drink it after lunch. Always wake up at the same time even on weekends to keep your rhythm in check. Eat real food. Dr. Breus told us that kiwis promote serotonin to help you relax before bed, bananas (nature's sleeping pills loaded with magnesium) and Greek yogurt packed with calcium and

FIGURE 10.1 *Sleep. Illustration by Zain Ansari.*

pineapple have a lot of melatonin. Dr. Breus makes a banana tea that helps to improve sleep. Put half a banana with the skin into boiling water. Once the water cools, drink the water.

Make sure to exercise in the morning or afternoon. Grounding, spending time in nature, meditation, breathing exercises can lower our stress throughout the day and help us sleep. No phone notifications a couple of hours before bed. Keep the phone out of the bedroom.

There is so much we can do to improve our sleep. How do we know if we are getting enough sleep? If you are tired all the time, you need more sleep. Focus on all the tips we gave you to get the best sleep of your life (Figure 10.1).

What Do the Holistic Kids Do?

We try our hardest to prioritize sleep. We do not have social media, so it is easier for us to stay off our devices and limit blue light. We live for sleep. We have developed a sleep routine, where we slow down before bed, eat four hours before we sleep, and listen to scripture before we sleep. Our bedding, our mattress, our pillows are all organic. We have snake plants and air filters in each room. Our curtains are darkening. We pray and meditate throughout the day and before we go to bed.

Sleeping is the easiest thing we can do to help our brain and our body. If you cannot sleep, remember that it is your body talking to you. Talk to a doctor and investigate what is off balance.

Revolution Recap: Invest in Sleep

- Stay away from blue light at least one to two hours before you go to sleep.
- Live for a successful snooze.
- Create a bedtime routine.
- Make a dedicated sleep schedule (at least eight hours).

11

O—Open to Gratitude and Purpose

 Our perspective can be our power or our pain.

There is so much negativity in the world. When we spend hours in a virtual world that only highlights the good in people's lives, it is easy to look at our lives as less. This is where trouble starts to brew. We start to have negative talk. The negative self-talks from a negative subconscious world led us to sickness.

No, do not pick up your phone and start scrolling TikTok . . . I know it is easier than facing reality . . . but we need to change.

We need to change our subconscious mind from thinking about the things we cannot control, to things we can do! There is so much hope! To change that, we need to change our perspective. Focus on our attitude of gratitude . . . we know it is cliche, but it works!

Is Gratitude Important?

Short answer . . . *yes!* We should be practicing gratitude every day, not just at Thanksgiving. Gratitude means the quality of being thankful and expressing appreciation. In the feeling of gratitude, spirituality is experienced. Gratitude helps us connect with our purpose and our soul, and it positively affects our brain and behavior as a teen.

Gratitude helps to create a subconscious world of positivity, which governs 90 percent of our thoughts and actions. Gratitude has the power to improve genetics, traumatic experiences, and years of learned behaviors. When we start to focus on all the good, it will shift our internal world to a world of positivity, leading to positive behaviors. This practice lowers the threshold for feel-good circuits to discharge in our brains, improves immune function, heart rate variability, lowers stress, improves mental health, and raises happiness indexes. Along with yoga, meditation, prayer, and mindfulness, gratitude can slow brain activity and lessen the negative thoughts that permeate our lives.[1]

An attitude of gratitude is powerful. We need to change our subconscious from being negative and train it to be positive by:

1. Keeping a gratitude journal.
2. Place sticky notes of all the things you are thankful for all over your communal areas. This will train your subconscious subliminally to concentrate on the blessings of your life.
3. Express gratitude to those in your life.
4. Immediately when you wake up, say ten things you are thankful for daily.

Gratitude improves our self-esteem. Self-esteem is how we feel and think about ourselves. Low self-esteem has the power of altering a person's physical, mental, and spiritual health. It may change our academic or professional success because we may avoid undertaking challenges and breaking new roads due to fear of failure and rejection. It is estimated that 85 percent of people worldwide have low self-esteem.[2] There are a lot of things that can influence our self-esteem, like negative experiences in our lives, peer pressure, social media, and so on.

Gratitude can help to build self-esteem as it can lead to having more positive feelings about ourselves. When a teen's subconscious thinks positively, their brain is now free to make its own decisions and figure out its own personal values. If we can keep our subconscious positive, it helps to build connections through strong and satisfying relationships. With gratitude, we are always good enough.

Building positivity in a world of negativity will take daily conscious training to change our subconscious. Self-love or self-compassion means treating your own thoughts, actions, and needs with gentleness and caring consideration, instead of criticism that comes from deep within. Find ways to feel successful, finding success on your own Appreciate that you have failures, as we all do. Our failures do not define us, they make us better. Gratitude helps us be open to purpose.

Find a Higher Purpose

For thousands of years, humans have had religious traditions to help guide them for life's answers. You have been put on this planet for a unique purpose, which is different for everyone. Mindfulness and gratitude will help us develop a positive attitude and reframe our stress. We can eat right, sleep, and exercise, but if we do not have a sense of purpose, a belief in something bigger than ourselves—we will be missing a large chunk of health. On our podcast, we had the pleasure of speaking to doctors and mental health professionals who have seen the power of purpose and spiritual health to improve overall health and wellness.

Purpose drives us to be the best we can be. A strong "purpose in life" reduces the chances that our self-esteem will fluctuate with the number of likes we get on social media. A lack of purpose has been linked to higher levels of the stress hormone cortisol, more abdominal fat, and other negative health markers.[3]

Discover Your Purpose

The creator economy is currently at $250 billion and is predicted to grow to half a trillion dollars in the next four years, according to Goldman Sachs. Eighty-six percent of young Americans want to become a social media influencer according to CBS News.[4] Especially with social media contributing to a decline in teen mental health, this is not the best purpose for us teens. Think about the ways our life would be better if we were spending more of our day aligning with our values and purpose.

We can help create meaning in our lives by asking questions such as why is the world a better place because I am here? What can I contribute? How does our work connect us to others? Are there hurts from our past that we can turn around to help others? What do others want or need from us? How do others change because of what we do? How do we want to be remembered after we die? What gives us joy, meaning and motivation?

Purpose is personal. The practice of finding purpose with something bigger requires deep intentionality, it does not just happen. We need to make it happen by setting intentions to look for and act.

Your Spiritual Health Matters

We are mind, body, and soul. There is something bigger than all of us, that we must either believe in, rely on, or connect with. Something bigger than what we can see with our eyes, something we can rely on in times of stress and despair. Just like with purpose, you need to define this yourself. For some people, it may be that we are deeply connected at a vibrational and spiritual level, to love other people and do good. For us, something bigger is God. For most, there is a larger force at work that is guiding our every move and helps us keep our faith that we are making positive ripples in the world that extend far beyond our line of sight. When we put our bodies back into balance with our lifestyles, we create a body that can easily connect with our higher purpose, source, a higher being, or God.

Engaging with this broader perspective is crucial for overall well-being, leading to inner contentment and enduring life satisfaction. We interviewed Dr. John Delony, mental and emotional health expert and author of *Building a Non-Anxious Life*, who emphasized that we have a society now where people do not believe in a higher power or anything bigger than them. They think they are the center of the universe, but the body knows we cannot hold up the universe; it is not our job. He said that we must be in service and believe in something bigger than us. Studies have shown that religiosity/spirituality is 80 percent protective against depression in high-risk individuals.[5] Children have been shown to be five times less likely to be depressed when spiritual life was shared with a mother.[6]

Spirituality is a major protective factor over the course of an entire lifetime. Feeling solely as a physical being, born, and destined to die alone, can foster loneliness, especially during challenging times. Without a connection to a higher purpose, individuals may be more susceptible to pursuing fleeting fame and power.

Dr. Jill Carnahan, physician and author of *Unexpected*, describes the importance of faith. She describes faith as how we deal with uncertainty, or when things come that we might not be expecting, like falling off our bike and breaking our arm. The unexpected can happen and it can mess us up. If we know there is a greater purpose, that there is something to learn even in those difficult circumstances, it can make the unexpected a little easier.

Connect and Be Whole

 With a grateful mindset anything is possible.

We all have an emptiness inside of us that we yearn to fill. If we do not fill it with something elevated, society will fill it with degraded garbage. We need to connect. We need to believe. We need to have faith. Build connections, find community, strengthen our spiritual connection, show kindness and empathy.

Know that we cannot do it all on our own; the universe and its problems were not meant for us to fix. We need to take those stresses off our shoulders and give it to the universe, nature, or a higher power. Find what works best for you, live by your morals and ethics.

Navigate life's challenges with resilience. Know that you are not alone, you are just a part of a greater whole. There is so much goodness in the world. You just need to see it. Developing a grateful mindset will help you connect with your higher purpose and improve your spiritual health (Figure 11.1).

What Do the Holistic Kids Do?

We practice gratitude daily and focus on our positives. We have a strong connection with God. Abdullah has memorized the whole Quran (the holy book for Muslims). We are all memorizing it regularly to stay connected with something bigger than ourselves, our creator. That is how we improve our spiritual health, and it has changed our lives inside and out. We have found our purpose, and you are reading it.

FIGURE 11.1 *Open to gratitude and purpose.* Illustration by Zain Ansari.

Revolution Recap: Open to Gratitude and Purpose

- When you wake up in the morning, say or think about ten things for which you are grateful.
- Explore your beliefs and life purpose.
- Set aside personal ego to connect with something larger.

12

N—Navigate Decisions with Mindfulness

Wow! Thank you for still being with us on this journey to create a teen health R-E-V-O-L-U-T-I-O-N! This is where the rubber hits the road. We have so many decisions we make daily. Some good, some not so good. These teenage years are training us for real adult life. The older we get, the more independent we should become. We need to be in charge, no one should be telling us what to do. Our choices can either help us or hurt us. We need to navigate those choices with mindfulness.

Let's be honest—as teenagers, our decision-making skills are still a work in progress. Our hormones, our emotions, and the rational part of our brain are still developing and pruning connections until we turn twenty-five. Research suggests that teens may be more likely to take risks during this pruning phase and are more likely to engage in high-risk behavior[1] and we may misinterpret social cues. To make rational decisions, we need to stay mindful of all these factors.

Live a Balanced Life for Balanced Decisions

We discussed earlier in the book the need to keep our lives balanced to balance our brains and decisions. To keep our decisions working for us,

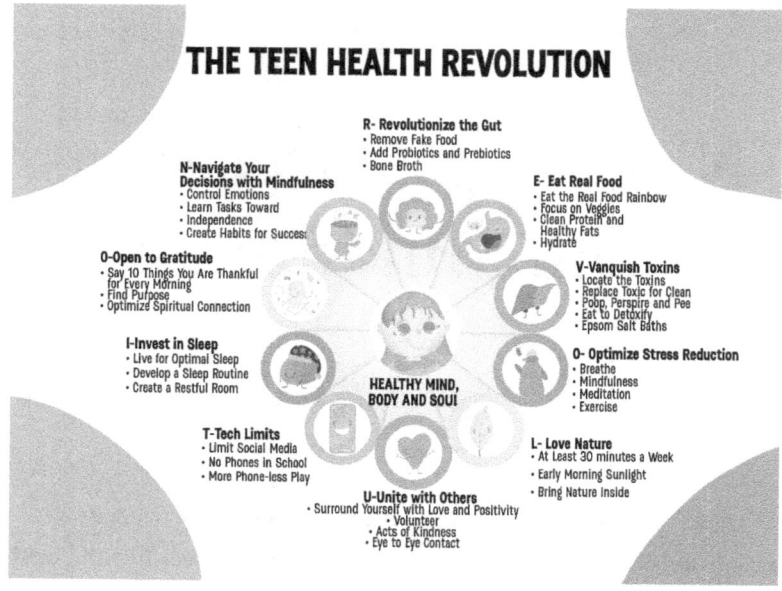

FIGURE 12.1 *The teen health revolution—Healthy mind, body, and soul. Illustration by Zain Ansari.*

we need to work on what we just talked about—R.E.V.O.L.U.T.I.O.N. Let us recap in Figure 12.1.

Listen to Your Body—Connect with Your Emotions

As a teenager, our environment, our relationships, and our emotions can drive our decisions. To make a well-thought-out decision, listen to your body. Being mindful of our emotions and feelings is especially important for making good decisions.

When a feeling we have gets triggered, there is a rush of biochemicals that go into our bloodstream. Those same biochemicals flush out of our bloodstream in ninety seconds. These feelings are like waves that come up and then go down. It takes ninety seconds for the wave to pass; if we stay present and breathe, we can defeat the wave.

We spoke to Dr. Joan Rosenberg, psychologist, author of *90 Seconds to the Life You Love*, who explained that the more we notice what we notice, or the greater we are aware of what we are aware of—we can be more mindful. When we are mindful, we can move away from having quick, mean reactions. Mindfulness helps people switch from reacting to responding. It is an important skill for teens to develop.

How are we going to manage our emotions? Dr. Rosenberg describes pleasant feelings and unpleasant or difficult feelings like sadness, shame, helplessness, anger, vulnerability, embarrassment, disappointment, and frustration. She says that these feelings exist for protective purposes. The pleasant feelings, like being happy or content, at ease, joyful—these guide us to lean into or toward something. These feelings lead to connections with others or to creativity. The unpleasant feelings are protective—they suggest that we should move away from something because it might be painful. When boys are raised to not express themselves, Dr. Joan believes that it is very damaging to them, as it keeps them feeling suppressed. Think of feelings as a source of information. If we are shutting down emotions, we are losing signal and cannot stay connected with ourselves.

Emotions and their bodily sensations can be uncomfortable, and it is easy to react or grab our phone. Unfortunately, that is what we are all doing. When we want to run away, our phones have become our pacifiers. Running away is not going to help us navigate the world.

Dr. Joan gives us five steps to manage our emotions and increase our confidence.

1. She wants us to feel our feelings, both pleasant and unpleasant emotions. Get good at that first. Know what you are feeling and ride the emotion. It is like body surfing in the ocean; ride your

emotions till they subside. Be present at that moment, lean in. Look at how, what, and why you are having this feeling.

2. Learn to express your thoughts and feelings to other people, the pleasant and unpleasant. Reflect on these emotions.

3. Be willing to take important steps and risks to pursue things that are important to you.

4. Stop being mean to yourself. Stop talking harshly to yourself. Know when you are being mean to yourself, and know you are running away from an unpleasant feeling. Ask yourself what difficult feeling you are experiencing.

5. Accept and take in compliments.

Mr. Dave Asprey explains to us that when you feel the emotion in your body, like a tension in the chest or a feeling in the stomach, ask for a minute to process that emotion. Step away and do some box breaths and regulate yourself. Once we have an awareness of our feelings, we can make use of them to make mindful, nonreactive decisions, express ourselves, connect, and grow.

One Decision at a Time to Adulthood

Teenage years are for us to work on ourselves before adulthood. We need to be mindful of our emotions, our feelings, and then subsequently our decisions. We spoke to NYT best-selling author Ms. Julie Lythcott-Haims and author of *Your Turn: How to Be an Adult*, about how teens can really build a life with which they are happy.

 Life is your canvas. Do not paint it for others.

Live the Life *You* Love

She emphasized that there is no right track—you need to create your own track. You will make mistakes. Do what calls to your soul, figure yourself out, and go be that person. You are worthy if you do not become a doctor, an engineer, or a lawyer. The world needs artists, chefs, priests, rabbis, imams, and businesspeople. Success is different for everyone. Life is a wide-open landscape. She recommends figuring out who you are, what you are good at, what you want, what you love—and go be that person.

You have permission to craft the life you want. You can live the life you love; you just need to be mindful about who you are. What do you love? Ask yourself, where could you work that would make you thrive? She recommends letting go of perfectionism and stop living the life that others want you to live. Stop pleasing others—they have no idea who you are.

Become More Independent

When you are a teen, working toward becoming a successful adult, you will become more independent, more in charge of your body, bills, and belongings. Ms. Julie emphasized that we could do it! She addressed the need to learn more for ourselves. Slowly learn everything. When we get out of high school, we should have all the skills we need to survive. As we get older, we need to become more independent.

Do chores . . . we know we said it. Seriously, chores help you learn things that are super useful when we get out in the world. Chores teach us that there is unpleasant work to be done, and we must do it. Chores teach us work ethics. Ms. Julie emphasized that chores help us feel a sense of belonging to our family and that gives us a sense of satisfaction.

Do you know how to groom yourself?

Do your laundry and fold it?

Do you know how to cross the street and take an Uber by yourself?

Can you cook something for yourself?

You need to have the confidence to figure it out as you go. You may not be able to figure it all out, but with time it will come. "You can be this A plus student, who doesn't know how to do the stuff of life, and you will be useless out there," says Ms. Julie.

Habits of Success

Create an environment that makes behavior change fun. To build the life you love, you need to create your own environment to help nurture that life for success. Restock the pantry with all your favorite, fun, real foods. Get a large glass water bottle for hydration. Lay out your workout clothes the night before. Place your water by the back door, which will trigger you to get some sunlight and drink water outside.

This is known as habit stacking. Before you get into the shower use the dry brush and do a hot/cold shower before you get out. Stock your car and backpack with nuts, water, seeds, beef jerky so that you are never in a pinch. This way you are giving your brain everything it needs to make a mindful thought-out decision.

Remember to start with one new habit that does not seem so overwhelming—then start to build on that. Overtime these small habits can create huge changes. You have self-control and power to do anything you put your mind to! Self-control gives us the ability to push the brakes before doing something we will regret.

Build the Life You Want

We have taught you so much in this part of the book, but how are we going to make those changes a reality? How do we build the life we love? We asked this very question to Mr. Jason and Ms. Colleen from mindbodygreen, a multimillion-dollar wellness online media business, and authors of *The Joy of Wellbeing*. They emphasized that small habits you instill now, no matter how old you are, can help to improve your life. Make sure to embrace the journey. It is never too early or late to start. They said that at the end of the day, everyone has different definitions of success.

Mold You Mindset—Believe in Yourself

Change your perspective on how you see yourself. Why do you want to do this today? Create your goals around that desire. Your perspective can be either your pain or your power. Gratitude can turn pain into power. Ms. Katie Wells, Wellness Mama, with a podcast of one thousand episodes, recommends waking up and writing three things you are thankful for and before you go to sleep, ask yourself: What am I grateful for today? What hard things did I try today and what did I learn today? She says that your mindset drives your physical health!

Enjoy the Journey

Remember to take it one step at a time, one meal at a time, one day at a time. Have practices or modalities to help you be happier and healthier. Any lifestyle change in the right direction is better than no lifestyle change. There will be setbacks. Mr. Jason and Ms. Colleen emphasized getting back up, it is okay to slow down. Always try harder, have faith, and do not give up. You will figure a way out. Remember, struggle is normal, that is how we learn and succeed. Do not worry about failure and rejection. Get out of your comfort zone and into your growth zone. Ms. Wells states to always be curious and be a problem solver.

Have Fun!

Find fun alternative real foods of all your favorite foods. Join an exercise class that is fun. Find an exciting book that you will want to read before you go to bed. When you make it fun, you will get better results and be more apt to stick to it.

What Do the Holistic Kids Do?

We work hard to be mindful teens. It is not easy, but we make it a priority. We do chores, we have a list of responsibilities, and we do them. Qasim handles taking the dishes out of the dishwasher, Emaad puts them up, Zain puts the dishes into the dishwasher and makes lunches. Abdullah takes out the trash. We all make our beds. All these chores need to be done before we leave for school, which leaves the rest of the day to do what we want. We wake with gratitude, we are as independent as teens can be, we iron our own clothes, and we have a podcast and now this book.

We habit stack. Along with the ones we told you above, when we pray, we also breathe, meditate, and practice mindfulness. We create goals and work toward them. We are making every decision with mindfulness. We have learned to listen to our emotions. Before we lash out, we take a step back and look, listen, and feel. If we start getting angry, we sit with the emotion, figure out why and manage it appropriately . . . we are not perfect . . . because our brains are still growing (yes, we say that to our mom so we do not get in trouble). We cannot imagine where all kids could go if we all were able to do that.

The decisions that we make daily can have significant impacts on our present and future well-being. Let us learn to navigate everyday decisions not reactively but with mindfulness.

Revolution Recap: Navigating Decisions with Mindfulness

- Listening to your body and emotions.
- Work on becoming an adult.
- Build a life you love.
- Be present, grateful, and mindful.

PART THREE

REAL-LIFE REVOLUTION

13

Revolutionize Your Physical Health

We GET IT! Everything we just discussed may be too much right now. There is way too much going on in your life. We are also in your shoes. Some of you may have picked up this book looking for answers for a specific condition that may be affecting your life. That is why we compiled a list of common real-life dilemmas teens deal with. Teens are not doctors or specialists, but we asked the experts so you do not have to. We are all dealing with something. The biggest first step is to recognize it and then seek solutions to improve your life. Look at everything you have done, not feeling your absolute best. Then look at everything you can be—when you ARE feeling your best, the world is yours!

Let us now revolutionize your physical and mental health, so you can really do anything you put your mind to!

Sickness Is Annoying!

Yup, you can say that again. You cannot really have fun when you are sick. The number of things that sickness holds you back from is crazy. In this section, you are going to learn how to crush physical sickness and use what we taught you in real life.

We are speaking from experience, listening to our mother and all the experts. This is what we have learned, and we hope it gives you as much hope as it has given us. We were suffering from multiple chronic conditions, and we no longer deal with them. Our mother has been practicing for over sixteen years and has helped thousands improve their health with these simple principles. Those with autoimmune conditions, chronic pain, mood disorders, hormonal imbalances, digestive issues, skin issues, all gone. How? By putting our body back into balance. We need healthy teens to change the world.

Healthy teens are full of fun and excitement, engaged, with the energy to keep up with those around them; they have eyes that are clear and bright with no dark circles, swelling, or redness; they can fall asleep in less than thirty minutes; they are eating a variety of foods including vegetables and fruit; they have little to no gas or bellyaches.

If you start having any symptoms of gas, indigestion, congestion, rash or hives, cough, difficulty breathing, constipation or other digestive issues, chronic ear infections, projectile vomiting, fits/tics, sinus issues, or adenoids, these may be risk factors for developing bigger health problems down the road like autoimmune diseases or mood disorders. These are symptoms that your body may be off balance.

Listen to Your Body

 Your symptoms are your body's way of telling you that something is off balance.

Listen to what your body is telling you. Look to see what is off balance in your lifestyle. Work on R.E.V.O.L.U.T.I.O.N!

- Look for a functional, integrative, and holistic practitioner that is willing to collaborate with you. Build your support system.

Get your parents on board. Give them this book. We also have references of other practitioners in the appendix to research further.

- Look for the root cause. Ask oneself: What is making me out of balance? What changes can I make today to start moving a little closer to a more balanced lifestyle that will help my body heal?

- Before you start on this healing journey, write down all the symptoms you are experiencing in a list. Then put it away. After two weeks, see how many symptoms have improved. Remember, healing takes time. Focus on the symptoms that are improving, not the ones that are not.

Where to Start

These are the steps toward healing (according the all the experts we have interviewed and our own mother, a board-certified family physician):

Step 1: Focus on Gratitude.
Sickness sucks. Tomorrow, as soon as you wake up, say ten things you are thankful for. If you cannot come up with 10, start with 3 (remember you have nothing to lose, so just start). Do this every morning. Bonus points if you focus on gratitude again before you go to bed.

Step 2: Heal the Gut.
Our gut is the gateway to our health. If you are dealing with a chronic health condition, you are likely dealing with an unhealthy gut. Let us work on the 5 R program to heal your gut. We will brief them here:

1. *Remove* the foods or bugs that may be causing a problem like gluten, grains, dairy, sugar, soy, all fake foods such as

nutrient-depleted foods, processed foods (full of poor-quality fats and oils [commercial liquid vegetable oils, hydrogenated oils, and trans fats] and GMOs) and any specific food sensitivities you may have. *Remove* chronic infections. Talk to your doctor about viruses, parasites, and bacteria that could be adding to you not feeling well.

2. *Replenish* with real food. First, you should replenish with nourishing food which is packed with fiber, polyphenols, prebiotics, and probiotics. Make sure to eat vegetables, clean protein, and healthy fat at every meal and make sure you are hydrated. Eating the rainbow is key to giving your body the nutrients it needs to heal. Eat as organic as possible. Improve your ability to digest with digestive enzymes, lemon water, and apple cider vinegar.

3. *Repopulate* with probiotics and prebiotics. You might need to take a supplement. Look for a mixture with at least ten strains, like lactobacilli (especially plantarum and brevis), bifidobacteria (longem and lactis), and soil-based organisms, such as endospore probiotics like bacillus subtilis and bacillus coagulans. Choose a product that is condition appropriate when it is available. Mushroom mycelia and Saccharomyces boulardii are good yeasts that fight the bad yeast and restore normal flora in the intestinal tract. Just like with everything else, everyone is different. What works for one teen may not work for the other teen. The CFU (colony forming unit) is the number of live and active microorganisms that are present in one serving of probiotics. Look for around 5 billion to 25 million CFU daily. Consult a professional to know what is best for you.

4. *Repair* the gut lining for improved healing. Eat food with key nutrients that help to repair the gut lining like bone broth (one cup per day) and foods with zinc, vitamin A, C, D, omega-3, vitamin E, and selenium.

5. *Revolutionize* the gut. Improve your overall health and wellness by limiting toxins, lowering stress, making sure you are sleeping, getting in nature, limiting technology, and making mindful decisions (Figure 13.1).

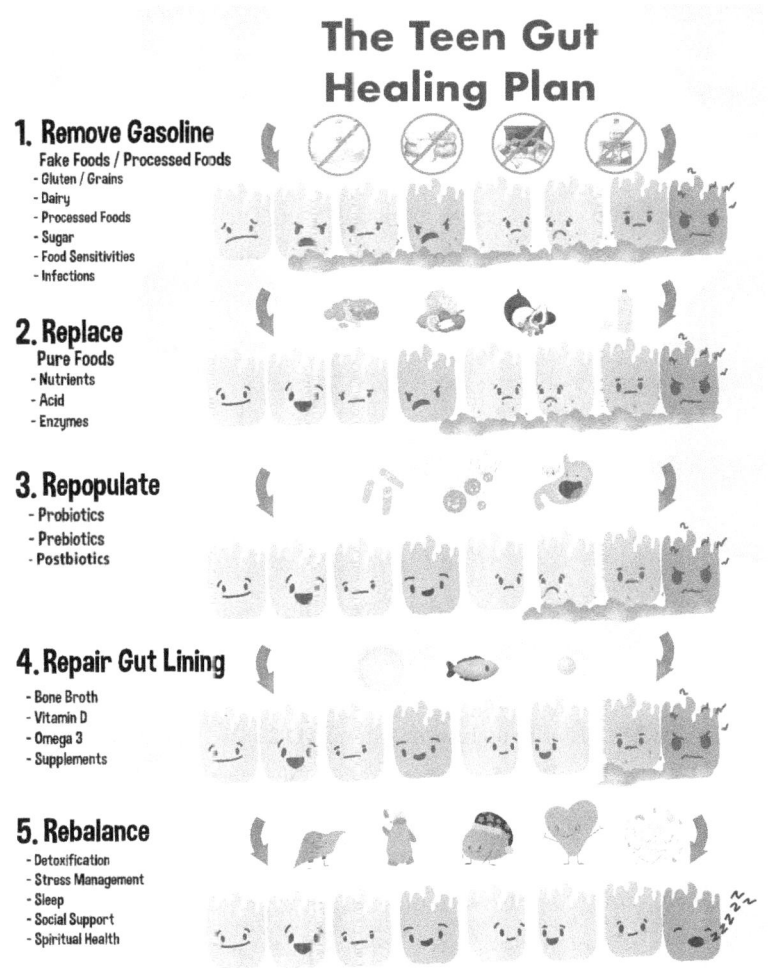

FIGURE 13.1 *The teen gut healing plan. Illustration by Zain Ansari.*

Step 3: Optimize Detoxification, Stress, Sleep, and Social and Spiritual health.

Clean up your surroundings. Detoxification is particularly important for improving every health condition, helping the body maximize glutathione. Make sure you are working hard to lower toxins in your environment, moving your fluids regularly, taking an Epsom salt bath a couple times a week, eating to detoxify and swapping out toxic for clean.

Are you incorporating a stress management technique into your life, like breathing, meditation, mindfulness, respecting your boundaries, spending time in nature, laughing, playing, engaging in some type of fun exercise daily, and making sure you have tech limits that don't impact your sleep? You need sleep to heal. Are your friends having a positive influence on you? Look into these factors as we discussed in the first part of the book. Are there toxins in your environment?

You can have the best gut health, but if you do not also focus on your social environment or stress, you can still get sick.

Step 4: Take Healing a Little Further.

Fix Deficiencies

Teens, like adults, have a lot of deficiencies. Ask your primary care doctor or a holistic practitioner to help you get a blood test. Have your practitioner run a set of labs like a complete blood panel, complete metabolic panel, lipid panel, HbA1c, fasting insulin, vitamin D 25 OH, magnesium (RBC), RBC zinc, vitamin B12, ferritin, uric acid, homocysteine, hsCRP, ANA, antithyroglobulin antibody, and antiTPO antibody, TSH and full thyroid panel, and reverse T3. Dr. Elizabeth Boham, author and physician at the UltraWellness Center, also recommends getting a full iron panel, vitamin A, serum zinc, copper levels, and even omega-3 levels. Please check out our mom's books, *The Holistic Rx* and *The Holistic Rx for Kids: Parenting*

Healthy Brains and Bodies in a Changing World, which will go through these in a lot more detail about these labs and what the results should be.

Nutritional Supplements

You might need to take a supplement to fix your deficiencies. Why do we have deficiencies? Sometimes certain medications can deplete vitamin levels, like antidepressant medications like SSRIs, which diminish melatonin, iodine, selenium, and folate; oral contraceptive pills that diminish zinc, vitamin B2, vitamin B3, B6, B12, folic acid, magnesium, vitamin C, and tyrosine; and even thyroid replacements like Synthroid that diminish calcium. Our soil now lacks certain nutrients, so certain supplements are necessary for most teens to take:

Vitamin D is an essential precursor to hundreds of disease-preventing proteins and enzymes. Vitamin D regulates vital components of hormones and neurotransmitters like serotonin, helps control cell growth, is a cancer fighter, is essential in mineral metabolism, is a major player in bone strength, and regulates the absorption and transport of calcium, magnesium, and phosphorus for bone mineralization and growth. Foods that are rich in vitamin D include sea vegetables, fish (especially sardines, salmon, and mackerel), beef liver, some cheeses, mushrooms, eggs, raw milk, and cod liver oil. We look for a range of about 50–80 mg/ml to improve health. It is best to have your physician check your vitamin D 25 OH lab value. If you work closely with a professional, they can prescribe the appropriate dose to quickly increase your vitamin D level.

Magnesium is an essential mineral, especially for your nerve cells, muscles, and bones and immune function. Magnesium is needed for over six hundred functions in the body. Sources of magnesium are green leaves, like frozen spinach, Swiss chard, avocados, dark chocolate, artichoke hearts, almonds, cashews, pumpkin and squash seeds, salmon, halibut, and meat. Soaking in a bath with magnesium sulfate will help increase our magnesium and glutathione levels!

Omega-3 fish oil. Fish oils are rich in essential fatty acids, like omega-3 and omega-6 fatty acids, which are needed for our cell membranes to work. These cannot be produced by our body, so they need to be consumed. Their use has been beneficial for a wide range of medical conditions. Sixty percent of your brain weight is made up of fat, and 25 percent of that fat is DHA. Omega-3 foods are cold-water fatty fish like sardines, herring, wild-caught salmon, lake trout, mackerel, shellfish, clams, oysters, mussels, pasture-raised chickens, grass-fed meat, antelope, shrimp, squid, eggs, walnuts, and flax and chia seeds.

Zinc is also a common deficiency. It is an essential trace element because your body cannot make it, so you need to give it to your body. It is a powerful antioxidant, important for hormone health, immune support, it helps to balance blood sugar, maintains the health of cells, muscles, eyes and even the liver. Zinc is found in oysters, pumpkin seeds, red meat, liver, garlic, watermelon, and even shellfish.

Iron is an important mineral needed for brain development. It is found in grass-fed beef, pumpkin seeds, spinach, Swiss chard, olives, beets, Brussel sprouts, chickpeas, lentils, organ meats, and even dark chocolate.

Further Testing

If you continue to have issues despite the above, your doctor may need to do further gut tests like a diagnostic stool evaluation, food sensitivity or a lactose breath test that will check for imbalances in your gut bugs called small intestinal bacterial overgrowth. Your doctor might order a nutritional evaluation like a nutrEval that will check for overall health and nutrient levels. In some cases, chronic infections can trigger the wildfire in your body. Examples include viruses, herpes (e.g., 1, 2, 6), Epstein-Barr virus, certain bacterial infections like Lyme, fungal and/or parasitic infections can cause autoimmune conditions. Genetic testing can also evaluate to see what genes are and are not working the way they should.

Are you being exposed to something in your environment that is putting you out of balance? There are so many tests to see what exact toxin you may be exposed to. A common toxin affecting teens is mold. For those with a high toxic load, it may be beneficial to add supplements to optimize healing, like doses of methylated B vitamins and glutathione that will help optimize function and detoxification as we discussed previously.

The Elephant in the Room—Trauma

In today's day and age, most teens are dealing with trauma—assault, parental divorce, bullying, and more.[1] Child trauma occurs more than you think. More than two-thirds of children report at least one traumatic event by the age of sixteen.[2] That is a lot of kids! Adverse childhood experiences are linked to chronic health problems, mental illness, and substance misuse/abuse in adulthood. We spoke to physician and expert trauma specialist Dr. Aimie Apigian, author of *The Biology of Trauma* who helped us understand what trauma is and how we can deal with it. She first explained to us the difference between stress and trauma. Stress is something we can learn from. Trauma is what overwhelms us and what make us feel confused. Dr. Apigian states that although trauma might occur around an event, it is not about the event. Trauma is the experience your body had going through the event, or through a period of time. For some teens it could be accumulated life experiences. At the end of the day, no matter what happened, the effect on the nervous system and the body is the same.

Every teen is different, everyone can respond in two ways to life's experiences. Some people respond with a stress and they grow from that experience. While another person can get overwhelmed, push the emotions and feelings away, that then leads to a trauma response with negative effects in the body. If trauma is happening inside of us, it can make us sick and diseased over time. These experiences can change our biology. Dr. Apigian states, "Trauma is not what happened to you in the past; it is what is happening in your body right now."

Are You Dealing with Trauma?

Trauma is a response of the body. When we do not know how to process something in the moment, it can stay with us and make us feel sick.

To know if you are dealing with trauma, let us take the ACEs quiz[3] (According to the Adverse Childhood Experiences Questionnaire):
Before your eighteenth birthday:

1. Did a parent or other adult in the household often swear at you, insult you, put you down, or humiliate you? Act in a way that made you afraid that you might be physically hurt?

2. Did a parent or other adult in the household often push, grab, slap, or throw something at you? Or ever hit you so hard that you had marks or were injured?

3. Did an adult or person at least five years older than you ever touch or fondle you or have you touch their body in a sexual way? Or attempt to or have oral, anal, or vaginal intercourse with you?

4. Did you often or very often feel that no one in your family loved you or thought you were important or special?

5. Did you often feel that you did not have enough to eat, had to wear dirty clothes, and had no one to protect you? Or were your parents too drunk or high to take care of you or take you to the doctor if needed?

6. Was a biological parent ever lost to you through divorce, abandonment, or other reason?
7. Was your mother or stepmother often pushed, grabbed, slapped, or had something thrown at her? Or sometimes, often, or very often kicked, bitten, hit with a fist, or hit with something hard or threatened with a gun or knife?
8. Did you live with anyone who was a problem drinker or alcoholic, or who used street drugs?
9. Was a household member depressed or mentally ill, or did a household member attempt suicide?
10. Did a household member go to prison?

Add up the number of responses you have. For each "yes" answer, add one. That is your ACE score. Scores range from zero to ten. The higher the score the higher the trauma, the higher the risk for long-term mental and physical consequences.

0 = indicates no exposure

10 = significant level of trauma prior to eighteen years of age.

If you got a high score, we are sorry for everything you had to deal with or are still dealing with. Healing from trauma takes more work once you have stored trauma. If your body gets overwhelmed by stress, your body can break. Stress is something we can do something about. With trauma, you are often stunned, unable to move, and unable to act. According to Dr. Apigian, there are so many tools we can bring in to help our healing journey.

Healing starts with connecting our mind and our body. Body-based somatic work (a treatment focusing on the body and how emotions appear within the body) can help, but we need to first feel safe in our body. Ask yourself: What do you think of feeling safe? How do you know if you are feeling safe or aren't feeling safe? That way, when you don't feel safe, then you can do something about that. Knowing what it feels like when our body feels safe will help us connect our mind and our body.

> Trauma will create a disconnection between our mind and our body and so part of healing from trauma is repairing that connection.
> —Dr. Aimie Apigian, physician, trauma specialist

Your feelings are important. Dr. Apigian discusses the importance of expressing your emotions and feelings to someone you feel safe with like your parents, a therapist, or a trusted adult. When you can address it and have someone validate you, that can help you feel better; we feel like we have someone on our team, helping us from being too overwhelmed. You are not your trauma. You aren't in this alone. Dr. Apigian says in order to heal from trauma, know how you feel loved. Go be with someone who you feel safe with, as they can help you connect your mind and body. Then once that connection is repaired, then I am going to think about a time I felt joy, connected with someone, and we can notice those sensations and then pay attention to that connection. It takes a lot of bravery to reach out to an adult that you feel safe with about how you feel. We can turn your trauma in to your gift.

If you are dealing with physical or mental health challenges, it could be stored trauma and that may take more work. A book our mother really likes to help those with stored trauma is called *the Emotion Code* by Bradley Nelson. Dr. Apigian also stressed the importance of addressing our thinking patterns, beliefs and thoughts and then strengthening the cycle of health and wholeness and address the root cause. Developing self-compassion is key. Remember, it can be overwhelming doing this on your own, so it is important to see a licensed practitioner to help you with your journey. Turn that pain into power.

Revolutionize Specific Conditions

If you are dealing with a certain condition, your doctor likely prescribed medication. Are meds all the hype? Certain medications are worth it. For an acute condition, conventional medicines are very important. But what about chronic conditions? For teens, there are certain medications we recommend you talk to your practitioner about:

Birth control pills Any hormonal problems, doctors will give you a birth control pill that shuts off your own hormone production. Birth control can change the microbiome, increase inflammation and yeast. These can often cause more problems once stopped. It is often not the best solution, as it does not deal with the root cause.

NSAIDs help with pain and fever, lowering inflammation but they also affect your gut bugs. They have many side effects like gastrointestinal issues, cardiovascular problems, and neurological effects. NSAIDs like ibuprofen and naproxen can contribute to leaky gut.

Acetaminophen, or Tylenol, has been thought to be safe, but depletes glutathione, lowering our ability to detoxify. Acetaminophen is one of the leading causes of liver failure. Chronic use of acetaminophen greater than 2,000 mg has been associated with a 3.7 times increased risk of bleeding in the upper digestive tract, which can lead to intestinal permeability. A 2019 study by the National Institutes of Health found that pregnant women who took acetaminophen during pregnancy had increased risk of their baby having ADHD and autism.[4]

Antibiotics sometimes need to be used but always ask about the risks versus the benefits. Even a single course of antibiotics can permanently alter our gut flora. If you do need antibiotics, there is hope in repairing your gut flora. It takes one to two months for most microbiota to get back to where they were before you took the antibiotics. Heal the gut and take probiotics during and after your treatment. When you take the probiotic, take it away from the antibiotic. For example, if you take the antibiotic twice a day, morning, and evening, take the antibiotic in the middle of the day.

Antidepressants are prescribed for a lot of different mood disorders. Just like with all these meds, they can be lifesaving for some, but for others they can lead to side effects and other symptoms. They have a black box warning of suicidal ideation. Antidepressants can contribute to leaky gut by altering the composition and function of gut bacteria.

Acid-blocking drugs. There are so many problems with these medications. You need acid in your stomach to make sure the harmful stuff does not go into your intestines. When we lower stomach acid it can lead to impaired bacterial overgrowth, impaired nutrient absorption, decreased resistance to infection and increased risk of cancer and other diseases.

Chronic Disease: The Basics

For Every Condition: Basics for Healing

When our bodies are sick, or we have symptoms, it means our bodies are off balance.

With any condition, we need to start with the basics. Our mother has started every patient she sees with these basic tips, and 90 percent of her patients have improved with these simple lifestyle changes:

- Say ten things you are thankful for every morning.
- Remove grains, dairy, sugar, processed foods, fake foods, and GMOs.
- At every meal, focus on vegetables, clean protein, and healthy fats. Focus on the real food rainbow.
- Drink one cup of bone broth per day.

- Meditate, mindfulness, and belly breaths.
- Epsom salt baths a couple times a week.
- Get out in nature for thirty minutes a week.
- Replace toxic products for clean products.
- Invest in your sleep.
- Surround yourself with love and positivity.
- Supplements—vitamin D3, magnesium, probiotics, and fish oil.

After implementing these changes, one can integrate different modalities like supplements, homeopathy, acupressure, and aromatherapy that can support our conventional care.

Supplements are products that are intended to supplement your diet. They include minerals, vitamins, herbs, enzymes, and others. They are usually safe for teens but always collaborate with a practitioner.

Homeopathy is a medical system, developed in the late 1700s, based on the belief that the body can cure itself. It uses tiny amounts of natural substances from plants and minerals and is an excellent and effective choice for teens. There are constitutional remedies and acute symptomatic remedies, please see *The Holistic Rx: Your Guide to Healing Chronic Inflammation and Disease* for more information. In that book, our mother has gone through over eighty chronic conditions and different remedies in a great amount of detail. We have found that the combination of remedies is beneficial. You will notice the homeopathic remedies have the name of the remedy followed by a number like 30C or 6C. This refers to the potency, how many times the remedy has been diluted and shaken.

Acupressure works by placing pressure on specific points on the body that lies along the meridians or channels in your body. Apply pressure for ten to fifteen minute-sessions, in small circular motions with light pressure for ten to thirty seconds at a time (Figure 13.2).

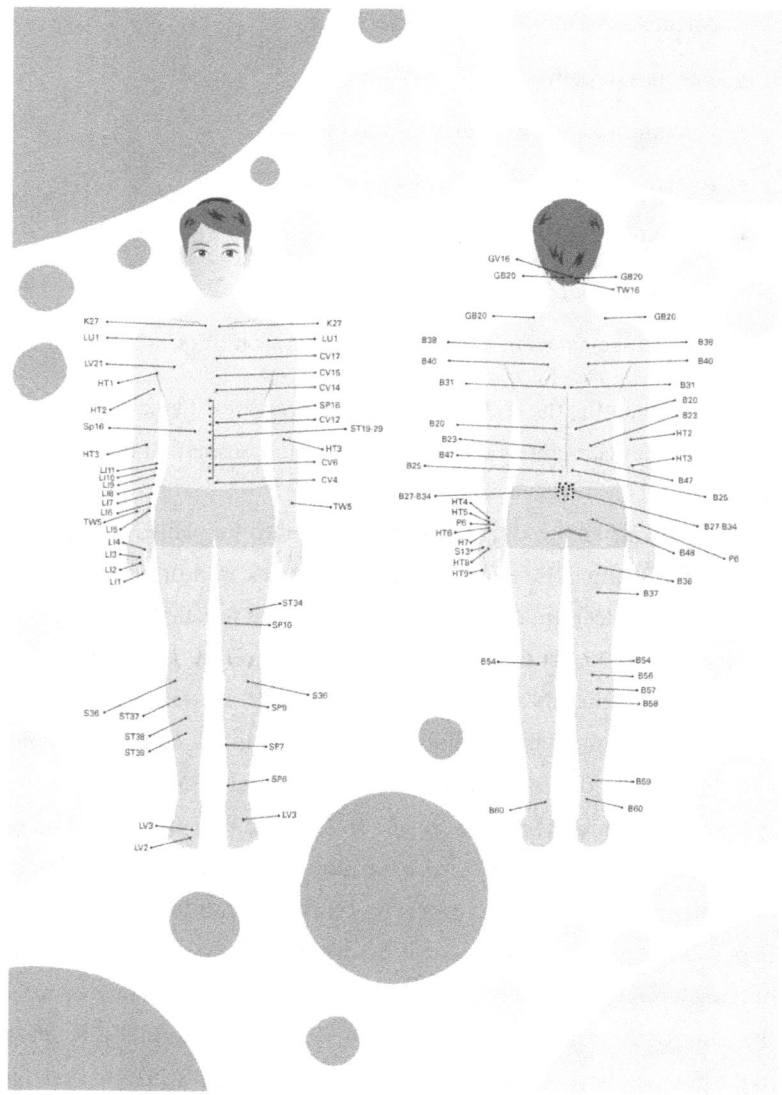

FIGURE 13.2 *Acupressure points. Illustration by Anna Cunningham.*

Aromatherapy or essential oils is very helpful for teens and is very potent, a little goes a long way. Dilute in the carrier oil before applying to the skin. Find what scent works best for you.

Other methods that are greatly beneficial for healing are cupping, chiropractic care, acupuncture, and reiki.

With the help of our mother, a board-certified physician, and the experts we have interviewed, we will dive briefly into the common conditions teens deal with. We will start with what they are, common root causes, and then after you have implemented the basics (as we discussed above), we can integrate other modalities that might help. This section may get overwhelming, but we wanted to show you that there is so much out there to help you. It is a MUST that you consult with your practitioner first before implementing anything. What may work for one person may not work for another. Working with someone who can help you navigate this road toward healing may decrease frustration and confusion. Our mother has written a book called *The Holistic Rx: Your Guide to Healing Chronic Inflammation and Disease*, where she discusses these in more detail.

Acne

Teenage years are already difficult, and acne can be devastating! Acne is a state of inflammation. Your skin also has a microbiome. There are millions of little bugs on your skin that determine your health. Your skin also reflects how your insides are doing, so healing your gut and balancing your hormones by lowering your sugar intake is important. Dairy is high in hormones and encourages acne growth. Optimizing your gut microbiome and getting rid of dairy from the diet is very helpful for your skin.[5]

Supplements

- Probiotics (like bacillus), fish oil or omega-3, vitamin D, and magnesium
- Berberine helps to improve sugar levels[6]
- Zinc (30 mg daily with meals copper [3–5 mg] along with the zinc; zinc sulfate is not easily absorbed)[7]
- Milk Thistle[8]

Homeopathy

- Boiron has a great acne relief kit.

Acupressure

- L14, L11, SP6, and GV14

Aromatherapy

- Tea tree oil[9]: Add two to three drops to a clean cotton ball and apply to the area of concern. This can also be added to your daily body wash or face wash. Lavender oil, clary sage, geranium, and bergamot can help to improve inflammation.

Asthma

Asthma is a chronic inflammatory condition of the lungs that leads to narrow airways and affects breathing. Working with a functional medicine practitioner is important to look for root causes like food allergies, sensitivities, mold, and other environmental toxins/allergens.

Healing the gut and managing stress is important. Please discuss these with your trained practitioner.

Supplements

- Probiotics,[10] fish oil, vitamin D[11], and magnesium
- Vitamin C (500–1,000 mg daily)
- B vitamins
- Zinc[12]
- Quercetin[13]

Homeopathy

Please discuss with your doctor before trying these homeopathy options.

- Aconitum napellus (30C) is for attacks that come suddenly, especially after exposure to cold, dry wind, fear of dying, and anxiety. Attacks occur at night. Discuss with your practitioner the best way to take this treatment.
- Antimonium tartaricum helps with asthma that is accompanied by exhaustion, weakness; mucus in the lungs which causes a rattly breathing that cannot be coughed up; skin is pale, cold, and clammy.
- Arsenicum album helps those with an attack between midnight and 2:00 a.m. These people feel restless, anxious, and cold, thirsty for sips of warm water; symptoms improve when sitting up.
- Ignatia is for when an attack comes on after an emotional breakup, after grief, or other emotional upset.
- Ipecac is a remedy for those with nausea and whose chest feels heavy. It is helpful when a lot of mucus formation causes coughing, gagging, and vomiting.

- Kali carbonicum is for asthma that is bad between 2:00 a.m. and 4:00 a.m.; the person sits with their face on knees and leaning forward helps relieve symptoms; the person is usually chilly, tired, and pale-looking.

Acupressure (see Figure 13.2)

- LU1, LU6, LU9, LU10, K27, LU7, ST13, ST16, B36, CV17, B12, B13, K6, and Ding Chuan point
- Allergic Asthma: LI4 and K6

Aromatherapy

- Essential oils can help manage allergies and mucus production. Make a homemade vapor rub with eucalyptus oil, lemon, and peppermint oil, which will help to open airways. Others can be frankincense oil, sandalwood, lavender, chamomile, helichrysum, thyme, and rosemary.

Allergies and Sinus Issues

In allergic rhinitis, or hay fever, your body overreacts to a substance that you inhale. Sinus issues occur when the inflammation is in the sinuses. Healing the gut is important. Getting your doctor to order a food sensitivity test (Genova diagnostics) will help you find out what foods may lead to symptoms. In some cases, a low histamine diet can be the most helpful to lower the histamine response.

Supplements

- Probiotics (soil-based), fish oil, vitamin D and magnesium

- Digestive enzymes
- Quercetin (1,000 mg daily)[14]
- Vitamin C (2,000 mg per day)
- Butterbur (500 mg per day)[5]
- Spirulina (1,000-2,000 mg per day)

Homeopathy

- Combination of homeopathics for allergies and sinus issues are incredibly helpful by Boiron and Genexa.

Acupressure

- Allergies: LI20, ST20, B2, LI4, SP5, B13, GB20

Aromatherapy

- Peppermint oil, eucalyptus oil, lemon oil, tea tree oil, lavender, peppermint oil, and frankincense can all be helpful. Find what works best for you.

Back Pain

Back pain can come on suddenly and can last six weeks (acute) or can last more than three months (chronic). Back pain is a shooting, stabbing, or aching pain in the back that may radiate down the leg, limiting range of motion. Causes of back pain may be due to muscle or ligament strain, bulging/prolapsed/ruptured disk, osteoporosis, skeletal irregularities, and/or arthritis.

Chronic pain is due to chronic inflammation. Lowering stress and dealing with trauma or underlying emotional issues can help to lower chronic pain. There is an amazing book called *The Emotion Code* that can help to release those trapped emotions that can lead to pain.

Supplements

- Vitamin D, probiotics, magnesium, omega-3
- Turmeric (1,000 mg daily)
- Proteolytic enzymes and bromelain (500 mg three times a day in between meals) and papain (500 mg three times per day)
- MSM (2,000–8,000 mg daily)[16]
- Calcium (500 mg)
- Collagen (40 mg daily), ginger (1,000 mg/day)
- Topical: Castor oil packs

Homeopathy

- Combination homeopathics for pain are extremely helpful like Arnicare arthritis by Boiron.

Acupressure

- B25, B31, B40, B20 (for middle back pain), GB20 and GV14 (upper back pain), B48 (to reduce stress)
- Upper and mid-back pain: B13, B38, B18, B42, SI11, SI10
- Lower back: B23, B47, B28, B48, B54, GB30, B60, GV4

Aromatherapy

- Peppermint and wintergreen oil help to cool the inflamed area. Frankincense and cypress oil reduces inflammation. Lemongrass essential oils can help back spasms. Peppermint oil and lavender oil to further penetrate the area which can help relax the inflamed area and help with cramps.

Cancer

Cancer refers to diseases that can be characterized by the growth of abnormal cells in the body that divide without control and can potentially invade and destroy other normal tissues. By receiving this diagnosis, most are left with a deep sense of hopelessness, but it can also be accompanied by a new revival of your inner self. The immune system plays an extremely key role in helping us defend and remove cancer. We spoke to Dr. Elizabeth Boham, author of *Breast Wellness: Tools to Prevent and Heal From Breast Cancer* and functional medicine practitioner and physician at the UltraWellness Clinic who specializes in seeing those with cancer. From her book and the *Chris Beat Cancer* book, we learned the following.

Maintaining an acid/alkaline balance by drinking alkaline water (add lemon or lime juice and/or hydrogen peroxide), increasing your intake of raw veggies, and removing grains and dairy will all improve detoxification. Increase omega-3 fatty acids, calcium, vitamin D like cod liver oil, blue green algae, conjugated linoleic acid, mushrooms, folic acid (effective against breast, pancreatic, and colorectal cancer), melatonin, vitamin B pyridoxine, and vitamin C. Low-carbohydrate diets with intermittent fasting help to stabilize insulin, which improves estrogen dominance. Tumor cells overexpress insulin receptors, allowing more glucose in to feed the tumor, so it is important to manage any insulin resistance. Fiber is best to lower the amount of estrogen and estrogen metabolites, which are available to stimulate the breast tissue and lower insulin and glucose levels that feed the tumor cells. Incorporate anticancer foods like cruciferous vegetables, pomegranate, turmeric, garlic, green tea, oolong tea, olive oil, bean sprouts, strawberries, figs, olives, selenium, tomatoes, dietary fiber, ginger, onions, and quercetin (can be found in capers, cocoa, hot chili peppers). It is important to keep your body mass index (BMI) below 25. Intermittent fasting can help to lower the risk of cancer but always talk to your doctor.

> Processed foods are a big problem, and too much meat and dairy and the sugary drinks and fast food which is a processed food are definitely big problems and they're definitely contributing to disease and the environmental pollution is definitely contributing to cancer.
> —Chris Wark, best-selling author of *Chris Beat Cancer*

We need to look at your whole life, not just cancer.

Supplements

Though it is best to get most of your nutrition from food, there are some situations where you can add a dietary supplement. Several supplements have been shown to reduce the risk of developing cancer.[17]

- Probiotics, vitamin D, magnesium, omega-3 fatty acids
- Vitamin C
- Turmeric
- Green tea and green tea catechins
- Omega-3 fatty acids
- Probiotics

- Resveratrol
- Berberine
- Sulforaphane (from cruciferous vegetables)
- Selenium
- Ganoderma, Maitake, and Shiitake mushrooms
- L-glutamine
- NAC, glutathione, and liver support supplements after a round of chemotherapy, not during

Be careful with what you choose and always check with your doctor about supplement-pharmaceutical interactions, as botanicals can decrease the concentration and efficacy of the cancer treatment (like Echinacea, grapeseed, kava, St. John's wort, and possibly garlic). Gingko can lead to increased toxicity of chemotherapeutic interventions.

Homeopathy

The homeopathic view is that cancer represents a profound breakdown at every level. For acute symptoms, take a 30C potency four times daily. Again, consult with a doctor first.

- Arsenicum can help with restlessness, burning pains, anxiety, and nausea.
- Arnica montana helps bruises or restless sensations.
- Cadmium sulphuratum can help with symptoms of vomiting, hair loss, and fatigue.
- Eupatorium can help with aching bone pain that is worse with motion and is often accompanied by stiffness and chills.
- Ipecacuanha can be used for patients with persistent vomiting and nausea, especially when vomiting does not relieve any symptoms.

- Nux vomica works best for those who complain of GI symptoms, like indigestion, nausea, or constipation.
- Radium bromatum is specific for radiation poisoning, especially when it is followed by arthritic complaints.

Acupressure

- P6, LI4 (reduces pain)
- extra 1 acupoint (anxiety)
- Others to improve your immune system and the liver are B23, B47, CV6, K27, and ST36.

Aromatherapy

- Combine bergamot, chamomile, and lavender in aromatherapy applications. Frankincense is powerful in cancer aromatherapy.

Constipation

Constipation is a symptom of hardened feces in persons who are having difficulty emptying the bowels; it is important to get to the root cause, optimize the gut microbiome, avoid common food sensitivities like dairy and gluten and make sure you are getting enough fiber.[18]

Supplements[19]

- Vitamin D, probiotics, magnesium, and omega-3 fatty acids (DHA/EPA)
- Psyllium (5 g psyllium husk twice daily)

- Flax seed oil or flax seeds (1–2 tbsp daily)
- Pectin
- Aloe vera juice
- Vitamin C

Homeopathy

- Find a combination for constipation, like TRP The Relief Products.

Acupressure

- LV3, LI4, LI11, ST36, CV12

Aromatherapy

- Carrot seed, orange, spearmint, ginger, and fennel help to soothe the effects of the digestive system.

Diabetes, Prediabetes, or Insulin Resistance

Diabetes is a chronic condition that is marked by abnormally elevated levels of glucose in the blood because the body either stops producing insulin or can't use the insulin that the body does produce. There are multiple types of diabetes. Type 1 is also known as juvenile or insulin-dependent diabetes, an autoimmune disease that occurs when the immune system destroys the cells that make insulin; Type 2 occurs when the pancreas cannot make enough insulin to keep blood glucose levels normal and is made worse by poor food choices.

Prediabetes occurs when the blood glucose levels are higher than normal but not enough to be diagnosed as diabetes; it is also known as impaired fasting glucose, impaired glucose tolerance, or insulin resistance.

Supplements

- Vitamin D, probiotics, magnesium, and omega-3 fatty acids (DHA/EPA)
- Berberine[20]
- Chromium[21] (600 mcg daily) helps with insulin sensitivity and balances blood sugar levels
- Cinnamon (2 tsp per day): add to food, smoothie, or tea
- Alpha lipoic acid[22] (300–1,200 mg daily) improves insulin sensitivity
- Fiber powder from veggies and seeds can control glucose levels
- Bitter melon

Homeopathy

- Argenticum nitricum is a remedy for diabetes with the symptom of swollen ankles.
- Codeinum helps relieve diabetes that presents with restlessness, depression, and skin irritation.
- Phosphoric is indicated for diabetes that is associated with symptoms brought on by nervous exhaustion from grief or working too hard.
- Uranium nitricum can help with symptoms of weakness, bedwetting, and digestive upsets.

- Insulin dependent: Natrum muriaticum, sulfur
- Non-insulin dependent: Sulfur

Acupressure

- Obesity: ST25, ST36, ST40, SP6, B20, B21, CV12
- ST36, LI4, B40, H7, P6, SP6, K3, GV24.5, GB21 (improve circulation)

Aromatherapy

- Essential oils like coriander and cinnamon can help your liver and pancreas to balance blood sugar levels. Obesity/metabolic syndrome can be helped with grapefruit essential oil that can break down body fat. Cinnamon oil can regulate blood glucose level; ginger oil reduces sugar cravings and reduces inflammation.

Dysmenorrhea (Painful Periods)

Painful periods can occur due to numerous issues, including hormonal imbalances and endometriosis. Diagnosis can be investigated via history and examination, along with imaging like ultrasound or even more invasive techniques. Endometriosis is when the uterine tissue lands on the pelvic tissue, leading to dysmenorrhea, painful stools. Insulin resistance and hormonal imbalances can lead to period issues. There is a lot that can be done to improve menstrual cramps.[23]

Supplements

- Vitamin D, probiotics, magnesium, and omega-3 fatty acids (DHA/EPA)

- Vitamin E
- Vitex (Chasteberry)[24] (400 mg twice daily) balances hormones; do not take with oral contraceptive pills
- Gamma linoleic acid from evening primrose oil or borage oil[25] (300 mg) can be helpful
- B complex (50 mg daily) with vitamin B-1 and B-6
- Milk thistle (150 mg twice daily)
- Vitamin C (6–10 g per day)

Homeopathy

- Combination homeopathy like Cyclease Cramps and PMS by Boiron

Acupressure

- CV4, LV3, SP6, LI4 (pain anywhere)

Aromatherapy

- Clary sage helps to balance hormones and has been shown to reduce symptoms of endometriosis.

Eczema

Eczema is a chronic skin condition, where an itchy, red rash appears all over the body. Eczema is related to chronic inflammation and gut health, healing the gut is key. Get a food sensitivity test or an environmental toxin test to see what sensitivities are in your food or your environment which could be leading to your symptoms can help. If your skin gets infected, you may need antibiotics. Sometimes a stricter elimination diet is needed like the *Gut and Psychology Syndrome Diet* by Dr. Natasha Campbell McBride, MD, without dairy or even a low histamine diet for a short amount of time.

Supplements

- Vitamin D with K2, probiotics, magnesium, and omega-3 fatty acids (DHA/EPA)
- Zinc[26]
- Digestive enzymes
- Saccharomyces boulardii
- Vitamin E (400 IU) helps the body use fatty acids and promotes wound healing
- Itch support: quercetin,[27] N-acetyl cysteine,[28] vitamin C, magnesium

Homeopathy

Depending on the stage of eczema, a different homeopathic is used.

- Arsenicum album is best used for tender skin eruptions that are also very dry itchy and swollen; condition is worse in the winter; itching is intense between midnight and 2:00 a.m. Patient feels restless.
- Alumina is for skin that is dry and itchy, and the person is constipated.
- Calendula can be used for affected inflamed areas and can be applied to soothe the skin.

- Graphites is for those with eczema mainly affecting the palms and areas behind the ears. The skin is dry, thick, and has a honey-like discharge. A warm bed intensifies itching. Cold makes the skin feel better.
- Petroleum is for dry, cracked skin with itching worse at night. Areas affected are the palms and hands.

Acupressure

- LI11 (helps with itching)
- B40, SP10, B23, B47, ST36, B10, LI4, LU9, B13
- Weeping eczema: SP9, B52, CV9
- Severe itching: LU7, SP10, LV5, B13

Aromatherapy

- Essential oils can help to soothe inflammation and itching. These include juniper, peppermint, bergamot, carrot, jojoba, lavender, frankincense, thyme, benzoin, sweet marjoram, geranium, and chamomile.

GERD

Gastroesophageal reflux disease (GERD) and acid reflux symptoms include heartburn, burping, bitter taste in mouth, and regurgitation of acid foods. Acid reflux can be due to not enough acid (I know that sounds crazy). Look into the baking soda test to see if you have enough acid. Healing your gut is key to improving acid reflux. Avoid common food sensitivities like dairy and gluten. Sometimes GERD can be due to small intestinal bowel overgrowth (when the good gut bugs are located in the wrong place).

Supplements

- Vitamin D, probiotics, magnesium, and omega-3 fatty acids (DHA/EPA)
- Focus on gut healing supplements like probiotics, digestive enzymes, and HCL with pepsin, L-glutamine, and so on
- Sometimes GERD can be due to SIBO, so try soil-based probiotics
- Specific formulations for acid relief, like Acid Soothe by Enzymedica

Homeopathy

- Combination homeopathics like Acidil by Boiron or Forces of Nature.

Acupressure

- HP6, ST36, CV12, SP4

Aromatherapy

- Peppermint and a ginger massage can be helpful to relieve symptoms of reflux.

Hashimoto's or Hypothyroidism

Hashimoto's is an autoimmune disease of the thyroid. Most cases of hypothyroidism are due to Hashimoto's. Symptoms include fatigue, depression and mood disorders, weight gain, feeling cold easily, digestive issues, muscular pain, stiffness and swelling in the joints, hair loss, frequent urination and excessive thirst, and changes in menstrual period. Healing the gut, lowering chronic inflammation, balancing hormones, lowering toxins and, even looking for chronic infections can help to improve the autoimmune condition.

Supplements

- Probiotics, fish oil, vitamin D, and magnesium
- Multivitamin with vitamin A (5,000–10,000 IU per day)
- Vitamin E (400 IU)
- B vitamins
- Zinc (25–50 mg per day)
- Vitamin C (1,000 mg per day)
- Iodine (50–900 mcg daily)
- Selenium (20–200 mcg daily)

Homeopathy

- Calcaria carbonica helps those with constipation and perfuse menses.
- Graphites can help those who tire easily, are obese, become sad easily when listening to music, and are constipated and timid.
- Lycopodium can be used for those who suffer from gastric problems with excessive gas, crave hot foods, and are weak and irritable.
- Sepia can be used with patients who are weak, have a pale yellow face and feel cold. It helps to control excessive hair loss. These patients crave acid foods and pickles.

Acupressure

- ST36, P6, KD3, GV7, KD7, SP6, LI10, LI11

Aromatherapy

- Frankincense can help to lower thyroid antibodies when used in conjunction with other modalities. Peppermint oil can help to reduce brain fog, depression, headaches, and digestive issues. Lavender and myrtle may help to restore hair and calm anxiety.

Headaches

Headaches are pains that can occur anywhere in the region of the head or neck. Magnesium deficiency can often cause headaches. Lowering inflammation, lowering stress, insulin resistance, and healing the gut are key.

Supplements[29]

- Vitamin D, probiotics, magnesium, and omega-3 fatty acids (DHA/EPA)
- B-complex vitamin
- 5-HTP (50–100 mg three times per day)
- Coenzyme Q10 (100 mg three times daily)

Homeopathy

- Look for a combination homeopathic for headaches

Acupressure

- Migraine: B10, TW16, GB12, GB6–11, GB14, LI4
- Tension: GB21, GB20, GB12, GB6–11, B 3–9, LI4

Aromatherapy

- Essential oils that may be beneficial: peppermint, lavender, eucalyptus, frankincense, rosemary, rosewood, grapefruit, coriander, lemongrass, bay laurel, lemon balm, marjoram, ginger, sandalwood, wintergreen, anise, basil, linalool, and Roman chamomile.

Irregular Periods

A woman's menstrual cycle involves a normal functioning ovary releasing an egg every twenty-five to twenty-eight days. When your body is working properly, you are having regular, moderately pain-free periods each month; this is a sign that your hormones are balanced. Irregular periods, missed periods, or very painful and intense PMS symptoms are signs that one or more of your hormones are imbalanced.

Balancing hormones is key to balancing irregular periods. Lowering insulin resistance will help to balance hormones. Incorporate a stress management technique into your daily routine. Try seed cycling to balance hormones. First two weeks of menstrual cycle: 1 tbsp of flax and 1 tbsp of pumpkin seeds. Second two weeks of menstrual cycle: 1 tbsp sesame seeds, 1 tbsp sunflower seeds. Make sure you are incorporating enough fat in your diet.

Supplements[30]

- Vitamin D, probiotics, magnesium, and omega-3 fatty acids (DHA/EPA)
- Vitamin C (500–1,000 mg three times per day)
- Evening primrose (2–4 g daily)
- Chasteberry (5 percent vitexin, 20–40 mg daily)
- Inositol
- Berberine

Homeopathy

- Calcarea is helpful for women with fatigue, feelings of legs being heavy, swollen, painful breasts, and anxiety.
- Ferrum is for women whose periods have stopped and are weak, tired, face is usually pale. Their symptoms are also accompanied by occasional hot flashes, and they want to sit down all the time.
- Ignatia is for those women whose periods have stopped because of loss or grief.
- Natrum muriaticum is for women who experience constipation, irritability, headaches, thinning hair, and recent emotional shock.
- Sepia is for women who feel weak, irritable, and weepy with abnormal vaginal discharge.

Acupressure

- LI4 (pain and inflammation)
- SP10, SP6

Aromatherapy

- Basil can improve delayed menstruation and scanty periods. Cypress can relieve stagnation associated with heavy bleeding or mid-cycle bleeding. Geranium can have an overall balancing effect on female hormones.

Irritable Bowel Syndrome

Irritable bowel syndrome leads to diarrhea, constipation, and pain after bowel movements, mucus in your stool and immediate need to go to the bathroom when you wake up and during or after meals. One may also have the feelings of incomplete emptying. Healing the gut and lowering stress are key to improving IBS. Some IBS can be due to SIBO (as discussed above), so it is important to get testing and see a professional to help guide treatment. For SIBO, one should avoid fermented foods. Look for the cause of SIBO, like stress, lower stomach acid, antibiotic use, food poisoning, or acid-suppressing medications. You can confirm SIBO with a lactulose hydrogen and methane breath test that looks for excessive gas generations by the overgrowing bacteria when they ferment sugar and starches in the diet.

Supplements[31]

- Vitamin D, probiotics, magnesium, and omega-3 fatty acids (DHA/EPA)
- Sometimes IBS can be due to SIBO, so try soil-based probiotics
- Digestive enzymes
- Tryptophan (1–5 g daily)
- Melatonin

Homeopathy

- General combination of homeopathics can help with IBS, like TRP Natural Relief or ones for diarrhea relief like Diaralia (by Boiron) or Lycopodium for bloating and gas relief.

Acupressure

- CV12 (prevents indigestion, so use before meal) and CV6 (soothes abdominal pain, constipation, and gas)

Aromatherapy

- Peppermint, fennel, and ginger can be used to improve symptoms of IBS.

14

Revolutionize Your Mental Health

One of the biggest problems teens are dealing with today is feeling unwell mentally. Follow the R.E.V.O.L.U.T.I.O.N. Just like our physical health, our mental health can also improve with the basic steps we highlighted in the previous chapter. A lot of mental health practitioners do not get your blood work done—make sure you ask your practitioner to order them for you. Always look for the root cause. Lowering inflammation and insulin resistance, healing the gut, addressing trauma, lowering stress, improving sleep, and focusing on gratitude are key. Seeing a therapist and discussing these issues is also extremely helpful, and make sure that teens should discuss with their pediatrician before trying anything new or adding supplements.

See Figure 14.1 for an overview of mental health help.

Now let us dive into common mental health challenges us teens deal with daily.

ADHD

Attention deficit hyperactivity disorder (ADHD) is characterized by difficulty concentrating and being easily distracted, irritable, disorganized,

FIGURE 14.1 *Mental health help. Illustration by Zain Ansari.*

unable to sit still, and impulsive. As always, please consult with your pediatrician before trying anything new or adding supplements.

Supplements

- Vitamin D, probiotics, magnesium, and omega-3 fatty acids (DHA/EPA)

- B complex (50 mg daily), Zinc 30 mg daily
- GABA (250 mg twice daily)
- Inositol (2–6 g twice daily) if anxious, sleep issues, or overfocused; use powder.
- Phosphatidylserine (100–300 mg) can be used if learning or memory problems are present.

Homeopathy

- General homeopathy for concentration.

Acupressure (see Figure 13.2)

- CV12, LI11, P6, H7, LU1, and SP6

Aromatherapy

- Vetiver, cedarwood, frankincense, cardamom, peppermint basil, thyme, orange, and chamomile can help to improve focus and alertness.
- Calming oils are ylang-ylang, neroli, orange, lavender, rose and sandalwood, chamomile, and vetiver.

Anxiety Disorders

Anxiety is a normal feeling that many people feel, but anxiety disorders are much more. An anxiety disorder is a condition that causes excessive worry that persists over time and interferes with daily life. Anxiety disorders include social anxiety disorder, panic disorder, and others. Dr. Uma Naidoo, Harvard psychiatrist and author of *Calm Your Mind with Food*, recommends B.R.A.I.N C.H.I.L.D. for those dealing with anxiety:

- B is for b vitamins and berries
- R is for rainbow veggies and fruit
- A is for antioxidants
- I is for iron and iodine, as some kids are deficient
- N is for nutrients (omega-3 foods, zinc folate and vitamin A)
- C is for choline and vitamin C
- H is for hydration
- I is for insulin and blood sugar control
- L is for the removal of ultra-processed foods, soda, and trans fats
- D is for vitamin D

Supplements

- Fish oil, vitamin D, probiotics, magnesium, B complex
- Vitamin C (1,000 mg in the morning)
- L-theanine (100–300 mg) per day
- GABA (125–500 mg)
- Adaptogenic herbs like Ashwagandha
- Inositol (3–5 g twice or three times daily)

Homeopathy

- The combination of homeopathic remedies for stress by Boiron and Genexa are both great.

Acupressure

- HP7, HP6, TW5, H7, H5, LU1

Aromatherapy

- Essential oils can provide a relaxing effect. These include lavender, rose, vetiver, ylang-ylang, bergamot, chamomile, and frankincense, neroli, sandalwood, and orange.

Depression

Depression is a mood disorder that gives someone an overwhelming feeling of loneliness, emptiness, and lack of interest. Dr. Austin Perlmutter, physician, *New York Times* best-selling author of *Brain Wash*, says today, we are building our brains with the wrong Legos; they are less stable. Look for an underlying root cause like insulin resistance, thyroid, autoimmune conditions, and even nutrient deficiencies that can lead to similar symptoms. Dr Perlmutter recommends questioning your emotions. Emotions are not bad or good, they give us an awareness of what is going on in our body. And remember, always talk with your own doctor before trying anything new.

Supplements

- Probiotics, fish oil, magnesium, and vitamin D. B complex, saffron (10–30 mg), curcumin (100–400 mg), zinc 30 mg/day

Homeopathy

- Arsenicum album is indicated for those with intense fatigue, restlessness, worry, hopelessness, pessimism, exhaustion, always feeling cold, and OCD. Depression causes weight loss, anxiety, and insomnia between 1:00 and 3:00 a.m.

- Aurum metallicum is for deep depression, disgust with oneself, and even suicidal tendency. Symptoms improve by being in the sun. Note: Suicidal tendencies should always be discussed with a doctor or suicide hotline.

- Ignatia amara aids depression that follows emotional trauma, often indicated with constant sighing and a sensation of a lump in the throat.

- Kali phosphoricum is indicated for fatigue, irritability, listless depression, fear of crowds; symptoms follow overwork or grief.

- Nux vomica is a remedy for those who find fault with everyone and are extremely irritable.

- Sepia helps depression in those who complain of memory problems, want to be alone, are irritated by consolation; symptoms worsen with menses.

Acupressure

- GB20, GB21, LV3, LV5, LV14, K27, B38, B23 (accompanied by fear or fatigue), B47, GV24.5, K27, CV17 (relieve depression made worse by grief or anxiety)
- ST36 (depression with digestive problems and fatigue)

Aromatherapy

- Essential oils have been proven to elevate mood; these include bergamot oil, lavender, Roman chamomile, and ylang-ylang.

Suicide

Suicide is a complex and tragic issue that affects family, friends, and the entire world. If you are thinking of or have a plan of suicide, please put down this book and seek help NOW. Dial 988 Suicide and Crisis Lifeline. You are worth it; we are here for you! We love you! The world needs you in it! You are a huge blessing.

Eating Disorders

Eating disorders, like anorexia, bulimia, and binge eating disorders, can be caused by an obsession with food, body weight, and shape and can lead to serious and fatal consequences. A diagnosis can be made through detailed history and physical with basic labs that can find the specific nutrient deficiencies (like zinc) and root cause (according to Dr. Greenblatt MD in the book *Answers to Anorexia*).

The following labs can be drawn: zinc taste test, amino acids, CBC with differential, celiac screening, cholesterol panel, CMP, copper, essential fatty acids, folate and vitamin B12, homocysteine, iron and ferritin, magnesium, methylmalonic acid, red blood cell trace minerals, thyroid, urinary organic acids, urinary peptides, vitamin D 25OH, zinc, and referenced-EEG.

Please consult with your doctor before trying anything new.

Supplements

- Vitamin D, EPA/DHA, magnesium, and probiotics.
- Vitamin C (1,000–2,000 mg per day).
- High-potency multivitamin.
- Zinc chelate (30–90 mg daily), along with 3 mg of copper.
- 5-Hydroxytryptophan (5-HTP) (100 mg two or three times daily) Do not use in combination with pharmaceutical antidepressant or antianxiety medications.

Homeopathy

- Argentum nitricum is useful for eating disorders that may also have claustrophobia and fear of tall buildings.
- Lycopodium is useful for digestive issues like bloating, also for those who get low blood sugar, who have irritability and low self-esteem.
- Natrum muriaticum is for someone with long-standing grief and depression. The person craves salty foods.

Acupressure

- CV12, ST36, SP6, LI4, LV3, LI11, P6, SP16 (can help bring appetite back to balance)

Aromatherapy

- Oils that are used for appetite loss are bergamot, buchu, galangal, dill, tarragon, cinnamon, lemon, lemongrass, fennel, wintergreen, peppermint, nutmeg, and ginger. Others for anorexia are rose, clary sage, lavender, and ylang-ylang.

Insomnia

Insomnia is a common sleep disorder that can make it hard to fall asleep or stay asleep. Practicing good sleep hygiene, healing the gut, and lowering insulin resistance and stress are key. Fix nutrient deficiencies.

Supplements

- Vitamin D, EPA/DHA, magnesium, and probiotics.
- Melatonin (1–3 g half an hour before bed, for a short time, if needed it longer to talk to your pediatrician).
- Passionflower (500 mg before bed or 1–2 ml a half hour before bedtime).
- Valerian (600 mg before bed or 2 ml a half hour before bedtime).
- 5HTP (50–100 mg before bed), taurine (1,000 mg before bed), GABA (750 mg before bed), chamomile tea and valerian tea (one cup before bed).

Homeopathy

- General homeopathic by Quietude by Boiron.

Acupressure

- B38, P6, H7, B10, GV15, GV20, GV24.5, CV17, K6, B62, SP6, H7
- Disturbed sleep: B5, B20, P6
- Difficulty falling asleep: B15, B23, K3

Aromatherapy

- Essential oils can help you relax and get to sleep. Examples include lavender, Roman chamomile, bergamot, cedarwood, cistus, clary sage, jasmine, and frankincense.

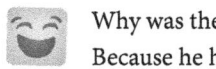 Why was the doctor always calm?
Because he had a lot of patients!

Substance Abuse/Addiction

If you find yourself in despair, we are here for you. Substance abuse means misusing a legal substance or using an illegal substance. There are many forms of addiction that teens are dealing with in today's world. With gambling, porn, internet usage, shopping, video gaming, tech addictions, and so much more. There is a physical addiction, when your body becomes dependent on a particular substance, and when you build a tolerance, you need more of a dose to get the same high.

Could You Be Addicted?

Do You: spend a lot of time figuring out how to get drugs, steal or sell belongings to be able to afford the drugs, feel shaky or sick when trying to stop, need to take more of a substance to get the same effect? Have your habits changed (like sleeping, eating, or mood), are your grades suffering at school, losing interest in activities that used to be important or are you dealing with relationship problems?

Just like everything we talked about in the first part of the book, start with the basics and look for a root cause. Is it peer pressure or trauma?

Kicking Addiction to the Curb!

Getting out of any addiction is difficult. Once you are stuck, it is extremely hard to get out. It is difficult but possible.

You are strong, and because you want to get out, this is the first step to success. There is nothing wrong with you. We need to look for the root cause and ask the question why?

Self-Acknowledgment

Facing the reality of addiction can be a challenging but important first step. It often involves a deep look at how your addiction has influenced various aspects of life—relationships, work, health, and mental well-being.

Strengthen Your Prefrontal Cortex

Remember the prefrontal cortex from the previous chapter? A strong prefrontal cortex is essential for impulse control, setting goals, adequate sleep, high intensity exercise, prayer and meditation, healthy diet with protein at every meal, finding meaning and purpose. Remember your prefrontal cortex does not fully mature until you are in the mid- to late twenties, so you are more vulnerable to developing unhealthy habits that can lead to addictions. Getting out of addiction also means finding different coping strategies to help you. Examples include practices such as mindfulness, meditation, or exercise. Doing this can help manage emotions and reduce reliance on drugs.

Seek Help

Recovering from drug addiction is rarely found in the world, especially alone. Building a support network can give encouragement and guidance. This may include family, friends, support groups, therapists, or mentors who understand the challenges of addiction. Addiction professionals can help stop cravings and keep you away from drugs.

Get Up and Get Busy

Do chores, clean, cook, run errands for your family. Find a part-time or full-time job. Find positions in leadership where you can learn to improve your leadership qualities like camp counselor, assistant coach or even babysitting.

Change the Toxic Environment

The environment of people you hang out with really makes a difference. We have talked about how peer pressure can make you do things that you may not do by yourself. If you go back to an environment where drugs are forced on you then you will continue the path of addiction. It is better to find a supportive friend group to hang out with.

A Note For Parents

You will not always see eye to eye with your teen. Especially if they are dealing with addiction, and if you try to talk to them, but instead they storm off and slam the door, let them have their moment. Once the amygdala is in full control, there is no way to reason with them. Once they cool off, then you can sit down and listen to what they are feeling. Figure out why they are doing what they are doing and look to see what is "off balance" in their lives. Just like anyone else, teens need respect, want to know they are valued and heard. Though teens are older, they need more time from you, to listen to what is going on in their lives. Let them know you are there for them and love them despite their "slips." It is important to empower them to turn their pain into power. It is easy to always talk about their problems and addictions, focus on what makes them special. Focus on their positive qualities.

Continue to look for root causes like insulin resistance, thyroid issues, and nutrient deficiencies.

Supplements

- Fish oil, vitamin D, probiotics, magnesium.
- Inositol (3–6 g two or three times per day), B complex (50 mg with 1 mg of folate).
- Vitamin C (500–1,000 mg of vitamin C).

- If true dependence, glutamine (1,000 mg or more three times daily) and glutathione are great for lowering cravings.

Homeopathy

- General homeopathy like Stress Calm by Boiron or Stress and Anxiety homeopathy from Genexa can help to lower the anxiety and stress associated with substance abuse.

Acupressure

- ST36, SP10 will help in the detoxification process.
- LU1 will help with depression or anxiety.

Aromatherapy

- Essential oils like peppermint, clove, cinnamon, cilantro, and grapefruit can help curb cravings; and lavender, sandalwood, orange, marjoram, and grapefruit can help improve withdrawals.

You are not your diagnosis. Your diagnosis is just your body telling you that something is off balance. When you put your body back into balance, your mind, body, and soul can work the best they can, allowing you to reach your dreams. You are amazing!!!

Conclusion

We as a society try to avoid darkness and challenges. People are like, Life is scary, must stay safe, but actually it is facing those challenges, and going through the heroes' journey, where you can come out the other side smarter, fitter, faster. If you don't go through these heroes' journeys, you get stuck, and you don't want to be stuck as a human . . . you need to overcome your fears, by running into them not running away from them.

—Dr. Molly Maloof, physician, author of *The Spark Factor*

The world we teens live in today is far different than the world our parents were raised in. This world comes with its own luxuries but also its own challenges. No one will understand those challenges more than us teens. We live in a world with rights, wrongs, challenges, hurdles, ups, and downs. This is our path to choose. We need to be in control. We need to get back into the driver's seat of our health.

Why are we just sitting around and allowing others to control our bodies, minds, souls, and choices? We are the future leaders, engineers, politicians, doctors, musicians, teachers, influencers, cooks, mothers, and fathers. We are ready to take center stage.

Start Asking Questions and Act

We are ready to take on that light, that torch to blaze a trail for all of us. A trail that leads to a better future, more peace in our bodies, more peace in our homes, more peace in the world We can create a better future. But we need to get off our devices. We need to start taking action! TODAY!

Ms. Katie Wells, Wellness Mama, podcaster of over one thousand episodes, recommends that we "stay curious." If you ask better questions, you are going to get better answers. We have access to a universe of information at our fingertips all the time. All the information is out there. You can learn almost everything and anything overnight. We can continue to ask better questions, raise our voices, build community, and bring people together for the common good.

We are being lied to by the agencies that we trust. We need to call out ultra-processed food companies. We need to call out these large organizations that are taking donations from ultra-processed food companies! We need to have our agencies clearly mark GMOs and what foods are harmful to us, just like they did for the tobacco industry. We need to take the characters and celebrities off the boxes of sugary cereals! Why are they luring us to get sick? Why are we listening to authorities like the American Diabetes Association that is taking money from Coca Cola,[1] and why are they not raging a war on sugar?!

Why is our government making recommendations from those that have accepted millions of dollars from processed food companies and drug companies? With diabetes, prediabetes, and mental health challenges on the rise, why aren't they removing ultra-processed foods from school lunches? We need a whole foods cafeteria! Why are we learning about math, science, and social studies, but not learning how to live, learning how to read a label, learning about what ingredients are doing to us?!? Why aren't we learning simple stress management techniques? Why aren't we learning to create lasting friendships? Why aren't we learning to manage our emotions?

Doctors and practitioners should be all over this, but instead they are not talking about how to improve health with lifestyle. Doctors need to stop pushing us to take lifelong medications for obesity and teach us how we can live our lives. Why aren't doctors screaming from the rooftops that we need to reduce ultra-processed foods as they are the number one contributor to heart disease?

> A sick teen or child is so profitable for the economy . . . they don't die, but they take more resources, hospital visits, and medications—sick kids are a business that makes money!
>
> —Calley Means, New York Times best-selling author of *Good Energy*

We need to have tighter regulations on more than 8,000 toxic fake chemicals that teens are drowning in. We need clear scientific guidelines that say kids should not eat junk food. We need to get them to clearly mark that the products we are using have xenoestrogens that affect our hormones.

Why aren't we learning to manage stress? We need to put warning signs on technology that is harming our minds, bodies, and souls. Why are parents being pressured to give young kids phones? They are messing us up by giving us these devices at a young age! Then they complain about how much time we spend on them. We need to act against all the technology that is making us addicted to their products! We need to start asking questions because when we are not critical thinkers, we are the only ones that suffer. Mr. Calley Means emphasizes the "need to vote with our wallet. Kids speaking out and kids driving change makes a big difference." Time to take action!

Create a Ripple Effect for Change

There is so much goodness in the world, there is so much in the world that unites us. Together we can create change. Teens are on a journey. We are discovering ourselves, learning how we fit into the world. We are also on that journey with you. We have our ups and downs, our good days and bad days. Life's stressors will throw us off that path, place hurdles that we need to climb; just get back on that path and continue one day at a time, one meal at a time, one thought at a time. The hurdles in your life were placed strategically for you so you can become the absolute best version of yourself. Once you have overcome a hurdle, you are the beacon of light for others so you can guide them. Be intentional about learning and absorbing all that life and its lessons have to offer, because we need you.

> You get to choose how you show up at school, you get to choose how you feel, you get to choose to have your emotions all over the place or whether you feel grounded, happy and focused.
>
> —Dave Asprey, NYT best-selling author, father of biohacking

We need to have the courage to stand up for ourselves. By taking care of our bodies, minds, and souls, which allows emotional regulation, which gives us power. Courage comes from having power, then we can become leaders to create that ripple effect for change. The world needs you. How you show up in the world matters, and there is so much in your control.

We navigated you through the R.E.V.O.L.U.T.I.O.N. We gave you the tools you need to start today. Create your own path. This is your journey. Find people you can rely on to help you through the challenges. These are easy things we can do every single day to make a difference in ourselves and our world. We do them. When we have applied this to our own lives, we have seen how the communities around us, our families, our friends, our places of worship have all changed. They are also starting to ask questions, we are opening their eyes to the world around us, making others look up from their phones. One teen can influence their friend circle, and so on. Our voices can be a powerful voice for change. Send letters to your elected voices that we teens demand change today!

We were that drop in the ocean, and now we are bringing this to you. We are just four kids, but we can create that ripple effect in our communities, in our homes, and our world. You can do that too. You have more power than you think. We are ready to take control over our mind, body, and soul. We are ready to take control over our emotions and actions. The world is ours. We are the future leaders. We are ready for a better future. We are ready to change our world. Are you in?

Gratefully,
Abdullah, Zain, Emaad, and Qasim
The Holistic Kids

Appendix A
The Teen Health Revolution Resources

Podcast: The Holistic Kids' Show

The Holistic Kids' Show

Basic Kid's Health Books

A Compromised Generation: The Epidemic of Chronic Illness in America's Children by Beth Lambert
The Dirt Cure by Dr. Maya Shetreat
Healthy Kids, Happy Kids by Elisa Song
The Rule of Five: A Parent's Guide to Raising Healthy Kids in an Unhealthy World by Dr. Ana Maria Temple

The Wellness Mama 5 Step Lifestyle Detox: The Essential DIY Guide to a Healthier, Cleaner, All-Natural Life by Katie Wells

Nutrition

The Pegan Diet: 21 Practical Principles for Reclaiming Your Health in a Nutritionally Confusing World by Dr. Mark Hyman

Integrative, Functional, Holistic Therapies

The Autism Revolution: Whole Body Strategies for Making Life All It Can Be by Dr. Martha Herbert and Karen Weintraub
Brain under Attack: A Resource for Parents and Caregivers of Children with PANS, PANDAS and Autoimmune Encephalitis by Beth Lambert and Maria Rickert Hong
Gut and Psychology Syndrome by Dr. Natasha Campbell
Healing the New Childhood Epidemics: Autism, ADHD, Asthma and Allergies: The Groundbreaking Program for the 4-A Disorders by Dr. Kennith Boch and Cameron Stauth
Healing ADHD: The Breakthrough Program That Allows You to See and Heal the 7 Types of ADD by Dr. Danial G. Amen
Healthy Kids, Happy Moms: 7 Steps to Heal and Prevent Common Childhood Illness by Dr. Sheila Kilbane
The Holistic Rx: Your Guide to Healing Chronic Inflammation and Disease by Dr. Madiha Saeed
Nourishing Hope for Autism: Nutrition and Diet Guide for Healing Children by Julie Mathews
Teletherapy Toolkit: Therapist Handbook for Treating Children and Teens by Dr. Roseann Capanna-Hodge

Picture Books

Adam's Healing Adventure Series by Dr. Madiha Saeed
A Healthy New Me & ADHD Free by Jennifer Giustra-Kosek, LPC, NCC
The Incredible Microbiome by Sean Davies FNP-C and Tori Davies

Cookbooks

Against All Grain: Delectable Paleo Recipes to Eat Well and Feel Great by Danielle Walker

Junior Chef: 100 Super Delicious Recipes for Kids by Kids by Will Bartlett, Katie Dessinger, Paul Kimball, Abigail Langford, and Anthony Spears

The Paleo Kids Cookbook: Transition Your Family to Delicious Grain and Gluten Free Food for a Lifetime of Healthy Eating by Jennifer Robins

The Wellness Mama Cookbook by Katie Wells

Appendix B
Sample Shopping List

We know we have bombarded you with a lot. It starts with shopping for real food. Here is our Teen Health Revolution shopping list:

- Vegetables (frozen veggies most cost-effective at Costco) like asparagus, bok choy, celery, kefir, kimchi, sauerkraut, and fermented vegetables, cruciferous vegetables (broccoli, Brussels sprouts, beets, cauliflower, watercress, cabbage, kale, Swiss chard, and collard greens, onions, mushrooms, prebiotic, and probiotic foods)

- Clean protein (most cost-effective at Costco and Trader Joe's) like wild-caught seafood, smoked salmon, eggs (preferably organic and pasture-raised), chicken (preferably organic and pasture-raised), turkey (organic turkey slices found at Costco only have TWO ingredients), beef (preferably grass-fed), grass-fed lamb, goat, no-nitrate jerkies, bones for broths, no-nitrate organic hot dogs, beans, lentils, and protein powders like beef gelatin, collagen, pea protein powder, and egg white protein powder

- Healthy fats (cost-effective at Costco) like avocados, olives, coconut, nuts and seeds, nut/seed butter, olive oil, grass-fed butter and ghee, avocado oil

- Fruits (most cost-effective frozen berries and fruit found at Costco) all rainbow fruit

- Condiments like mustard, ketchup (no sugar), avocado mayonnaise (Costco), apple cider vinegar, coconut aminos, sriracha with limited ingredients (Yellow Bird), paleo salad dressings (Primal Kitchen), and paleo dips (Primal Kitchen and Siete)
- Spices, all rainbow spices/seasoning blends, and sea salt or Himalayan salt
- Pastas made with organic lentils or chickpea or lentil pasta, and almond flour lasagna sheets, organic wheat pasta
- Bread and bagels like organic sourdough, organic wheat flour, buckwheat (Live Pacha), or almond flour bread (Base Culture, Unbun)
- Taco shells or burrito wraps made with cassava flour (Siete) or organic corn
- Cheese like raw, organic, pasture-raised cheese or nut cheeses (Miyoko's)
- Beverages like herbal teas (like green, dandelion, milk thistle, chamomile, turmeric, etc.), filtered water, and sparkling water
- Milk like almond milk (with only two or three ingredients), canned coconut milk (BPA free, full fat, no guar gum), hemp milk, walnut milk, cashew milk, coconut milk, hazelnut milk, raw milk, organic A2 cow milk. Malk, Elmhurst, Kiki milk, Three Trees all have milk with simple ingredients
- Snacks like seed and nut crackers (Simple Mills), no-grain chips (usually made with cassava flour) (Lesser Evil or Siete), seaweed with olive or avocado oil, chips fried in coconut oil, like plantain chips
- Bars like nut and seed bars, paleo bars

- Flours, like almond flour (Costco), coconut flour, tapioca starch, chickpea/garbanzo bean flour (found in Pakistani/Indian stores (organic)), arrowroot, cassava flour, tigernut flour and Himalayan Tartary buckwheat, and sprout flours
- Baking items like unsweetened cocoa powder, dairy-free, sugar-free chocolate chips (Hu chocolate, Navitas, Just Dates), raw honey, organic stevia, maple sugar, maple syrup, coconut sugar, and date sugar
- Sweet treats like paleo cookies (Siete and Simple Mills), graham crackers, and cake boxes (Simple Mills), and candy (organic by YumEarth)
- Swap fake food for real food, all-natural soaps, lotions, shampoo, makeup, cleaners, toilet paper, laundry detergent (organic Whole Foods brand), dishwashing detergent, unbleached parchment paper, nontoxic shower curtain liners, and so on
- Cast iron, glass, and ceramic cookware
- Epsom salt, baking soda, and sea salt for baths
- Household plants
- Water and air filters for the main area and bedrooms

Appendix C
Holiday Swaps

Remember fun food is real food, even on the holidays. Simple replacements can help to make your dish healing and delicious! We love to work with our mom in the kitchen and come up with clean recipes . . . we turn it into a game! We come up with our favorite dishes and find ways to make it super nutrient-dense. Here is how we make our favorites healthier:

- Protein with Stuffing → Organic/Grass-fed/Pasture-Raised with organic paleo stuffing
- Gravy and Sauces → Make at home, avoid sugar and flour
- Breads → Organic, sprouted, sourdough, almond flour, cassava flour
- Potatoes → Organic, with organic butter and milk (dairy-free with coconut milk and cashew butter), purple potatoes and sweet potatoes are a bonus
- Casseroles → No canned soups, make at home, clean ingredients, use avocado oil/coconut oil/ghee, organic veggies, thicken with arrowroot, cassava, tapioca flour, add sprouts
- Veggie side → Organic
- Pie → organic flour or cassava flour, avoid sugar
- Fried food → chickpea flour or cassava flour

Appendix D

Teen Health Revolution Recipes

Breakfast

Cassava Flour Pancakes

Ingredients:

- ¾ cup of cassava flour
- 1 tablespoon honey
- ½ teaspoon baking soda
- ¼ teaspoon salt
- 3 eggs
- ½ cup of water
- 1/4 cup of avocado oil
- 1/8 cup Himalayan Tartary Buckwheat

Directions: Mix batter and ladle into a pan to form a circle. Flip when mixture starts to bubble.

Blueberry Cake

Ingredients:

- 3 cups of almond flour
- ½ cup honey
- 1 teaspoon of baking soda
- 1 teaspoon salt
- 6 eggs
- ½ cup of avocado oil
- Blueberries

Directions:

Preheat the oven to 350 degrees F. Stir together the ingredients. Pour batter onto an unbleached parchment paper baking tray.

Green "Hulk" Smoothie

Ingredients:

- Frozen power greens/dandelion greens
- Frozen blueberries
- Frozen strawberries
- Frozen cauliflower, riced
- Water or non-dairy milk
- ½ avocado
- Banana
- 1 scoop collagen

- Spirulina
- 1 scoop of amla

Directions:

Add the quantity of ingredients as desired. Mix in a blender. Add stevia if needed to add sweetness. We will also add supplements into the smoothie, like glutathione, glutamine, and zinc. We also have powders like maca, Camu Camu, organ meat, aronia, acerola, probiotics, prebiotic fibers like green banana, Jerusalem artichoke, sea veggies, and other things that we will alternate.

Everything Bagel Smoked Salmon Toasts

Ingredients:

- Smoked wild-caught salmon
- Arugula, ½ cup, optional
- One tablespoon of cashew cream cheese or organic cream cheese
- Capers
- Unbun everything bagel
- Microgreens

Directions:

1. Slice and toast bagel on a heated, oiled skillet.
2. Add cream cheese to the bagel.
3. Top with arugula, smoked salmon, capers, and top with microgreens.
4. Add fried eggs on top.
5. Garnish with dill, salt, and pepper and serve.

Lunch

Chicken Bites

Ingredients:

- 1 pound of chicken, bite-sized pieces
- 1/2 teaspoon garlic
- ½ teaspoon salt
- ¼ teaspoon black pepper
- 2 tablespoons of lemon juice
- ¼ teaspoon paprika
- 2 tablespoons chickpea flour

Directions: Mix. With one tablespoon of oil, cook each side for 2–3 minutes over medium heat.

Pasta

Ingredients:

- 1 pound ground grass-fed beef or organic turkey
- 1 onion, chopped
- 1 teaspoon salt
- ½ teaspoon black pepper
- 1 tablespoon of Italian seasoning
- 1 teaspoon garlic
- 1 jar of pasta sauce

- 1 packet broccoli sprouts
- 1 cup of riced cauliflower
- 1 tablespoon avocado oil
- 1 box lentil pasta

Directions:

1. In a large saucepan, sauté chopped onions in a little bit of avocado oil until translucent.
2. Combine ground beef, spices, and vegetables until tender.
3. Add pasta sauce and cook until thickened.
4. Boil and cook lentil pasta according to the instructions on the box.
5. When pasta is cooked, drain pasta and add it to sauce.

Chicken Burrito

Ingredients:

- 1 pound of chicken, diced
- 1 bell pepper, sliced
- 1/2 onion, diced
- 1 teaspoon garlic powder
- 1 teaspoon salt
- 1 teaspoon of taco seasoning
- Cassava flour burrito tortillas
- 1 can of refried organic beans
- Cabbage, sliced

- Salsa
- Almond milk cream cheese, optional

Directions:

1. Dice chicken and cook over a medium skillet with vegetables and spices.
2. Once cooked, move aside.
3. Warm tortilla in an oiled skillet just till it is soft and pliable.
4. Take off the skillet onto a plate. In the center of the tortilla, add cabbage slices, topped with the chicken mixture, refried beans, salsa, and almond milk cream cheese.
5. Fold both sides in and then the top in, like a burrito style.
6. Add oil to a ceramic skillet over medium-high heat for two minutes on each side to make the tortilla crispy.
7. Can serve with veggies, avocado, and even enchilada sauce.

Yellow Soup

Ingredients:

- 3 cups of chicken bone broth
- 1 large onion, diced
- ½ teaspoon salt
- 1 can of butternut squash
- 1 can of pumpkin
- 1 cup of frozen cauliflower rice
- 1 cup of frozen carrots

- 1 tablespoon rosemary
- 1 teaspoon garlic
- Two tablespoons of avocado oil
- Optional spices—sage and ginger

Directions:

1. Heat the oil in a large pot over medium heat.
2. Add the onions till soft.
3. Add bone broth, veggies, and spices. Bring to boil.
4. Cover and simmer until veggies are tender.
5. Let cool slightly, then pour the soup into a blender and blend till smooth. You may need to do this in smaller batches.

Egg Roll

Ingredients:

- Whole chicken, rotisserie, shredded
- 1 bag of coleslaw
- 1/4 onion, sliced
- 1/2 cup peanut butter
- 3 tablespoons of coconut aminos
- 1/2 teaspoons of sesame oil
- 1 teaspoon of garlic
- Salt, to taste
- Konjac noodles, optional
- Chickpea or cassava flour wraps

Directions:

1. In a skillet, add oil and sliced onions and soften.
2. Add chicken, coleslaw mix, coconut aminos, sesame oil, and spices.
3. Once the cabbage has wilted down and cooked, add peanut butter.
4. On another heated skillet, slightly toast the wraps just so it is malleable, then take it off the grill.
5. Add the egg roll mixture into the middle of the wrap and fold as you would a burrito.
6. Toast the folded wrap on the same heated skillet until it develops a golden-brown tint on each side.
7. Serve hot.

Dinner

Coconut Shrimp Curry

Ingredients:

- 1 cup of chicken bone broth
- 1 large onion, diced
- ½ teaspoon salt
- 2 tablespoons of avocado oil
- 2 cans of coconut milk
- 1 teaspoon curry powder
- 1 teaspoon of turmeric

- ½ teaspoon of paprika
- Sliced mushrooms
- Sliced carrots
- Or any other veggies

Directions:

1. Heat the oil in a large pot over medium heat.
2. Add the onions till soft.
3. Add bone broth, coconut milk, veggies, and spices. Bring to boil.
4. Cover and simmer until veggies are tender and the soup thickens.

Chicken Wings

Ingredients:

- 4 pounds of chicken wings cut into flats and drumettes
- ½ teaspoon salt
- 2 teaspoons of garlic powder
- Pinch of cracked pepper

Directions:

1. Toss chicken wings in spices and air fry till done.
2. Serve with my favorite sauce and salad. Our favorite sauce is sriracha mixed with a little maple syrup! Yum!

Rainbow Pasta Salad

Ingredients:

- 1 box of lentil pasta
- 1 can of black olives
- ½ yellow bell pepper, chopped
- 1 red bell pepper, chopped
- 2 cups of cherry tomatoes
- 1 green bell pepper, chopped
- 1 cup of spinach, chopped
- 1 can of palms of heart, chopped
- 2 tablespoons of olive oil
- Squeeze of lemon, as desired

Directions:

1. In a large pot of salted boiling water, cook pasta according to box.
2. Once done, drain and rinse under cold water.
3. Add vegetables, spices, oil, and lemons.

Fish Fingers

Ingredients:

- 6 pieces of halibut or cod
- ½ cup of chickpea flour
- 1 teaspoon salt

- 1 teaspoon garlic
- ½ teaspoon paprika
- Water
- Oil

Directions.

1. Heat up ½ inch of avocado oil in a pan over medium heat.
2. Slice up fish into strips.
3. Combine chickpea flour, water, and spices until it makes a thick paste.
4. Dip fish into chickpea flour mixture.
5. Place battered fish into hot oil and cook both sides till crispy.

Note: we have also used 1/4 cup of cassava flour, 1 egg, and water just to create a paste, and used that also as a coating instead of the chickpea flour.

Green beans

Ingredients:

- ½ onion, diced
- One bag of green beans
- 1 container of shiitake mushrooms
- 1 tablespoon coconut aminos
- 1 teaspoon garlic
- 1 teaspoon salt
- 2 tablespoons of oil

Directions

1. In a skillet, heat up the oil.
2. Add onions, cook till soft.
3. Add vegetables, coconut aminos, and spices.
4. Serve as a side dish.

Lasagna

Ingredients:

- 1 pound ground beef
- ½ onion, diced
- 1 jar of tomato sauce
- 1 teaspoon Italian seasoning
- 1.5 teaspoons of basal
- Salt
- Mushrooms, diced
- Broccoli sprouts
- Cauliflower, riced
- Almond flour lasagna sheets
- Black olives, sliced
- Large tomatoes, sliced

Cheese layer

- ½ cup of parsley, chopped
- 2 tubs of almond milk or whole milk ricotta, 8 ounces
- 1 egg

Directions:

1. Brown the beef, onion, diced mushrooms, riced cauliflower, broccoli sprouts, and garlic over medium-high heat until no pink remains.
2. Stir in pasta sauce and spices. Let the sauce simmer.
3. Mix ricotta, parsley, and egg.
4. Add one cup of meat sauce to a 9 x 13 pan. Top with lasagna noodles.
5. Layer with 1/3 of cheese mixture and one cup of meat sauce.
6. Repeat and top the final noodle layer with sauce.
7. Slice up tomatoes and olives to garnish on top.
8. Cover with parchment paper and foil and bake for 45 minutes.
9. Rest for 15 minutes before cutting.

Homemade Pizza

Ingredients:

- Simple Mills Pizza Mix
- Oil
- Apple cider vinegar
- Pizza sauce
- Cashew or Organic Cheese
- Toppings, per your preference

Directions:

1. In a large mixing bowl, mix the batter as instructed on the box.
2. Form into a pizza on a baking pan.
3. Bake for 10 minutes at 350°F.

4. Take out and top with pizza sauce, your favorite toppings, and then your preferred cheese.
5. Bake for another 30 minutes until you get your desired pizza consistency.
6. Take out and enjoy.

Dessert

Banana Bread

Ingredients:

- 3 cups of almond flour
- ½ cup honey
- 1 teaspoon of baking soda
- 1 teaspoon salt
- 6 eggs
- ½ cup of avocado oil
- 5 bananas
- ½ cup of walnuts, chopped

Directions:

1. Preheat oven to 350 degrees F.
2. In a large mixing bowl combine all the ingredients until smooth.
3. On an unbleached parchment lined cookie sheet, pour out the batter and top with chopped walnuts.
4. Bake for 15 minutes
5. Remove and let cool before cutting it to serve.

Pineapple Upside Down Cake

Ingredients:

- 3 cups almond flour
- 1/2 cup of oil
- 1/2 cup of honey
- 6 eggs
- 1 teaspoon of baking soda
- 1 teaspoon salt
- Canned or fresh pineapple
- ½ cup juice of canned pineapple (100 percent)
- Sliced red fruit to place within the pineapple circles

Directions:

1. Preheat oven to 350 degrees F.
2. In a large mixing bowl combine all the ingredients until smooth, leave some pineapple slices for the top.
3. On an unbleached parchment lined cookie sheet, place the remaining pineapple circles as desired on the cookie sheet, with either cherries, raspberries, or strawberries placed in the middle of the pineapple circles.
4. Pour the mixture over the pineapple circles.
5. Bake for 15 minutes.
6. Remove, flip, and let cool before cutting to serve.

Chocolate Chip Peanut Butter Cookies

Ingredients:

- 3 cups almond flour
- 1/4th Himalayan Tartary buckwheat
- 1/2 cup peanut butter or another nut butter
- 1/2 cup of honey
- 3 eggs
- 1 teaspoon of baking soda
- 1 teaspoon salt
- No sugar chocolate chips

Directions:

1. Preheat oven to 350 degrees F.
2. In a large mixing bowl combine all the ingredients until smooth.
3. On an unbleached parchment lined cookie sheet, roll out the cookies.
4. Bake for 15 minutes.

Chocolate Covered Strawberries

Ingredients:

- Strawberries
- No sugar chocolate chips

Directions:

1. Melt chocolate chips in a bowl over a pan with boiling water.
2. Dip strawberries into the chocolate and lay them on parchment paper.
3. Add toppings as needed.
4. Refrigerate till solid.

Cheesecake

Ingredients:

- 5 packages of cream cheese
- ¼ cup of sour cream
- 6 eggs
- 1 cup of maple sugar

Crust

- 1.5 cups of Simple Mills honey cracker crumbs
- ½ tablespoon maple sugar
- 6 tablespoons unsalted butter, melted

Directions:

1. To make the cheesecake crust, crush all the honey crackers into crumbs.
2. Combine together with melted butter and maple sugar.
3. Press crumbs together into a 9-inch springform pan.
4. Bake at 350°F for 8 minutes then take it out.

5. Change the temperature of the oven to 450°F.
6. In a blender, mix cream cheese, maple sugar, eggs, and sour cream.
7. Pour the batter on top of the cooled crust.
8. Place the springform pan into a slightly larger round cake pan. Place the round cake pan in another larger pan. Pour hot water into the last largest pan, so it goes halfway up the cake pan.
9. Cover the top of the cake with a small sheet of parchment paper.
10. Bake at 450°F for 15 minutes, then reduce the heat to 225°F without opening the door.
11. Bake for another 75 minutes until the center of the cheesecake wobbles slightly when you tap the pan.
12. Remove the cheesecake from the oven and let it rest in the larger roasting pan with water for 45 minutes, then transfer pan to a cooling rack.
13. Chill overnight before serving.

Note: This recipe has been adapted from Natasha's Kitchen recipes. We have used this same recipe but changed up the cracker we used. We used the chocolate brownie Simple Mills sweet thins for the crust, and in the cheesecake batter, we crushed different candies and cookies and threw them into the batter. So delicious!

NOTES

Introduction

1. Harris, E. "More Than 1 in 10 US Children Diagnosed With ADHD." *JAMA* 331, no. 17 (2024): 1440. https://doi.org/10.1001/jama.2024.5159.

2. "'Dying Young' in the USA: New Report Shows Lower Life Expectancy for Young Americans." *Carolina Population Center*, University of North Carolina at Chapel Hill, December 7, 2022. https://www.cpc.unc.edu/news/dying-young-in-the-usa-new-report-shows-lower-life-expectancy-for-young-americans/.

Chapter 1

1. Langan, S. M., A. R. Mulick, C. E. Rutter, et al. "Trends in Eczema Prevalence in Children and Adolescents: A Global Asthma Network Phase I Study." *Clinical and Experimental Allergy* 53, no. 3 (2023): 337–52. https://doi.org/10.1111/cea.14276.

2. Centers for Disease Control and Prevention. "Childhood Obesity Facts." Last modified January 9, 2025. https://www.cdc.gov/obesity/childhood-obesity-facts/childhood-obesity-facts.html.

3. Centers for Disease Control and Prevention. "Diabetes Data and Statistics." Last modified January 9, 2025. https://www.cdc.gov/diabetes/php/data-research/index.html.

4. Jonas, D. E., E. B. Vander Schaaf, S. Riley, et al. "Screening for Prediabetes and Type 2 Diabetes in Children and Adolescents: Evidence Report and Systematic Review for the US Preventive Services Task Force." *JAMA* 328, no. 10 (2022): 968–79. https://doi.org/10.1001/jama.2022.7957.

5. American Academy of Pediatrics. "AAP-AACAP-CHA Declaration of a National Emergency in Child and Adolescent Mental Health." Accessed June 21, 2024. https://www.aap.org/en/advocacy/child-and-adolescent-healthy-mental-development/aap-aacap-cha-declaration-of-a-national-emergency-in-child-and-adolescent-mental-health/.

6   Harris, E. "More Than 1 in 10 US Children Diagnosed With ADHD." *JAMA* 331, no. 17 (2024): 1440. https://doi.org/10.1001/jama.2024.5159.

7   Centers for Disease Control and Prevention. "CDC Reports on Youth Risk Behavior Survey Data for 2023." Last modified February 13, 2023. https://www.cdc.gov/media/releases/2023/p0213-yrbs.htm.

8   American Psychological Association. "Psychologists Take Action to Prevent Teen Suicide." *APA Monitor*, July 2023. Accessed June 21, 2024. https://www.apa.org/monitor/2023/07/psychologists-preventing-teen-suicide.

9   American Psychological Association. "Psychologists Take Action to Prevent Teen Suicide." *APA Monitor*, July 2023. Accessed June 21, 2024. https://www.apa.org/monitor/2023/07/psychologists-preventing-teen-suicide.

10 National Aeronautics and Space Administration. "Climate Change: How Do We Know?" *NASA Science*. Accessed June 21, 2024. https://science.nasa.gov/climate-change/evidence/.

11 Statista. "Fertilizer Consumption Worldwide by Nutrient 2021." Accessed October 5, 2024. https://www.statista.com/statistics/438967/fertilizer-consumption-globally-by-nutrient/.

12 Román-Palacios, Cristian, and John J. Wiens. "Recent Responses to Climate Change Reveal the Drivers of Species Extinction and Survival." *Proceedings of the National Academy of Sciences* (2020): 201913007. https://doi.org/10.1073/pnas.1913007117.

13 "Animal Populations Plummeted by Nearly 70% in last 50 Years, New Report Says." *CBS News*, last modified October 14, 2022. Accessed June 21, 2024. https://www.cbsnews.com/news/animal-populations-plummeted-by-nearly-70-percent-last-50-years-new-report/.

14 Scientific American. "Only 60 Years of Farming Left If Soil Degradation Continues." Accessed June 21, 2024. https://www.scientificamerican.com/article/only-60-years-of-farming-left-if-soil-degradation-continues/.

Chapter 2

1   Harris, E. "Ultra Processed Foods Linked With 32 Types of Health Problems." *JAMA* 331, no. 15 (2024): 1265. https://doi.org/10.1001/jama.2024.2088.

2 Centers for Disease Control and Prevention. "Fruits and Vegetables: A Key to Healthy Living." Last modified October 30, 2018. Accessed October 5, 2024. https://archive.cdc.gov/www_cdc_gov/nccdphp/dnpao/division-information/media-tools/dpk/vs-fruits-vegetables/.

3 New York Health Foundation. "Fact Sheet: Potentially Toxic Chemicals in Personal Care Products." Accessed October 5, 2024. https://nyhealthfoundation.org/resource/fact-sheet-potentially-toxic-chemicals-in-personal-care-products/.

4 "Student Stress Statistics." *Research.com*. Accessed June 28, 2024. https://research.com/education/student-stress-statistics.

5 Centers for Disease Control and Prevention. "Sleep and Sleep Disorders." Accessed June 21, 2024. https://www.cdc.gov/healthyschools/sleep.htm.

6 Centers for Disease Control and Prevention. "Physical Activity Facts." Accessed June 21, 2024. https://www.cdc.gov/healthyschools/physicalactivity/facts.htm.

7 Gao, W., M. Sanna, Y. Chen, M. Tsai, and C. Wen. "Occupational Sitting Time, Leisure Physical Activity, and All-Cause and Cardiovascular Disease Mortality." *JAMA Network Open* 7, no. 1 (2024): e2350680. https://doi.org/10.1001/jamanetworkopen.2023.50680.

8 "Social Media Affects Mental Health." *Center for Research on Education Outcomes*. Accessed June 28, 2024. https://www.center4research.org/social-media-affects-mental-health.

9 Mayo Clinic. "Tween and Teen Health." Accessed June 21, 2024. https://www.mayoclinic.org/healthy-lifestyle/tween-and-teen-health/basics/tween-and-teen-health/hlv-20049436.

10 Riehm, K. E., K. A. Feder, K. N. Tormohlen, et al. "Associations Between Time Spent Using Social Media and Internalizing and Externalizing Problems Among US Youth." *JAMA Psychiatry* 76, no. 12 (2019): 1266–1273. https://doi.org/10.1001/jamapsychiatry.2019.2325.

11 American Psychological Association. "Teen Social Media Use and Mental Health." *APA Monitor*, April 2024. Accessed June 21, 2024. https://www.apa.org/monitor/2024/04/teen-social-use-mental-health.

12 American Psychological Association. "Teen Social Media Use Linked to Mental Health Concerns." *APA Monitor on Psychology*, April 2024. https://www.apa.org/monitor/2024/04/teen-social-use-mental-health.

13 Comaford, Christine. "Got Inner Peace? 5 Ways to Get It Now." *Forbes*, April 4, 2012. Accessed October 5, 2024. https://www.forbes.com/sites/christinecomaford/2012/04/04/got-inner-peace-5-ways-to-get-it-now/.

14 Soroka, Stuart, Pierre Fournier, and Liran Nir. "Cross-National Evidence of a Negativity Bias in Psychophysiological Reactions to News." *Proceedings of the National Academy of Sciences of the United States of America* 116, no. 38 (2019): 18888–92. https://doi.org/10.1073/pnas.1908369116.

15 "Purpose in Life: Less Stress, Better Mental Health." *American Psychiatric Association*. Accessed June 23, 2024. https://www.psychiatry.org/news-room/apa-blogs/purpose-in-life-less-stress-better-mental-health.

16 Ratner, Kaylin, Qingyi Li, Gaoxia Zhu, Melody Estevez, and Anthony L. Burrow. "Daily Adolescent Purposefulness, Daily Subjective Well-Being, and Individual Differences in Autistic Traits." *Journal of Happiness Studies* (2023): https://doi.org/10.1007/s10902-023-00625-7.

17 "How Spirituality Affects Mental Health." *WebMD*. Accessed June 28, 2024. https://www.webmd.com/balance/how-spirituality-affects-mental-health.

18 Northwestern Medicine. "11 Fun Facts About Your Brain." Last modified August 31, 2023. Accessed October 6, 2024. https://www.nm.org/healthbeat/healthy-tips/11-fun-facts-about-your-brain.

19 "Child Addiction to Ultra-Processed Foods May Be a Concern." *CNN*. Accessed June 27, 2024. https://www.cnn.com/2024/06/27/health/child-addiction-ultraprocessed-foods-wellness.

20 Fazzino, T. L., D. Jun, L. Chollet-Hinton, and K. Bjorlie. "US Tobacco Companies Selectively Disseminated Hyper-palatable Foods into the US Food System: Empirical Evidence and Current Implications." *Addiction* 119, no. 1 (2024): 62–71. https://doi.org/10.1111/add.16332.

21 Gearhardt, A. N., and A. G. DiFeliceantonio. "Highly Processed Foods can be Considered Addictive Substances Based on Established Scientific Criteria." *Addiction* 118, no 4 (2023): 589–98. https://doi.org/10.1111/add.16065.

22 Arrona-Cardoza, P., K. Labonté, J. M. Cisneros-Franco, and D. E. Nielsen. "The Effects of Food Advertisements on Food Intake and Neural Activity: A Systematic Review and Meta-Analysis of Recent Experimental Studies." *Advances in Nutrition* 14, no. 2 (2023): 339–51. https://doi.org/10.1016/j.advnut.2022.12.003.

23 The Washington Post. "How Dietitians on Instagram and TikTok Get Paid by the Food Industry." Accessed June 21, 2024. https://www.washingtonpost.com/wellness/2023/09/13/dietitian-instagram-tiktok-paid-food-industry/.

Chapter 3

1 NPR. "Antibiotic Resistance in Children Is Becoming a Bigger Problem Around the World." *NPR*, November 7, 2023. https://www.npr.org/2023/11/07/1211329922/antibiotic-resistance-in-children-is-becoming-a-bigger-problem-around-the-world.

2 Fasano, A. "All Disease Begins in the (leaky) Gut: Role of Zonulin-mediated Gut Permeability in the Pathogenesis of Some Chronic Inflammatory Diseases." *F1000Research*, 2020, 9 Faculty Rev-69. Published January 31, 2020. https://doi.org/10.12688/f1000research.20510.1.

3 National Public Radio. "Study: U.S. Kids' Diets Dominated by Ultra-Processed 'Junk' Foods." *NPR*, August 11, 2021. https://www.npr.org/2021/08/11/1026816658/study-us-kids-diet-ultraprocessed-junk-food.

4 National Center for Biotechnology Information. "Research News: 2045." Accessed June 24, 2024. https://www.ncbi.nlm.nih.gov/search/research-news/2045/.

5 Lane, M. M., E. Gamage, S. Du, D. N. Ashtree, A. J. McGuinness, S. Gauci, et al. 2024. "Ultra-processed Food Exposure and Adverse Health Outcomes: Umbrella Review of Epidemiological Meta-analyses." *BMJ* 384. https://doi.org/10.1136/bmj-2023-077310.

6 Liu, S., C. Mo, L. Lei, et al. "Association of Ultraprocessed Foods Consumption and Cognitive Function among Children Aged 4–7 Years: A Cross-Sectional Data Analysis." *Frontiers in Nutrition* 10 (2023): 1272126. https://doi.org/10.3389/fnut.2023.1272126.

7 "Ultra-Processed Foods and Brain Health." *The Wall Street Journal*. Accessed June 24, 2024. https://www.wsj.com/health/wellness/ultra-processed-food-brain-health-7a3f9827.

8 "Study: Ultra-Processed Foods Linked to Higher Risk of Early Death." *CNN*. Accessed July 1, 2024. https://www.cnn.com/2024/07/01/health/worst-ultraprocessed-food-early-death-wellness/index.html.

9. "Food Additives Market." *Future Market Insights*. Accessed June 28, 2024. https://www.futuremarketinsights.com/reports/food-additives-market.

10. Whelan, K., A. S. Bancil, J. O Lindsay, and B. Chassaing. "Ultra-processed Foods and Food Additives in Gut Health and Disease." *Nature Reviews Gastroenterology & Hepatology* 21, no. 6 (2024): 406–27. https://doi.org/10.1038/s41575-024-00893-5.

11. Pipoyan, D., S. Stepanyan, S. Stepanyan, et al. "The Effect of Trans Fatty Acids on Human Health: Regulation and Consumption Patterns." *Foods* 10, no. 10 (2021): 2452. Published October 14, 2021. https://doi.org/10.3390/foods10102452.

12. Johns Hopkins Medicine. "Finding the Hidden Sugar in the Foods You Eat." *Johns Hopkins Medicine Health*. Accessed January 11, 2025. https://www.hopkinsmedicine.org/health/wellness-and-prevention/finding-the-hidden-sugar-in-the-foods-you-eat.

13. Beecher, K., Ignatius Alvarez Cooper, Joshua Wang, et al. "Long-Term Overconsumption of Sugar Starting at Adolescence Produces Persistent Hyperactivity and Neurocognitive Deficits in Adulthood." *Frontiers in Neuroscience* 15 (June 2021). Accessed June 24, 2024. https://www.frontiersin.org/articles/10.3389/fnins.2021.670430/full.

14. Fang, H., F. F. Anhê, and J. D. Schertzer. "Dietary Sugar Lowers Immunity and Microbiota that Protect Against Metabolic Disease." *Cell Metabolism* 34, no. 10 (2022): 1422–4. https://doi.org/10.1016/j.cmet.2022.09.006.

15. Liu, Ta-Chiang, Justin T. Kern, Umang Jain, et al. "Western Diet Induces Paneth Cell Defects Through Microbiome Alterations and Farnesoid X Receptor and Type I Interferon Activation." *Cell Host & Microbe* 29, no. 6 (June 2021): 988–1001E6. Accessed June 24, 2024. https://pubmed.ncbi.nlm.nih.gov/34010595/.

16. Rupérez, A. I., M. I. Mesana, and L. A. Moreno. "Dietary Sugars, Metabolic Effects and Child Health." *Current Opinion in Clinical Nutrition and Metabolic Care* 22, no. 3 (2019): 206–16. https://doi.org/10.1097/MCO.0000000000000553.

17. Zänkert, Sandra, Brigittte M. Kudielka, and Stefan Wüst. "Effect of Sugar Administration on Cortisol Responses to Acute Psychosocial Stress." *Psychoneuroendocrinology* 115 (May 2020). Accessed June 24, 2024.

18. "Diet Drinks May Affect Blood Sugar Levels, Insulin Resistance, and Gut Microbiome." *News Medical*, October 14, 2023. https://www.news-medical

.net/news/20231014/Diet-drinks-may-affect-blood-sugar-levels-insulin-resistance-and-gut-microbiome.aspx.

19 Argou-Cardozo, Isadora, and Fares Zeidán-Chuliá. "Clostridium Bacteria and Autism Spectrum Conditions: A Systematic Review and Hypothetical Contribution of Environmental Glyphosate Levels." *Medical Sciences* 6, no. 2 (June 2018): 29. https://www.ncbi.nlm.nih.gov/pmc/articles/PMC6024569/; Mao, Qixing, Fabiana Manservisi, Simona Panzacchi, et al. "The Ramazzini Institute 13-Week Pilot Study on Glyphosate and Roundup Administered at Human-Equivalent Doses to Sprague Dawley Rats: Effects on the Microbiome." *Environmental Health* 17 (2018): 50. https://www.ncbi.nlm.nih.gov/pmc/articles/PMC5972442/; Shehata, Awad A., Wieland Schrödl, Alaa A. Aldin, et al. "The Effect of Glyphosate on Potential Pathogens and Beneficial Members of Poultry Microbiota in Vitro." *Current Microbiology* 66 (2013): 350–8. https://link.springer.com/article/10.1007/s00284-012-0277-2.

20 De Araujo, Jessica S. A., Isabella F. Delgado, and Francisco J. R. Paumgartten. "Glyphosate and Adverse Pregnancy Outcomes, a Systematic Review of Observational Studies." *BMC Public Health* 16 (2016): 472. https://www.ncbi.nlm.nih.gov/pmc/articles/PMC4895883/;Ondine; von Ehrenstein, S., Chenxiao Ling, Xin Cui, et al. "Prenatal and Infant Exposure to Ambient Pesticides and Autism Spectrum Disorder in Children: Population Based Case-Control Study." *British Medical Journal* 364 (2019): 1962. https://www.ncbi.nlm.nih.gov/pmc/articles/PMC6425996/; Hyland, Carly, Patrick T. Bradshaw, Robert B. Gunier, et al. "Associations Between Pesticide Mixtures Applied Near Home During Pregnancy and Early Childhood with Adolescent Behavioral and Emotional Problems in the CHAMACOS Study." *Environmental Epidemiology* 5, no. 3 (June 2021): e150. https://www.ncbi.nlm.nih.gov/pmc/articles/PMC8196094/.

21 "How GMOs Are Regulated in the United States." *U.S. Food and Drug Administration.* Accessed June 24, 2024. https://www.fda.gov/food/agricultural-biotechnology/how-gmos-are-regulated-united-states.

Chapter 4

1 Oranika, Uchechi S., Oladapo L. Adeola, Theophilus O. Egbuchua, et al. "The Role of Childhood Obesity in Early-Onset Type 2 Diabetes Mellitus: A Scoping Review." *Cureus* 15, no. 10 (2023): e48037. Published October 31, 2023. https://doi.org/10.7759/cureus.48037.

2   O'Hearn, M., Lauren B. N., Wong, J. B., Kim, D. D., and Mozaffarian, D. "Trends and Disparities in Cardiometabolic Health Among U.S. Adults, 1999-2018." *Journal of the American College of Cardiology* 80, no. 2 (2022): 138–51. https://doi.org/10.1016/j.jacc.2022.04.046.

3   Calliari, Luis Eduardo, Fabiana de Jesus Almeida, and Renata Maria Noronha. "Infections in Children with Diabetes." *Jornal de Pediatria* (Rio J) 96, Suppl 1 (2020): 39–46. https://doi.org/10.1016/j.jped.2019.09.004.

4   "Study: Drinking Water May Reduce Childhood Obesity." *CBS Pittsburgh*. Accessed June 24, 2024. https://www.cbsnews.com/pittsburgh/news/study-drinking-water-reduce-childhood-obesity/.

5   Azagba, Sunday, Donald Langille, and Mark Asbridge. "An Emerging Adolescent Health Risk: Caffeinated Energy Drink Consumption Patterns Among High School Students." *Preventive Medicine* 62 (2014): 54. https://doi.org/10.1016/j.ypmed.2014.01.019.

6   Vigar, V., S. Myers, C. Oliver, J. Arellano, S. Robinson, and C. Leifert. "A Systematic Review of Organic Versus Conventional Food Consumption: Is There a Measurable Benefit on Human Health?" *Nutrients* 12, no. 1 (2019): 7. https://doi.org/10.3390/nu12010007.

7   Jung, M., Kim, J., Kwon, O., and Lee, J. "Sustainable Food Systems and Their Impact on Human Health: A Review." *Journal of Cleaner Production* (2023). https://doi.org/10.1016/j.jclepro.2023.137343.

8   Bhardwaj, R. L., A. Parashar, H. P. Parewa, and L. Vyas. "An Alarming Decline in the Nutritional Quality of Foods: The Biggest Challenge for Future Generations' Health." *Foods* 13, no. 6 (March 14, 2024): 877. https://doi.org/10.3390/foods13060877.

9   RTS. "Food Waste in America." *RTS*. Accessed January 11, 2025. https://www.rts.com/resources/guides/food-waste-america/.

Chapter 5

1   Donley, N. "The USA Lags Behind Other Agricultural Nations in Banning Harmful Pesticides." *Environmental Health* 18, no. 44 (2019). https://doi.org/10.1186/s12940-019-0488-0.

2   United Nations Environment Programme. "UN Report: Urgent Action Needed to Tackle Chemical Pollution Globally." Last modified February

14, 2023. https://www.unep.org/news-and-stories/press-release/un-report-urgent-action-needed-tackle-chemical-pollution-global.

3. U.S. Environmental Protection Agency. "EPA Releases First Major Update to Chemicals List in 40 Years." Last modified September 28, 2023. Accessed October 6, 2024.

4. "Teen Vaping Linked to Toxic Lead, Uranium Exposure." *CNN*, April 29, 2024. Accessed June 24, 2024. https://www.cnn.com/2024/04/29/health/teen-vaping-toxic-lead-uranium-exposure-wellness/index.html.

5. "Almost 1 Million People Die Every Year Due to Lead Poisoning, with More Children Suffering Long-term Health Effects." *World Health Organization*, October 23, 2022. Accessed June 24, 2024. https://www.who.int/news/item/23-10-2022-almost-1-million-people-die-every-year-due-to-lead-poisoning--with-more-children-suffering-long-term-health-effects.

6. Zhang, L., J. Chu, B. Xia, Z. Xiong, S. Zhang, and W. Tang. "Health Effects of Particulate Uranium Exposure." *Toxics* 10, no. 10 (2022): 575. Published September 30, 2022. https://doi.org/10.3390/toxics10100575.

7. Society for Risk Analysis. "Heavy Metals in Our Food are Most Dangerous for Kids." *ScienceDaily*. Accessed June 29, 2024. www.sciencedaily.com/releases/2023/12/231212112342.htm.

8. Yıldız, S., A. Gözü Pirinççioğlu, and E. Arıca. "Evaluation of Heavy Metal (Lead, Mercury, Cadmium, and Manganese) Levels in Blood, Plasma, and Urine of Adolescents With Aggressive Behavior." *Cureus* 15, no. 1 (2023): e33902. Published January 17, 2023. https://doi.org/10.7759/cureus.33902.

9. "Children are More Exposed to Microplastics than Adults, says Expert."*News-Medical.net*, February 1, 2022. Accessed June 24, 2024. https://www.news-medical.net/news/20220201/Children-are-more-exposed-to-microplastics-than-adults-says-expert.aspx.

10. Veidis, Emily M., LaBeaud, Adele D., Phillips, Angela A., and Barry, Matthew. "Tackling the Ubiquity of Plastic Waste for Human and Planetary Health." *American Journal of Tropical Medicine and Hygiene* 106, no. 1 (2021): 12–14. Published November 8, 2021. https://doi.org/10.4269/ajtmh.21-0968.

11. "Third Unregulated Contaminant Monitoring Rule (UCMR 3): Analytical Results of Drinking Water." *Environmental Protection Agency*. Accessed June 28, 2024. https://www.epa.gov/sites/default/files/2015-10/documents/ace3_drinking_water.pdf.

12. Johns Hopkins University. "Vaping Unknown Chemicals: What We Don't Know About the Health Risks." *Hub* (blog), October 7, 2021. https://hub.jhu.edu/2021/10/07/vaping-unknown-chemicals/.

13. "Women Put an Average of 168 Chemicals on Their Bodies Every Day, Consumer Group Says." *ABC News*. Accessed June 24, 2024. https://abcnews.go.com/Health/women-put-average-168-chemicals-bodies-day-consumer/story?id=30615324.

14. Suarez-Lopez, Jose R., Naomi Hood, José Suárez-Torres, Sheila Gahagan, Megan R. Gunnar, and Dolores López-Paredes. "Associations of Acetylcholinesterase Activity with Depression and Anxiety Symptoms Among Adolescents Growing Up Near Pesticide Spray Sites." *International Journal of Hygiene and Environmental Health* (2019). https://doi.org/10.1016/j.ijheh.2019.06.001.

15. Lanphear, B. P., P. Den Besten, and C. Till. "Time to Reassess Systemic Fluoride Exposure. Again." *JAMA Pediatrics*. Published online January 6, 2025. https://doi.org/10.1001/jamapediatrics.2024.5549.

Chapter 6

1. Nerurkar, A., A. Bitton, R. B. Davis, R. S. Phillips, and G. Yeh. "When Physicians Counsel About Stress: Results of a National Study." *JAMA Internal Medicine* 173, no. 1 (January 14, 2013): 76–7. https://doi.org/10.1001/2013.jamainternmed.480

2. "Stress Relief: Techniques to Tame Stress." *Mayo Clinic*. Accessed June 28, 2024. https://www.mayoclinic.org/healthy-lifestyle/stress-management/in-depth/stress-relief/art-20044456.

3. Adrian Buttazzoni and Leia Minaker. "Associations Between Real-time, Self-reported Adolescent Mental Health and Urban and Architectural Design Concepts." *Cities & Health* (2023). https://doi.org/10.1080/23748834.2023.2286741.

Chapter 7

1. Cazalis, Victor, Michel Loreau, and Gladys Barragan-Jason. "A Global Synthesis of Trends in Human Experience of Nature." *Frontiers in Ecology and the Environment* (2022). https://doi.org/10.1002/fee.2540.

2. Jo, H., C. Song, and Y. Miyazaki. "Physiological Benefits of Viewing Nature: A Systematic Review of Indoor Experiments." *International Journal of*

Environmental Research and Public Health 16, no. 23 (2019): 4739. Published November 27, 2019. https://doi.org/10.3390/ijerph16234739.

3   Li, Q. "Effects of Forest Environment (Shinrin-yoku/Forest Bathing) on Health Promotion and Disease Prevention—The Establishment of 'Forest Medicine'." *Environmental Health and Preventive Medicine* 27 (2022): 43. https://doi.org/10.1265/ehpm.22-00160.

4   "Title of the Article." *ScienceDirect* (2023). Accessed June 24, 2024. https://www.sciencedirect.com/science/article/abs/pii/S0272494423000439.

5   Van Wieren, Gretel, and Stephen R. Kellert. "The Origins of Aesthetic and Spiritual Values in Children's Experience of Nature." *Journal of the Study of Religion, Nature and Culture* 7, no. 3 (2013): 243–64.

6   "Hug a Tree, Relieve Your Stress." *Journal of Psychosocial Nursing and Mental Health Services* 37, no. 6 (1999): 9.

Chapter 8

1   Holt-Lunstad, Julianne, Timothy B. Smith, and Julianne B. Layton. "Social Relationships and Mortality Risk: A Meta-analytic Review." *PLoS Medicine* 7, no. 7 (2010): e1000316. Published July 27, 2010. https://doi.org/10.1371/journal.pmed.1000316.

2   *The Surgeon General's Advisory on Building a Healthy and Resilient Social Connection.* U.S. Department of Health and Human Services. Accessed June 24, 2024. https://www.hhs.gov/sites/default/files/surgeon-general-social-connection-advisory.pdf.

3   Pew Research Center. "Teens' Views About Social Media." *Pew Research Center,* November 16, 2022. https://www.pewresearch.org/internet/2022/11/16/2-teens-views-about-social-media/.

4   "Volunteering and Its Surprising Benefits." *HelpGuide.org.* Accessed June 24, 2024. https://www.helpguide.org/articles/healthy-living/volunteering-and-its-surprising-benefits.htm.

5   Psychology Today. "Two Key Reasons Why You Should Call Your Mom." *Psychology Today,* April 19, 2021. https://www.psychologytoday.com/us/blog/the-psychology-of-relationships/202104/two-key-reasons-why-you-should-call-your-mom.

Chapter 9

1. The Guardian. "Screen Time: How Much Should Kids Really Be Using Phones?" *The Guardian*, February 1, 2024. https://www.theguardian.com/lifeandstyle/2024/feb/01/screen-time-phones-kids-limit.

2. Afrotech. "New Study Shows Most Americans Use Their Smartphone on the Toilet." *Afrotech*, August 30, 2021. https://afrotech.com/new-study-shows-most-americans-use-their-smartphone-on-the-toilet.

3. Harvard Health Publishing. "Blue Light Has a Dark Side." *Harvard Health Blog*, December 1, 2020. https://www.health.harvard.edu/staying-healthy/blue-light-has-a-dark-side.

4. Lee, David S., Tao Jiang, Jennifer Crocker, and Baldwin M. Way. "Social Media Use and Its Link to Physical Health Indicators." *Cyberpsychology, Behavior, and Social Networking* (2022). https://doi.org/10.1089/cyber.2021.0188.

5. Yale Medicine. "Social Media and Teen Mental Health: A Parent's Guide." *Yale Medicine*. Accessed January 11, 2025. https://www.yalemedicine.org/news/social-media-teen-mental-health-a-parents-guide.

Chapter 10

1. Centers for Disease Control and Prevention. "Sleep." *CDC*. Accessed January 11, 2025. https://www.cdc.gov/physical-activity-education/staying-healthy/sleep.html.

2. Johns Hopkins Medicine. "Teenagers and Sleep: How Much Sleep Is Enough?" *Johns Hopkins Medicine Health*. Accessed January 11, 2025. https://www.hopkinsmedicine.org/health/wellness-and-prevention/teenagers-and-sleep-how-much-sleep-is-enough.

3. The Conversation. "It's Almost Impossible to Keep Teens Off Their Phones in Bed, but New Research Shows it Really Does Affect Their Sleep." *The Conversation*, December 7, 2023. https://theconversation.com/its-almost-impossible-to-keep-teens-off-their-phones-in-bed-but-new-research-shows-it-really-does-affect-their-sleep-237955.

4   BBC Future. "What You Can Learn from Einstein's Quirky Habits." *BBC Future*, June 12, 2017. https://www.bbc.com/future/article/20170612-what-you-can-learn-from-einsteins-quirky-habits.

5   American Academy of Pediatrics. "Only Half of US Children Get Enough Sleep During the Week." *ScienceDaily*, October 25, 2019. Accessed October 7, 2024. https://www.sciencedaily.com/releases/2019/10/191025075604.htm.

Chapter 11

1   Zhao, H., M. Zhang, Y. Li, and Z. Wang. "The Effect of Growth Mindset on Adolescents' Meaning in Life: The Roles of Self-Efficacy and Gratitude." *Psychology Research and Behavior Management* 16 (2023): 4647–64. https://doi.org/10.2147/PRBM.S428397.

2   Here is the Chicago-style citation for the provided URL: Langwell, Shawn. "Fact: 85% of U.S. Suffer from Low Self-Esteem." *Medium*, November 17, 2020. https://medium.com/@shawnlangwell/fact-85-of-us-suffer-from-low-self-esteem-364cf613148.

3   Boreham, I. D., and N. S. Schutte. "The Relationship Between Purpose in Life and Depression and Anxiety: A Meta-Analysis." *Journal of Clinical Psychology* 79, no. 12 (2023): 2736–67. https://doi.org/10.1002/jclp.23576.

4   "Social Media Influencers: 86% of Young Americans Want to Become One." Accessed June 21, 2024. https://www.cbsnews.com/news/social-media-influencers-86-of-young-americans-want-to-become-one/.

5   Svob, C., and M. M. Weissman. "The Role of Religiosity in Families at High Risk for Depression." *Ethics, Medicine, and Public Health* 2019, no. 9 (2019): 1–6. https://doi.org/10.1016/j.jemep.2019.03.007.

6   Here is the Chicago-style citation for the given article: Jacobs, M., L. Miller, P. Wickramaratne, M. Gameroff, and M. M. Weissman. "Family Religion and Psychopathology in Children of Depressed Mothers: Ten-Year Follow-Up." *Journal of Affective Disorders* 136, no. 3 (February 2012): 320–7. https://doi.org/10.1016/j.jad.2011.11.030.

Chapter 12

1   Spear, L. P. "Adolescent Neurodevelopment." *Journal of Adolescent Health* 52, no. 2, Suppl 2 (2013): S7–S13. https://doi.org/10.1016/j.jadohealth.2012.05.006.

Chapter 13

1. StopBullying.gov. "Facts About Bullying." *StopBullying.gov.* Accessed January 11, 2025. https://www.stopbullying.gov/resources/facts.

2. Lawrence-Sidebottom, D., L G. Huffman, A. B. Beam, R. Guerra, A. Parikh, M. Roots, and J. Huberty. "Rates of Trauma Exposure and Posttraumatic Stress in a Pediatric Digital Mental Health Intervention: Retrospective Analysis of Associations with Anxiety and Depressive Symptom Improvement Over Time." *JMIR Pediatrics and Parenting* 7 (February 27, 2024): e55560. https://doi.org/10.2196/55560.

3. https://www.oregon.gov/oha/PH/HEALTHYPEOPLEFAMILIES/WIC/Documents/modules/aces-childhood-questionnaire.pdf.

4. National Institutes of Health. "NIH-Funded Study Suggests Acetaminophen Exposure in Pregnancy Linked to Higher Risk of ADHD, Autism." *National Institutes of Health,* October 19, 2021. https://www.nih.gov/news-events/news-releases/nih-funded-study-suggests-acetaminophen-exposure-pregnancy-linked-higher-risk-achd-autism.

5. Alyoussef, Abdullah. "The Impact of Consuming Probiotics and Following a Vegetarian Diet on the Outcomes of Acne." *Cureus* 16, no. 1 (January 3, 2024): e51563. https://pmc.ncbi.nlm.nih.gov/articles/PMC10835645/.

6. Sun, Luyao, Qian Yu, Fu Peng, Chen Sun, Daibo Wang, Lin Pu, Fang Xiong, Yuncai Tian, Cheng Peng, and Qinmei Zhou. "The Antibacterial Activity of Berberine Against *Cutibacterium Acnes*: Its Therapeutic Potential in Inflammatory Acne." *Frontiers in Microbiology,* January 5, 2024. https://pmc.ncbi.nlm.nih.gov/articles/PMC10797013/.

7. Yee, Brittany E., Phillip Richards, Jennifer Y. Sui, and Amanda Fleming Marsch. "Serum Zinc Levels and Efficacy of Zinc Treatment in Acne Vulgaris: A Systematic Review and Meta-Analysis." *Dermatologic Therapy* 33, no. 6 (November 2020): e14252. https://doi.org/10.1111/dth.14252.

8. Draelos, Zoe D., Martina Kerscher, Stephen Lynch, Stacy White, and Hina Choudhary. "A Silymarin Antioxidant Serum Improves Facial Acne Alone and as Part of a Treatment Regimen." *Journal of Drugs in Dermatology* 23, no. 4 (April 1, 2024): 233–8. https://doi.org/10.36849/JDD.8120.

9. Nascimento, Tânia, Diana Gomes, Ricardo Simões, and Maria da Graça Miguel. "Tea Tree Oil: Properties and the Therapeutic Approach to Acne—A Review." *Antioxidants* 12, no. 6 (June 12, 2023): 1264. https://doi.org/10.3390/antiox12061264.

10 Drago, Lorenzo, Luigi Cioffi, Maria Giuliano, Marco Pane, Angela Amoruso, Irene Schiavetti, Gregor Reid, Giorgio Ciprandi, and the PROPAM Study Group. "The Probiotics in Pediatric Asthma Management (PROPAM) Study in the Primary Care Setting: A Randomized, Controlled, Double-Blind Trial with *Ligilactobacillus salivarius* LS01 (DSM 22775) and *Bifidobacterium breve* B632 (DSM 24706)." *Journal of Immunology Research* 2022 (January 17, 2022): 3837418. https://doi.org/10.1155/2022/3837418.

11 Fedora, Katherine, Retno Asih Setyoningrum, Qorri' Aina, Laili Nur Rosyidah, Nur Lailatun Ni'mah, and Feelin Fatwa Titiharja. "Vitamin D Supplementation Decreases Asthma Exacerbations in Children: A Systematic Review and Meta-Analysis of Randomized Controlled Trials." *Annals of Medicine* 56, no. 1 (December 2024): 2400313. https://doi.org/10.1080/07853890.2024.2400313.

12 Siripornpanich, S., N. Chongviriyaphan, W. Manuyakorn, and P. Matangkasombut. "Zinc and Vitamin C Deficiencies Associate with Poor Pulmonary Function in Children with Persistent Asthma." *Asian Pacific Journal of Allergy and Immunology* 40, no. 2 (June 2022): 103–10. https://doi.org/10.12932/AP-100620-0878. PMID: 33274952.

13 Jafarinia, M., M. Sadat Hosseini, N. Kasiri, N. Fazel, F. Fathi, M. Ganjalikhani Hakemi, and N. Eskandari. "Quercetin with the Potential Effect on Allergic Diseases." *Allergy, Asthma & Clinical Immunology* 16 (May 14, 2020): 36. https://doi.org/10.1186/s13223-020-00434-0. PMID: 32467711; PMCID: PMC7227109.

14 Mlček, J., T. Juríková, S. Skrovanková, and J. Sochor. "Quercetin and Its Anti-Allergic Immune Response."*Molecules* 21, no. 5 (May 12, 2016): 623. https://doi.org/10.3390/molecules21050623. PMID: 27187333; PMCID: PMC6273625.

15 Schapowal, A., and the Petasites Study Group. "Randomised Controlled Trial of Butterbur and Cetirizine for Treating Seasonal Allergic Rhinitis."*BMJ* 324, no. 7330 (January 19, 2002): 144–6. https://doi.org/10.1136/bmj.324.7330.144. PMID: 11799030; PMCID: PMC64514.

16 Butawan, M., R. L. Benjamin, and R. J. Bloomer. "Methylsulfonylmethane: Applications and Safety of a Novel Dietary Supplement." *Nutrients* 9, no. 3 (March 16, 2017): 290. https://doi.org/10.3390/nu9030290. PMID: 28300758; PMCID: PMC5372953.

17 Boham, Elizabeth. *Breast Wellness: Tools to Prevent and Heal Breast Cancer* (Amazon Self-Publishing, 2025). Goldman, Eric. "I Expect My Patients to Be Outliers: Applying Nutrition to Improve Cancer Outcomes." *Holistic

Primary Care, February 18, 2019. https://holisticprimarycare.net/topics/cancer-care/i-expect-my-patients-to-be-outliers-applying-nutrition-to-improve-cancer-outcomes/.

18. Salvatore, S., M. S. Battigaglia, E. Murone, E. Dozio, L. Pensabene, and M. Agosti. "Dietary Fibers in Healthy Children and in Pediatric Gastrointestinal Disorders: A Practical Guide." *Nutrients* 15, no. 9 (May 6, 2023): 2208. https://doi.org/10.3390/nu15092208. PMID: 37432354; PMCID: PMC10180776.

19. Medical News Today. "Vitamins for Constipation: Do they Work?" *Medical News Today*, November 25, 2019. https://www.medicalnewstoday.com/articles/327115.

20. Xie, Wei, Fei Su, Guang Wang, Zhi Peng, Yao Xu, Yun Zhang, Nan Xu, Kun Hou, Zhi Hu, Yanyan Chen, and Rui Chen. 2022. "Glucose-Lowering Effect of Berberine on Type 2 Diabetes: A Systematic Review and Meta-Analysis." *Frontiers in Pharmacology* 13 (November 16): 1015045. https://doi.org/10.3389/fphar.2022.1015045.

21. Kim, C. W., B. T. Kim, K. H. Park, K. M. Kim, D. J. Lee, S. W. Yang, and N. S. Joo. "Effects of Short-Term Chromium Supplementation on Insulin Sensitivity and Body Composition in Overweight Children Randomized, Double-Blind, Placebo-Controlled Study." *Journal of Nutritional Biochemistry* 22, no. 11 (November 2011): 1030–4. https://doi.org/10.1016/j.jnutbio.2010.10.001.

22. Gosselin, L. E., L. Chrapowitzky, and T. C. Rideout. "Metabolic Effects of α-Lipoic Acid Supplementation in Pre-Diabetics: A Randomized, Placebo-Controlled Pilot Study." *Food & Function* 10, no. 9 (September 1, 2019): 5732–8. https://doi.org/10.1039/c9fo00390h.

23. Mayo Clinic Staff. "Menstrual Cramps: Diagnosis and Treatment." *Mayo Clinic*. Last modified February 17, 2021. https://www.mayoclinic.org/diseases-conditions/menstrual-cramps/diagnosis-treatment/drc-20374944.

24. Höller, M., H. Steindl, D. Abramov-Sommariva, J. Kleemann, A. Loleit, C. Abels, and P. Stute. "Use of *Vitex agnus-castus* in Patients with Menstrual Cycle Disorders: A Single-Center Retrospective Longitudinal Cohort Study." *Archives of Gynecology and Obstetrics* 309, no. 5 (May 2024): 2089–98. https://doi.org/10.1007/s00404-023-07363-4.

25. Wu, C. C., M. Y. Huang, R. Kapoor, C. H. Chen, and Y. S. Huang. "Metabolism of Omega-6 Polyunsaturated Fatty Acids in Women with

Dysmenorrhea." *Asia Pacific Journal of Clinical Nutrition* 17, Suppl. 1 (2008): 216–19.

26 David, T. J., F. E. Wells, T. C. Sharpe, and A. C. Gibbs. 1984. "Low Serum Zinc in Children with Atopic Eczema." *British Journal of Dermatology* 111 (November): 597–601. https://doi.org/10.1111/j.1365-2133.1984.tb06630.x.

27 Beken, B., R. Serttaş, M. Yazıcıoğlu, K. Türkeşkul, and S. Erdoğan. "Quercetin Improves Inflammation, Oxidative Stress, and Impaired Wound Healing in Atopic Dermatitis Model of Human Keratinocytes." *Pediatric Allergy, Immunology, and Pulmonology* 33, no. 2 (June 2020): 69–79. https://doi.org/10.1089/ped.2019.1137.

28 Janeczek, M., L. Moy, A. Riopelle, O. Vetter, J. Reserva, R. Tung, and J. Swan. "The Potential Uses of N-Acetylcysteine in Dermatology: A Review." *Journal of Clinical and Aesthetic Dermatology* 12, no. 5 (May 2019): 20–6.

29 Streit, Lizzie, MS, RDN, LD, and Alina Sharon. "Best Vitamins and Supplements for Migraine." *Healthline*, May 29, 2024. https://www.healthline.com/health/migraine/migraine-vitamins.

30 CentreSpring MD. "Irregular Period? 10 Evidence-Based Ways to Help Regulate Your Cycles." *CentreSpring MD*. Accessed April 12, 2025. https://centrespringmd.com/irregular-period-10-evidence-based-ways-to-help-regulate-your-cycles.

31 Schaefer, Anna, and Kerry Weiss. "7 Natural Remedies for IBS." *Healthline*, December 23, 2024. https://www.healthline.com/health/irritable-bowel-syndrome/5-natural-products-for-ibs.

Conclusion

1 Caffrey, Mary. "Big Soda Sponsored 96 Health Groups Over a 5-Year Period." *The American Journal of Managed Care*, October 10, 2016. https://www.ajmc.com/view/big-soda-sponsored-96-health-groups-over-5-year-period.

Acknowledgments
We Cannot Thank God Enough!

So thankful for all the blessings in our lives. Our amazing parents, Omer and Madiha, opened our eyes and heart to this mission. So thankful for our grandparents, Mumtaz and Tahira Ansari, Muhammad and Nusrat Saeed—they were here to support us all with their hugs, love, and delicious food. Our parents, aunts, uncles, grandparents and cousins opened our hearts to the power of unconditional love and what it truly means to trust our heart when the world is telling you differently.

Grateful specifically to our aunts and uncles, Athar, Fasiha, Sophia, Atif, Sadaf, Usman, Sadia, and Shazia, who supported us through every hurdle, took on our family's "out of the box" ideas, respected us, and loved us through everything we have learned. When we adopted this healthy lifestyle, we had to change our lifestyles, change our foods, change our restaurants, change our outings and dietary habits, and our extended family supported us through it all. To the point, we do not have to worry about what we are eating at their homes because they take an extra step to make sure it is of the highest quality. Our aunt would even take us on vacation, find all the organic restaurants for us, take all the highest quality snacks for us. Our aunts spoil us with all the organic, clean treats. Even our grandmother will spend hours handpicking each of our outfits, 99 percent of our wardrobe since we were born, and all of our school supplies. She continues to look for the best deals on organic fruits and veggies, and even organic grass-fed meats, and brings them to us on a weekly basis.

We are forever thankful. We are forever grateful. Without family, we would be nowhere. Each and every one treats us with so much respect and love, we could never have asked for a more loving and supportive family. A special thanks to Tayibba khala, who gifted us her time and wisdom to edit this book for all of you. We can't thank her enough.

Grateful to our friends and family who support us, listen to our ideas on educating the world, and encourage us every step of the way. Grateful for Roman & Littlefield/Bloomsbury, my editor Christen, and our agent Jeff Herman for helping us make our dreams a reality.

Very thankful for all the leaders in functional, integrative, and holistic medicine who have guided us and supported us. Dr. Jeffrey Bland, Dr. Deanna Minich, Dr. Terry Wahls, Dr. Wendy Warner, Dr. Mark Hyman, Dave Asprey, Dr. Calley and Casey Means, Dr. Will Cole, Colleen and Jacob Wahcob, Dr. Tom O'Bryan, Vani Hari (Food Babe), Dr. Izabella Wentz, Dr. Elisa Song, Dr. Joel Gator, Dr. Maya Shetreat, Dr. David, and Austin Perlmutter, Beth Lambert, Erik Goldman, Kimberly Whittle, Katie Wells (Wellness Mama), Dhru Purohit, JJ Virgin, Dr. Amie Apigian, Dr. Rajka Milanovic Galbraith, Dr. Steven Masley, Dr. Uma Naidoo, Dr. Michael Breus, Dr. Sandra Scheinbaum, Dr. Romie, and so many more who have educated and opened our eyes to the holistic system of healing. They taught us the importance of a healthy lifestyle. We are so thankful specifically to MAS-ICNA, the Institute of Functional Medicine, A4M, and Dr. Dan Lukaczer for gifting us that platform for our voices to be heard. Thank you, Dr. Amy Myers, for teaching us how to autograph our names in our books, and as you waited patiently for us while fumbling through our signatures. We are so thankful to those at Physicians Holistic Health Alliance (Dr. Uthman Cavallo, Dr. Susan Cavallo, Krista, and Shelly) who inspired our mother to dedicate her and our lives to living holistically.

Thank you from the bottom of our hearts to all the podcast guests. Thank you for your time and wisdom helping us be the absolute best version of ourselves. Thankful to Mary Agnes and her team for the guidance and support. Thank you all for changing our lives forever!

The power of unconditional love and sacrifice can open doors that one could never have imagined. Love has brought us here today. Love has brought us to you. Love can save our future. Together we can raise each other up to create a healing teen revolution.

INDEX

Note: Page locators in italics refer to figures.

abstinence   133, 134
acetaminophen   187
acid-blocking drugs   188
acne   191
   acupressure   192
   aromatherapy   192
   homeopathy   192
   supplements   192
aconitum napellus   193
acupressure   189, *190*, 192
   acne   192
   anxiety disorders   218
   asthma   194
   attention deficit hyperactivity disorder   217
   back pain   196
   cancer   200
   constipation   201
   depression   220
   diabetes   203
   dysmenorrhea   204
   eczema   206
   gastroesophageal reflux disease   207
   headaches   210
   hypothyroidism   209
   insomnia   223
   irregular periods   211
   irritable bowel syndrome   213
   sinus   195
   substance abuse   227
   suicide   222
adenosine triphosphate (ATP)   15
adulthood   166

Adverse Childhood Experiences (ACE) Questionnaire   184–5
air pollution   101
Akkermansia muciniphila   77
alcohol   76
alpha lipoic acid   202
alumina   205
aluminum additives   53
American Academy of Child and Adolescent Psychiatry   12
American Academy of Pediatrics   12, 49, 76
American Diabetes Association   49, 230
American food supply   29
amygdala   28, 226
antibiotic resistance   43
antibiotics   43, 102, 187–8
antidepressants   188
antimonium tartaricum   193
anxiety disorders   217–18
   acupressure   218
   aromatherapy   219
   homeopathy   218
   supplements   218
The Anxious Generation   141, 142
apeel   78
aromatherapy   191
   acne   192
   anxiety disorders   219
   asthma   194
   attention deficit hyperactivity disorder   217

INDEX

back pain   197
   cancer   200
   constipation   201
   depression   220
   diabetes   203
   dysmenorrhea   204
   eczema   206
   gastroesophageal reflux disease   207
   headaches   210
   hypothyroidism   209
   insomnia   223
   irregular periods   212
   irritable bowel syndrome   213
   sinus   195
   substance abuse   227
   suicide   222
arsenic   99
artificial sweeteners   55, 68
asthma
   acupressure   194
   aromatherapy   194
   homeopathy   193–4
   supplements   193
attention deficit hyperactivity disorder (ADHD)   1, 215–16
   acupressure   217
   aromatherapy   217
   homeopathy   217
   supplements   216–17

back pain   195
   acupressure   196
   aromatherapy   197
   homeopathy   196
   supplements   196
balanced life   18, 35, 163, 177
   versus imbalanced life   28, 28
basil   212
berberine   192
big food companies   30

binge-watching   31, 32
biochemicals flush   164
birth control pills   187
blood sugar   24, 66, 68, 71, 81, 110, 222
blue light   119, 148, 154
blue-purple foods   70–1
bone broth   76
boredom   145
box breathing   112
brain derived neurotrophic factor (BDNF)   117
bread   53, 80–2
breathing   111–12, 116, 120, 193
brown foods   71
bullying   136
Burhenne, Mark   61
butylated hydroxytoluene (BHT)   53

cadmium   99
Campbell McBride, Natasha
   Gut and Psychology Syndrome Diet   205
cancer   197–8
   acupressure   200
   aromatherapy   200
   homeopathy   199–200
   supplements   198–9
carbon emission   87
carcinogen   54
carrageenan   53
CDC   12, 25, 147
cell   15, 17, 18, 20, 24, 41, 66
   brain cells   53, 117
   defined   14
   immune cells   58
   membranes   182
   tumor cells   197
child trauma   183
choices   8, 17, 27, 106, 163
chores   167, 170

Chris Beat Cancer 197
chromium 202
chronic health problems 6
chronic illness 110
chronic inflammation 18, *19*, *21*, 204
chronic stress 18, 25, 43, 109, 110
cinnamon 202
cinnamon oil 203
climate change 13, 87
Coca Cola 58, 230
coffee 43, 56, 76
colony forming unit (CFU) 178
color additives
    Blue 1 53
    caramel color 53
    Red 40 53
    Yellow 5 52
    Yellow 6 52
commitment 133, 134
common illnesses 12
common interest 135
constipation
    acupressure 201
    aromatherapy 201
    homeopathy 201
    supplements 200–1
conventional medicine 3, 39, 187
corn syrup 53, 56
cortisol 76, 110, 135, 136
cyberbullying 141
cypress 197, 212
cytokines 41, 45

dairy product 83–4
decisions 163
    adulthood 166
    balanced decisions 163–4
    build the life you want 168–9
    enjoy the journey 168–9
    find fun 170
    habits of success 168
    independent living 167–8
    live the life you love 167
    with mindfulness 170
    mindset molding 168
deep sleep 151
depression
    acupressure 220
    aromatherapy 220
    homeopathy 219–20
    supplements 219
detoxification 70, 75, 105–8, *107*, 180
diabetes 11
    acupressure 203
    aromatherapy 203
    homeopathy 202–3
    in kids 2
    prediabetes 202
    supplements 202
    type 1 201
    type 2 58, 201
    in US children 11
diet 6, 24, 68, 82
    intermittent fasting 85
    keto diet 85
    lectin diet 85
    mediterranean diet 84
    paleo diet 85
    raw food diet 85
    sugar diet 58
    vegan diet 84
    vegetarian diet 84
digestive system 24, 39, 40
digital detox 123, 143
digital foodprint 144
diverse microbiome 45
DNA 20, 59
dopamine 31, 32, 42, 114, 140
drug addiction 225
dysmenorrhea

acupressure 204
aromatherapy 204
homeopathy 204
supplements 203-4

eating disorders 221
e-cigarettes 99
eczema 3, 13, 17, 204-5
    acupressure 206
    aromatherapy 205
    homeopathy 205-6
    supplements 205
edible plants 24
Einstein, Albert 150
electromagnetic fields (EMFs) 102
EMF exposure limitation 104
emotions 110, 111, 164, 183, 186, 219
    management 165-6
endocrine-disrupting chemicals 100
endometriosis 203
Environmental Working Group 78, 103
epsom salt 105, 107, 119, 180
essential oils 122, 191, 194, 203, 206, 210, 219, 220, 227
exercise 43, 170, 225
    benefits 117
    breathing exercises 112, 153
    goals 117-18

faith 26, 114, 159
fake foods 48, 49, 68, 87
    to real food alternatives 94-5
feelings 140, 164-6, 186, 212
fertilizer use 13
fiber 61, 68, 80, 82, 106, 198
    powders 72, 202
    rich foods 71
5 R program *179*

Remove 177-8
Repair 178
Replenish 178
Repopulate 178
Revolutionize 179
food 63, 64
    dairy product 83-4
    diet 84-5
    fake to real food alternatives 94-5
    fiber importance 71-2
    fruits 76-7
    healing plate 64, *65*
    healthy fats 73, *74*
    herbs 78-9
    hydration 75-6
    industry 29, 31, 49, 56
    meal planning 87-91
    nutrient-dense foods 88
    nutrition 65
    organic food 77-8
    postbiotics 72
    prebiotics 72
    probiotics 72
    protein 72-3
    pyramid 85-6, *86*
    read food labels 92, *92*, 93
    real whole foods 87, *87*
    salt 79
    skittles 93
    spices 78-9
    sweets 79
    vegetables 69-71
    whole grains 79-83
    yumearth giggles 93-4
food additives 51
    aluminum additives 53
    butylated hydroxytoluene 53
    calcium propionate 53
    carrageenan 53
    color additives 52-3

corn syrup   53
monosodium glutamate   53–4
nitrates   54
nitrites   54
potassium bromates   54
preservatives   52
sodium benzoate   54
tartaric acid   54
tert-butyl hydroquinone   54
Food and Drug Administration (FDA)   51, 52, 60
The 48 Laws of Power   131
4-7-8 breathing technique   112
frankincense   197, 200, 209
friends   118, 126, 130–2, 134, 137, 138, 180
fruits   60, 76–7

gastroesophageal reflux disease (GERD)   206
   acupressure   207
   aromatherapy   207
   homeopathy   207
   supplements   207
generally recognized as safe (GRAS)   51
generosity   135
genes   20, 106
genetically modified organisms (GMOs)   55, 59–60, 230
genetic testing   182
Gen Zers   139
geranium   212
ghee   73
ginger oil   203
global warming   13
glucoraphanin   71
glucose   15, 58, 66, 201, 202
glutathione   83, 106, 183, 187, 226
gluten   81–3, 96
gluten free products   83

glycation   24
glycemic load (GL)   68
glyphosate   59, 60
graphites   206, 208
grass-fed butter   73
gratitude   7, 114, 120, 155, 156, 160, *161*, 169, 170
   failures   157
   mindfulness and   157
   self-esteem   156, 157
   self-love   157
green foods   70
gut   6
   bacteria   42
   bug balance   42–3
   bugs   24, 41, 42, 48
   cytokines   41
   digestive system   39, 40
   food-like substances   61
   health   180
   leaky gut   43–5, *44*
   microbiome   40–2, 47, 61, 105, 191
   oral microbiome   61
   pooping   45
   revolution   62
   sugar (*see* sugar)
   ultra-processed food (*see* ultra-processed food)
Gut Associated Lymphatic Tissue (GALT)   41

habit stacking   168, 170
harmonious sounds   115
headaches
   acupressure   210
   aromatherapy   210
   homeopathy   209
   supplements   209
healing plate   64, *65*
healthy fats   73, *74*

INDEX

healthy gut
  and brain   45, *46*
  versus leaky gut   43, *44*
healthy relationship   134
healthy teens   176
heart rate variability (HRV)   114
heavy metals   99–101
herbs   78–9
hidden toxins   97
Himalayan Tartary buckwheat flour   95
The Holistic Kids' Show   16
The Holistic Rx and The Holistic Rx for Kids: Parenting Healthy Brains and Bodies in a Changing World   179–80
The Holistic Rx: Your Guide to Healing Chronic Inflammation and Disease   189, 191
homeopathy   189, 192
  acne   192
  anxiety disorders   218
  asthma   193–4
  attention deficit hyperactivity disorder   217
  back pain   196
  cancer   199–200
  constipation   201
  depression   219–20
  diabetes   202–3
  dysmenorrhea   204
  eczema   205–6
  gastroesophageal reflux disease   207
  headaches   209
  hypothyroidism   208
  insomnia   223
  irregular periods   211
  irritable bowel syndrome   213
  sinus   195
  substance abuse   227

suicide   222
honey   79
hormesis   116
hormonal imbalance   65, 203, 210
hot chocolate breath   112
Hulk   112
human body   14, 81, 122
hydration
  bone broth   76
  coffee   76
  water   75
hypothyroidism
  acupressure   209
  aromatherapy   209
  homeopathy   208
  supplements   208

immune system   18, 40, 43, 82, 114, 130, 197, 201
inflammation   18, 20, 21, *21*, 22, 24, 45, 55, 194
Influence: The Psychology of Persuasion   131
insomnia
  acupressure   223
  aromatherapy   223
  homeopathy   223
  supplements   223
insulin   66, 67, 197, 201
insulin resistance   65, 66, 203, 210
  causes   68–9
intermittent fasting   85, 197, 198
intestines   41
iron   86, 182
irregular periods
  acupressure   211
  aromatherapy   212
  homeopathy   211
  hormonal imbalance   210
  supplements   211
irritable bowel syndrome (IBS)

INDEX

acupressure 213
aromatherapy 213
homeopathy 213
supplements 212

JAMA Pediatrics 11
Johns Hopkins pediatrician 147
junk food 18, 30, 31, 49

keto diet 85
kindness 129, 135

laughter 114
lavender oil 197
lead 99
leaky gut 43–5, *44*, 45, 73, 82
lectin diet 85
lemongrass essential oil 197
leptin 68
lifestyle 23–4, 28, 118
  changes 17, 169, 188–9
  choices 17–18
  modern lifestyle 16
loneliness 130
love 114, 129, 133
lycopodium 208, 222

magnesium 86, 181
mantra 114, 120
maple syrup 79
Mayo Clinic 26
meal planning 87
  breakfast 88–9
  dinner 91
  lunch 89–90
  snacks 90–1
medication 5, 14, 43, 181, 187
meditation 113–14, 116
mediterranean diet 84
melatonin 42, 153, 223
menstrual cycle 210

mental health 26, 140–1, 215
  anxiety disorders 217–19
  attention deficit hyperactivity
    disorder 215–17
  crisis 33
  depression 219–20
  insomnia 222–3
  substance abuse 224–7
  suicide 220–2
mercury 99
metabolic dysfunction 67–8
metabolism 14, 77, 78, 181
microbial diversity 124
microbiome 40–2, 45
  gut microbiome 40–2, 47, 61,
    105, 191
  oral microbiome 61
microplastics 100
milk 83, 84
mindful choices 7, 49
mindfulness 111, 113–14, 120, 157,
  165, 170
mitochondria 15, 20, 66, 102
mitochondrial dysfunction 16, *16*
monosodium glutamate 53–4
Morris, Philip 30
MSG 54
Murthy, Vivek 33
mushroom mycelia 178

nanoplastics 100
NASA 12
National Health and Nutrition
  Survey 56
National Institutes of Health 187
natural flavors 54–5
natural sweeteners 77, 79
nature 7, 115, 121
  connects with spiritually 122–3
  grounding 122
  healing 121–2

in home   125
mindful in   123–4
morning sunlight   123
in real life   123
trees   124
vitamin nature   126
negative ions   122
negative perspectives   26
negative self-talk   155
Nelson, Bradley
   the Emotion Code   186, 196
nervous system   15, 109, 113
neurotransmitters   42, 136, 181
New York Times   6, 17, 27, 219
nitrates   54
nitrites   54
non-GMO   78, 93
nonstick cookware   102–3
nutrient deficiencies   68, 219, 221
nutrient-dense foods   88
nutrition   63, 65
nutritional evaluation   182

obesity/metabolic syndrome   203
O'Bryan, Tom   82, 83
   Autoimmune Fix and *You Can Fix Your Brain*   72, 81
omega-3 fatty acids   73
omega-3 fish oil   182
oral health   105
oral microbiome   61
orange foods   69
organic food   77–8
oxidative stress reactions   20, 24
oxytocin   135, 136

paleo diet   85
peace   132, 229
peppermint oil   197, 209
physical addiction   224
physical health   140

acetaminophen   187
acid-blocking drugs   188
acne   191–2
acupressure   189, *190*
antibiotics   187–8
antidepressants   188
aromatherapy   191
asthma   192–4
back pain   195–7
birth control pills   187
cancer   197–200
constipation   200–1
conventional medicines   187
deficiency fixing   180–1
detoxification   180
diabetes   201–3
dysmenorrhea   203–4
eczema   204–6
5 R program   177–9, *179*
focus on gratitude   177
gastroesophageal reflux disease   206–7
genetic testing   182
headaches   209–10
heal the gut   177
homeopathy   189
irregular periods   210–12
irritable bowel syndrome   212–13
lifestyle changes   188–9
listen to body   176–7
NSAIDs   187
nutritional evaluation   182
nutritional supplements   181–2
sickness   175, 176
sinus   194–5
stress management technique   180
trauma   183–6
physical intimacy   133
physical sickness   175

phytoncide   122
play   98, 115, 123
pomegranates   77
pooping   45, 107
positive relationship   134
postbiotics   72
potassium bromates   54
prebiotics   61, 72
prediabetes   11, 66, 202
prefrontal cortex   27, 225
preservatives   52
pressure   132–3, 189
probiotics   72, 178, 187
processed foods   30, 31, 198, 230
protein   72–3, 77, 81, 82, 85, 98
purpose   7, 26, 156–60, *161*

rainbow color vegetables   69–71
raw food diet   85
read food labels   92, *92*, 93
real food   6, 23, 48, 61, 64, 69, 87, *87*, 106
red foods   69
relationship   130, 132
   healthy relationship   134
   physical intimacy   133
   positive relationship   134
   romantic relationship   133–4
REM sleep   151
Reynolds, R. J.   30
ripple effect   231–3
romantic relationship   133–4

Saccharomyces boulardii   178
salt   79
sea vegetables   70
self-compassion   186
self-control   134, 168
self-esteem   156–7
self-love   157
sepia   208, 211, 220
serotonin   42, 121, 123, 152

sickness   33, 175–7
sinus
   acupressure   195
   aromatherapy   195
   homeopathy   195
   issues   17
   supplements   194–5
skittles   93
sleep   7
   best to invest   152
   blue light   148
   deep sleep   151
   exercise   153
   food routine   152–3
   importance   149–51
   by Johns Hopkins pediatricians   147
   natural light exposure   152
   relaxation activities   151–2
   REM sleep   151
   restrictions   150
   routine   151, 153–4
   stages   151
   starting sleep   151
   stop the scroll   148–9
   successful sleep   152–3
Snack vs Chef   47
social connections   25–6, 129
The Social Dilemma   31
social media   5, 25, 118, 139–41
   influencer   158
   mindful use   142–3
   platforms   33
   safety and privacy   141–2
   teens usage   25, 26
soda   58, 94
sodium benzoate   54
spices   78–9
spiritual connection   26
spiritual health   26, 141, 158–60
spirituality   141, 156, 159
sprout powder   95

stevia 79
stress 18, 25, 58, 68, 76, 109, 185
stress management 7, 68, 109, 180
   apps/programs 115
   breathing 111–12, 120
   chronic illness 110
   chronic stress 109, 110
   exercise 117–18
   faith 114
   gratitude 114, 120
   harmonious sounds 115
   hormesis 116
   laughter 114
   love 114
   manifesting 114
   mantra 120
   meditation 113–14
   mindfulness 113, 114, 120
   nature 115
   play 115
   spend time with family 115
   stressors 109–10
   time management 115
   toxic thoughts management 116
   vagus nerve 109, 118
stressors 109–10, 232
subconscious mind 141, 155
substance abuse
   acupressure 227
   aromatherapy 227
   change toxic environment 226
   homeopathy 227
   network building 225
   physical addiction 224
   rid from addiction 224
   self-acknowledgment 225
   stay busy 225
   strengthen prefrontal cortex 225
   supplements 226
sugar 55
   affects brain 57–8
   chronic diseases 58
   damages immune system 58
   in drinks 58–9
   in food industry 56
   genetically modified organisms 59–60
   ultra-processed sugar 56, 57
   weight gain 58
suicide 2, 12, 220–1
   acupressure 222
   aromatherapy 222
   eating disorders 221
   homeopathy 222
   supplements 221
supplements
   acne 192
   anxiety disorders 218
   asthma 193
   attention deficit hyperactivity disorder 216–17
   back pain 196
   cancer 198–9
   constipation 200–1
   depression 219
   diabetes 202
   dysmenorrhea 203–4
   eczema 205
   gastroesophageal reflux disease 207
   headaches 209
   hypothyroidism 208
   insomnia 223
   irregular periods 211
   irritable bowel syndrome 212
   sinus 194–5
   substance abuse 226
   suicide 221
sweets 79

tartaric acid 54
technology limits 7
   affects teens life 139
   cyberbullying 141

mental health 140-1
phone-based life 139
physical health 140
positive subconscious 143
self care prioritization 143-4
social media (*see* social media)
spiritual health 141
teens 4, 6, 35, 49, 76, 81, 115, 139,
    140, 147, 148, 163, 166, 224,
    231, *see also individual entries*
  affects by technology 140
  brains and decisions 27-8
  decision-making skills 163
  education 7
  faith 26
  girls 12, 71
  healthy teens 176
  mental health 158
  negative perspectives 26
  out of control 27
  risk taking 163
  screen time 123
  social media usage 25, 26
  spiritual connection 26
  sugar harms 57
  with trauma 183, 184
  US 12, 25
tert-butyl hydroquinone
    (TBHQ) 54
time management 115
tobacco 29, 30, 101, 230
toxic chemicals 5, 24-5
toxic fake chemicals 231
toxic food 102-3
toxins 7, 98
  in air 101
  arsenic 99
  cadmium 99
  cleaning products 103
  detoxification 105-8, *107*
  electromagnetic fields 102
  EMF exposure limitation 104

  endocrine-disrupting
    chemicals 99
  hidden toxins 97
  lead 99
  mercury 99
  nonstick cookware 102-3
  oral health 105
  on our body 102
  plastics use limitation 104
  toxic food 102-3
  uranium 99
  ventilation 104
  in water 100-1
trauma 113, 183-4
  ACEs quiz 184-5
  emotions and feelings 186
  healing 185
  self-compassion 186
triclosan 102
tumor cells 197

ultra-processed food 23, 24, 29-31,
    68, 231
  artificial sweeteners 55
  companies 230
  fake foods 48
  food additives (*see* food additives)
  natural flavors 54-5
  risks 48-9
  US Nacho Cheese Doritos 47-8
  vegetable oils 55
ultra-processed grains 80-1
ultra-processed sugar 56, 57
UltraWellness Clinic 197
unbalanced life 18
unexpected 159
United Nations 13, 97
United States 49, 97
  banned chemicals 97
  children with diabetes 11
  food addiction 29
  food supply 87

INDEX

teens   12, 25
ultra-processed foods   29–31
unite with others   7, *137*
   abstinence   133, 134
   bullying   136
   commitment   134
   common interest   135
   friends   130
   generosity   135
   join group   135
   kindness   135
   love   129, 133
   pressure   132–3
   relationship   130, 132–4
   volunteer   135
unpleasant feelings   165
uranium   99
US Nacho Cheese Doritos   47–8

vagus nerve   42, 109, 112, 118
vegan diet   84
vegetables   69, 176
   oils   55
   rainbow color vegetables   69–71

vegetarian diet   84
villi   41
vitamin D   86, 181
vitamin nature   125
volunteer   135

water   13, 75, 108, 125
   filters   104
   toxins in   100–1
wheat   81, 82, 84
white bread   81
white foods   71
whole grains   79–80
   problem with gluten   81–3
   ultra-processed grains   80–1
wildfires, *see* inflammation
wintergreen oil   157
World Health Organization   99

yellow foods   70
yumearth giggles   93–4

zinc   182, 192, 221

ABOUT THE AUTHORS

Abdullah, Zain, Emaad, and Qasim are co-hosts of The Holistic Kids' Show podcast, speakers, and co-authors of four best-selling books (they write with their mother, Madiha Saeed, MD) titled *Adam's Healing Adventures from Sickness to Health*, *The Power of Rainbow Foods*, *Gratitude Is a Super Power* and *Real Food vs Fake Food*. The children's book series has been featured on Dr. Mark Hyman's Top 5 Picks. Zain illustrated the children's book *Adam's Healing Adventures: Real Food vs Fake Food*.

The Holistic Kids' Show podcast is a completely kid-run podcast—kids empowering kids. This one-of-a-kind podcast has featured over 200 experts, from *New York Times* best-selling authors, world-leading physicians, practitioners, Harvard professors, actors, *Wall Street Journal* White House correspondents, TV personalities, and more.

Abdullah and Zain have appeared on the Emmy Award-winning medical talk show, The Dr. Nandi Show. The kids have spoken at international conferences like The International Institute of Functional Medicine and A4M (as the first kids to have spoken at that event), MAS-ICNA, The Nourished Festival, as the keynote speakers for the YMCA's Interfaith Mayor's Breakfast, and speak on podcasts, summits, TV, and schools across the country.

The Holistic Kids co-created the first health course for kids by kids called Real Healing for Real Life Kids' Course.

Abdullah likes to play soccer and basketball. Zain is invested in cities, architecture, runs track, loves to eat, draw, and create maps. Emaad loves to cook and solve puzzles. Qasim loves to bake and to annoy his brothers while occasionally doing their laundry.

Madiha Saeed, MD, is a board-certified integrative holistic family physician—also known as HolisticMom, MD, and HolisticUrdu, MD, on social media—an international speaker, and a global best-selling author of *The Holistic Rx: Your Guide to Healing Chronic Inflammation and Disease*, *Adam's Healing Adventures* children's health book series, *The Pandemic Prescription: Restoring Hope from Quran, Sunnah and Science*, *The Quranic Prescription: Unlocking the Secrets to Optimal Health*, and *The Holistic Rx for Kids: Parenting Healthy Children to Save Our Future*. Her children are writing a book called *The Teen Health Revolution: Unlocking Lifestyle Secrets to Optimizing the Mind, Body, and Soul* and *The Fitna in Food: Redefining Halal Eating*.

Dr. Saeed is the director of education for Documenting Hope and KnoWEwell. She sits on multiple medical advisory boards, including Holistic Primary Care and Wellness Mama. Dr. Saeed and her children speak internationally at the most prestigious holistic conferences, summits, podcasts, TV (ABC, NBC, CNN, and CBS), radio, and newspapers.